POWER

ALSO BY JEFFREY PFEFFER

The External Control of Organizations

Managing with Power

Competitive Advantage Through People

New Directions for Organization Theory

The Human Equation

The Knowing-Doing Gap

Hidden Value

Hard Facts, Dangerous Half-Truths, and Total Nonsense

What Were They Thinking?

POWER

Why Some People Have It—and Others Don't

Jeffrey Pfeffer

HARPER
BUSINESS

An Imprint of HarperCollins*Publishers*
www.harpercollins.com

HarperCollins books may be purchased for educational, business, or sales promotional use. For information, please write: Special Markets Department, HarperCollins Publishers, 10 East 53rd Street, New York, NY 10022.

Designed by Cassandra J. Pappas

Library of Congress Cataloging-in-Publication Data

Pfeffer, Jeffrey.

Power : why some people have it and others don't / by Jeffrey Pfeffer.
p. cm.
ISBN 978-0-06-178908-3
1. Success in business. 2. Success. 3. Management. 4. Power (Social sciences).
I. Title.
HF5386.P5765 2010
650.1—dc22 2010015280

11 12 13 14 OV/RRD 10

To the Amazing Kathleen

CONTENTS

AUTHOR'S NOTE

This book is about real people who have been kind enough to share their stories with me over the years. In most instances, I have used their real names—in some instances they are public figures and some of the material comes from public sources. However, in a few cases, at the request of my sources, I have changed the names of people and, less frequently, other identifying information to protect their anonymity.

POWER

Introduction: Be Prepared for Power

ALMOST ANYTHING is possible in attaining positions of power. You can get yourself into a high-power position even under the most unlikely circumstances if you have the requisite skill. Consider the case of a real person we'll call Anne. Coming out of business school, Anne wanted to lead a high technology start-up. But Anne had no technology background. She was an accountant and had neither studied nor worked in the high-tech sector. Not only that, prior to her business education she had practiced public-sector accounting—she had been a senior accountant working in an important agency in a small foreign country and she was now focusing her aspirations on Silicon Valley in California. Nonetheless, Anne was able to accomplish her goal by making some very smart power plays.

Success began with preparation. While most of her compatriots took the entrepreneurial classes offered in the business school, Anne took a class in the engineering school on starting new ventures. With that one move she altered the power dynamics and her bargaining leverage. In the business school class, there were about three MBAs for every engineer, while in the engineering school course, there was only about one MBA for every four engineers. She explained that MBAs were unwilling to walk all the way over to the engineering building. Not only did she want to improve her bargaining position, Anne wanted to take a class closer to the laboratories, where technology was being developed and where she was more likely to run into interesting opportunities. Because of the pressure from the professor and the venture capitalists who judged the business plans that were the central part of the course to get MBA skills reflected in that work, Anne had bargaining leverage in her chosen environment.

After interviewing a number of project teams, Anne joined a group that was working on a software product that improved existing software performance without requiring lots of capital investment in new hardware. She had not developed the technology, of course, and joined the team notwithstanding some disdain for her skills on the part of her engineering colleagues.

Having found a spot, Anne was then very patient and let the others on her team come to recognize her value to them. The team—she was the only woman—initially wanted to target the product at a relatively small market that already had three dominant players. Anne showed them data indicating this was not a good idea, but went along with the group's wishes to focus on this first market in their class presentation. The presentation got creamed by the venture capitalists. As a result, the engineers began to think that Anne might know something of actual value. When the course was over, the team continued to work on their idea and got a small seed grant from a venture capital firm to develop the business over the summer. Anne, the best writer on the team, took the lead in putting together the funding pitch.

Anne was graduating with an offer from a major consulting firm. She told her team about the offer, thus letting them know she had much higher paid options so they would appreciate her and realize that she could make a credible threat to quit. She also intentionally let the engineers try to do things that she knew how to do proficiently—such as making presentations and doing financial projections—so they could see these tasks weren't as easy as they thought. Anne used her accounting and business expertise to review the articles of incorporation for the new company and the funding documents for its financing. Meanwhile, she gathered lots of external information and, being more social than the engineers, built a strong external network in the industry they were set to target. Her outside contacts helped the team get funding after the summer was over and the initial seed grant had run out.

Anne had more than business skills—she was also politically savvy and tough. When classes were over and the team was setting up the company, there was one other competitor for the CEO position. Anne told her colleagues she wouldn't join the company if he was named CEO. To show she was serious and to gain further leverage, she had her colleagues meet with other MBAs who might be possible replacements for her. Because she had spent lots of time working with the team, eating lots of pizza and bad Mexican food, the group felt much more comfortable with Anne. In the end she became co-CEO and found funding for the product at a hedge fund. Although there is no guarantee the business or product will be successful, Anne achieved her goal of becoming the leader of a promising high-tech start-up less than a year after graduating from business school, overcoming some significant initial resistance and deficits in her background along the way.

In contrast to Anne, you may have lots of job-relevant talent and interpersonal skills but nevertheless wind up in a position with little power, because you are unwilling or unable to play the power game. Beth graduated from a very high status undergraduate institution and an equally prestigious business school about 20 years ago. When

I caught up with her she had just left the nonprofit she was working for after a new executive director took over. The new boss was a friend of several of the nonprofit's board members and had once worked with Beth. He saw her competence as a threat and was willing to pay her a decent severance to get her out of the way.

Beth has experienced a "nonlinear" career after her MBA, punctuated by several spells of unemployment as well as some periods of great job satisfaction. She has yet to attain a stable leadership position in her chosen field, even though she has held senior jobs in government—on Capitol Hill and in the White House. The issue, as she explained it to me, was her unwillingness to play organizational politics, or at least to do so with the consistent focus and energy and maybe even the relentlessness evidenced in Anne's story. "Jeffrey, it's a tough world out there," Beth said. "People take credit for the work of others. People mostly look out for their own careers, often at the expense of the place where they work. The self-promoters get rewarded. Nobody told me that my coworkers would come to the office each day with a driving agenda to protect and then expand their turf. I guess I haven't been willing to be mean enough or calculating enough or to sacrifice things I believed in order to be successful, at least as success is often measured."

Systematic empirical research confirms what these two contrasting stories, as well as common sense and everyday experience, suggest: being politically savvy and seeking power are related to career success and even to managerial performance. For instance, one study investigated the primary motivations of managers and their professional success. One group of managers were primarily motivated by a need for affiliation—they were more interested in being liked than getting things done. A second group were primarily motivated by a need for achievement—goal attainment for themselves. And a third group were primarily interested in power. The evidence showed that this third group, the managers primarily interested in power, were the most effective, not only in achieving positions of influence inside companies but also in accomplishing their jobs.[1] In another example, Gerald Ferris of Florida State University and colleagues have developed an eighteen-item political skills inventory. Research on 35 school administrators in the midwestern United States and 474 branch managers of a national financial services firm showed that people who had more political skill received higher performance evaluations and were rated as more effective leaders.[2]

So welcome to the real world—not necessarily the world we want, but the world that exists. It *can be* a tough world out there and building and using power are useful organizational survival skills. There is a lot of zero-sum competition for status and jobs. Most organizations have only one CEO, there is only one managing partner in professional services firms, only one school superintendent in each district, only one prime minister or president at a time—you get the picture. With more well-qualified people competing for each step on the organizational ladder all the time, rivalry is intense and only getting more so as there are fewer and fewer management positions.

Some of the individuals competing for advancement bend the rules of fair play or ignore them completely. Don't complain about this or wish the world were different. You can compete and even triumph in organizations of all types, large and small, public or private sector, if you understand the principles of power and are willing to use them. Your task is to know how to prevail in the political battles you will face. My job in this book is to tell you how.

WHY YOU SHOULD WANT POWER

Obtaining and holding on to power can be hard work. You need to be thoughtful and strategic, resilient, alert, willing to fight when necessary. As Beth's story illustrates, the world is sometimes not a very nice or fair place, and while Anne got the position she wanted, she had to expend effort and demonstrate patience and interpersonal toughness to do so—to hang in with people who initially didn't particularly respect her abilities. Why not just eschew power, keep your head down, and take what life throws at you?

First of all, having power is related to living a longer and healthier life. When Michael Marmot examined the mortality from heart disease among British civil servants, he noticed an interesting fact: the lower the rank or civil service grade of the employee, the higher the age-adjusted mortality risk. Of course many things covary with someone's position in an organizational hierarchy, including the incidence of smoking, dietary habits, and so forth. However, Marmot and his colleagues found that only about a quarter of the observed variation in death rate could be accounted for by rank-related differences in smoking, cholesterol, blood pressure, obesity, and physical activity.[3] What did matter was power and status—things that provided people greater control over their work environments. Studies consistently showed that the degree of job control, such as decision authority and discretion to use one's skills, predicted the incidence and mortality risk from coronary artery disease over the next five or more years. In fact, how much job control and status people had accounted for more of the variation in mortality from heart disease than did physiological factors such as obesity and blood pressure.

These findings shouldn't be that surprising to you. Not being able to control one's environment produces feelings of helplessness and stress,[4] and feeling stressed or "out of control" can harm your health. So being in a position with low power and status is indeed hazardous to your health, and conversely, having power and the control that comes with it prolongs life.[5]

Second, power, and the visibility and stature that accompany power, can produce wealth. When Bill and Hillary Clinton left the White House in 2001, they had little money and faced millions in legal bills. What they did have was celebrity and a vast network of contacts that came from holding positions of substantial power for a long time. In the ensuing eight years, the Clintons earned $109 million, primarily from speaking fees and book deals, as well as through the investment opportunities made available to them because of their past positions.[6] Rudy Giuliani, following his tenure as mayor of New York City, became a partner in a security consulting firm, and through that firm and his speaking fees, he too quickly transformed his economic status for the better. Not all power is monetized—neither Martin Luther King Jr. nor Mahatma Gandhi traded on their celebrity to attain great wealth—but the potential is always there.

Third, power is part of leadership and is necessary to get things done—whether those things entail changing the U.S. health-care system, transforming organizations so they are more humane places to work, or affecting dimensions of social policy and human welfare. As the late John Gardner, the founder of Common Cause and former secretary of health, education, and welfare under President Lyndon Johnson, noted, power is a part of leadership. Therefore, leaders are invariably preoccupied with power.[7]

Power is desirable to many, albeit not all, people, for what it can provide and also as a goal in and of itself. The social psychologist David McClelland wrote about a need for power. Although the strength of that power motive obviously varies across individuals, along with a need for achievement, McClelland considered power seeking a fundamental human drive, found in people from many cultures.[8] If you are going to seek power, you will be happier if you are effective in that quest.

To be effective in figuring out your path to power and to actually use what you learn, you must first get past three major obstacles. The first two are the belief that the world is a just place and the hand-me-down formulas on leadership that largely reflect this misguided belief. The third obstacle is yourself.

STOP THINKING THE WORLD IS A JUST PLACE

Many people conspire in their own deception about the organizational world in which they live. That's because people prefer to believe that the world is a just and fair place and that everyone gets what he or she deserves. And since people tend to think they themselves are deserving, they come to think that if they just do a good job and behave appropriately, things will take care of themselves. Moreover, when they observe others doing things they consider to be inappropriate, self-aggrandizing, or "pushing the envelope," most people do not see anything to be learned, believing that even if those people are successful at the moment, in the end they will be brought down.

The belief in a just world has two big negative effects on the ability to acquire power. First, it hinders people's ability to learn from all situations and all people, even those whom they don't like or respect. I see this all the time in my teaching and work with leaders. One of the first reactions people have to situations or cases about power is whether or not the individual "likes" the person being studied or can identify with the object of study. Who cares? It is important to be able to learn from all sorts of situations and people, not just those you like and approve of, and certainly not just from people you see as similar to yourself. In fact, if you are in a position of modest power and want to attain a position of great power, you need to pay particular attention to those holding the positions you aspire to.

Second, this belief that the world is a just place anesthetizes people to the need to be proactive in building a power base. Believing that the world is fair, people fail to note the various land mines in the environment that can undermine their careers. Consider the case of Jim Walker, hired to build up Nomura Securities' Asian equity operation in Hong Kong in the late 1990s. By many measures, Walker was quite successful, recruiting outstanding analysts and garnering a strong ranking for the company's research team as well as increasing its profits. A charismatic leader who built a flat organization focused on merit and business results, he nevertheless failed to appreciate the political nature of the environment in which he was working. Confronted with opposition, rivalry, and some setbacks that cost him a degree of control, Walker left Nomura. "At the root of this latest departure is a misunderstanding. Walker misunderstood how unyielding and political Nomura can be."[9]

The pervasiveness of the belief in a just world, called in social psychology the "just-world hypothesis," was first described by Melvin Lerner decades ago.[10] Lerner argued that people wanted to think that the world was predictable and comprehensible and, therefore, potentially controllable. Or, as another psychologist described it, from early childhood "we learn to be 'good and in control' people."[11] How else could we navigate a world that is random and can't be controlled without feeling thwarted and frustrated much of the time? The desire for control and predictability results in a tendency to see the world as a just place because a just world is one that is also understandable and predictable. Behave by the rules and you will be all right; fail to follow the rules and bad things will happen.

The just-world hypothesis holds that most people believe that "people get what they deserve; that is, that the good people are likely to be rewarded and the bad to be punished. Most important, the phenomenon works in reverse: if someone is seen to prosper, there is a social psychological tendency for observers to decide that the lucky person must have done something to deserve his good fortune. He or she becomes a better person . . . simply by virtue of the observed rewards."[12] Conversely, if something bad happens to someone, "the belief in a just world causes the conclusion that the victim must have been a bad person."[13] This latter effect creates the frequently observed phenomenon of "blaming the victim," in which people find things that justify the bad events that happen to targets of crimes or corporate misfortunes. And the opposite is also true: success, however achieved, will promote efforts to find the many positive virtues in those who are successful—thereby justifying their success.

There are literally scores of experiments and field studies that show the just-world effect. Many of the original studies examined the opinions held by participants of people who were randomly chosen by the experimenter to receive an electric shock or some other form of punishment. The research showed that others were more likely to reject the (randomly) punished people and to see them as lacking in social worth—even though the observers *knew* those punished had received their bad outcomes purely by chance! Moreover, victims of random bad luck got stigmatized: "Children who receive subsidized school lunches are thought to be less able students than those not in the lunch program; ugly college students are believed less capable of piloting a private plane than pretty ones; welfare recipients are often treated as if they are untrustworthy or incapable of managing any aspect of their lives."[14]

As soon as you recognize the just-world effect and its influence on your perceptions and try to combat the tendency to see the world as inherently fair, you will be able to learn more in every situation and be more vigilant and proactive to ensure your own success.

BEWARE OF THE LEADERSHIP LITERATURE

The next obstacle you will need to overcome is the leadership literature. Most books by well-known executives and most lectures and courses about leadership should be stamped CAUTION: THIS MATERIAL CAN BE HAZARDOUS TO YOUR ORGANIZATIONAL SURVIVAL. That's because leaders touting their own careers as models to be emulated frequently gloss over the power plays they actually used to get to the top. Meanwhile, the teaching on leadership is filled with prescriptions about following an inner compass, being truthful, letting inner feelings show, being modest and self-effacing, not behaving in a bullying or abusive way—in short, prescriptions about how people *wish* the world and the powerful behaved. There is no doubt that the world would be a much better, more humane place if people were always authentic, modest, truthful, and consistently concerned for the welfare of others instead of pursuing their own aims. But that world doesn't exist.

As a guide for obtaining power, these recommendations are flawed. Most CEOs are not the level 5 leaders described by Jim Collins in *Good to Great* as helping to take companies up the performance curve—individuals who are "self-effacing, quiet, reserved, even shy," who get the best out of employees by not soaking up all the limelight and making all the decisions.[15] The rarity of such leaders may be why so few organizations go from good to great. And even Collins begins his story when these paragons were already in the CEO position—the road to the top may require different behavior than being successful once you have arrived. For most leaders, the path to power bears little resemblance to the advice being dished out.

The pablum in most leadership books and courses can be reduced to three causes. First, leaders such as former New York mayor Rudy Giuliani or former General Electric CEO Jack Welch, writing books and articles about themselves, may believe they are being inspirational and even truthful.[16] But leaders are great at self-presentation, at telling people what they think others want to hear, and in coming across as noble and good. This ability to effectively self-present is why successful individuals reached high levels in the first place. In the stories told either directly in autobiographies or indirectly in the case studies found in leadership books, leaders overemphasize their positive attributes and leave out the negative qualities and behaviors.

Two other factors help ensure that the positive stories persist. Those in power get to write history, to paraphrase an old saw. As we will discover in a later chapter, one of the best ways to acquire and maintain power is to construct a positive image and reputation, in part by coopting others to present you as successful and effective. Second, lots of research shows evidence of a particular manifestation of the just-world effect: if people know that someone or some organization has been successful, they will almost automatically attribute to that individual or company all kinds of positive qualities and behaviors. Although it is far from evident that doing the stuff in the leadership books will make you successful, once you become successful, odds are vastly increased that people will selectively remember and attend to the positive characteristics they believe make good leaders.[17] Stories of success that emphasize "positive" behaviors help us believe the world is a just place. Also, we see what we expect to see—imputing to successful individuals qualities that we think are associated with success, even if such qualities aren't actually there.

So don't automatically buy into advice from leaders. It could be accurate, but more likely it is just self-serving. People distort reality. One study found that out of 1,000 resumés, there were substantial misstatements on more than 40 percent.[18] If people make up educational qualifications and previous job experience—stuff that can actually be verified—do you think everyone is completely honest when they describe aspects of their behavior and character that are more difficult to discover?

What you *should* trust is the social science research that provides help on how to acquire power, hold on to it, and use it. And you should trust your own experience: Watch those around you who are succeeding, those who are failing, and those who are just treading water. Figure out what's different about them and what they are doing differently. That's a great way to build your diagnostic skill—something useful in becoming an organizational survivor.

GET OUT OF YOUR OWN WAY

The third big obstacle to acquiring power is, believe it or not, you. People are often their own worst enemy, and not just in the arena of building power. That's in part because people like to feel good about themselves and maintain a positive self-image. And ironically, one of the best ways for people to preserve their self-esteem is to either preemptively surrender or do other things that put obstacles in their own way.

There is an immense research literature about this phenomenon—called "self-handicapping."[19] The logic is deceptively simple. People desire to feel good about themselves and their abilities. Obviously, any experience of failure puts their self-esteem at risk. However, if people *intentionally* choose to do things that could plausibly diminish their performance, then any subsequent performance decrements can be explained away as not reflecting their innate abilities. So, for instance, told that a test is highly diagnostic of their intellectual ability, some people will choose to not practice or study the relevant material, thereby decreasing their performance but also providing an excuse for poor performance that doesn't implicate their natural ability. Similarly, if someone doesn't actively seek a powerful position, the fact that he or she doesn't obtain it will not signal some personal shortcoming or failure but instead a conscious choice. So, Beth's apparent unwillingness to "play the power game" protects her from the self-esteem consequences of possibly failing in that effort.

There is evidence that the tendency to self-handicap is an individual difference and predicts the extent to which people make excuses about their performance.[20] Research shows, not surprisingly, that self-handicapping behavior negatively affects subsequent task performance.[21] Therefore, our desire to protect our self-image by placing external impediments in our way so we can attribute any setbacks to things outside our control actually contributes to doing less well. Keep this idea about self-handicapping in mind as you read this book—you will be more open-minded about the content and also more likely to actually try some of the things you learn.

Self-handicapping and preemptively giving up or not trying are more pervasive than you might think. Having taught material on power for decades, I have come to believe that the biggest single effect I can have is to get people to *try to become powerful*. That's because people are afraid of setbacks and the implications for their self-image, so they often don't do all they can to increase their power.

So get over yourself and get beyond your concerns with self-image or, for that matter, the perception others have of you. Others aren't worrying or thinking about you that much anyway. They are mostly concerned with themselves. The absence of practice or efforts to achieve influence may help you maintain a good view of yourself, but it won't help you get to the top.

A GUIDE TO USING THIS BOOK

Not all organizations have identical political cultures, and not all individuals are the same, either. Unfortunately, we live in a world in which much of the management advice proffered is presented as universally true. And unfortunately, many people are looking for simple, universal formulas for action that will work equally well in all circumstances. How you behave and what you should do needs to fit your particular circumstances—the organizational situation and also your own personal values and objectives. So always place the ideas and examples of this book in context.

Second, except for certain laws in the physical sciences, we live in a world of probabilities. Just as no drug works well for everyone or all of the time, the same holds for ideas based on the best and most recent behavioral research. There will be exceptions and times when the advice offered in this book won't guarantee a good outcome. But as long as the odds are in your favor, in the long run you will be much better off heeding the research evidence and examples that illustrate that evidence.

Third, the learning process—in school and in the rest of life, too—is frequently too passive to be as helpful as it might be. There is only one way to become more effective in building power and using influence: practice. So don't just read this book and think about the examples—try some of the things you learn and see how they work. Model the behaviors of some of the effective people you read about. Turn knowledge into practice—it is the best way to develop the skills that make becoming powerful second nature.

I have organized this book as my colleagues and I organize the course we teach—using a path or developmental metaphor. The introduction and chapter 1 provide some orienting thoughts to help you reconsider taken-for-granted assumptions about the sources of power and success. Chapter 1 considers the evidence on job performance and power and how you can define job performance criteria in ways that are beneficial to you. Chapter 1 also provides a conceptual framework—some simple ideas—you can use to guide your reading of the subsequent material.

Chapter 2 treats the personal qualities you might develop that produce power. Many of these attributes are not inborn but learned. As such, you can diagnose your strengths and weaknesses and build a personal development plan to strengthen those personal characteristics that both research and logic argue are related to obtaining influence. Chapter 3 considers how to decide where to begin your career, the organizational locations most favorable for successfully launching your journey to power. Chapter 4 provides some advice on how to obtain the initial positions you want at the place where you want to begin—how to land a place on the first rung of the ladder to power.

The next chapters explore the sources of power and how to develop them. These power sources include resources (chapter 5), social networks and network position (chapter 6), the ability to act and speak in ways that both convey and produce power (chapter 7), and building a reputation as a powerful individual—a reputation that actually can become self-fulfilling and an important source of power (chapter 8).

Regardless of how successful and effective you are, sooner or later you will encounter opposition and setbacks. Chapter 9 analyzes how, and when, to fight and other ways to cope with opposition. It also provides some insight on the inevitability of reversals of fortune and how to cope. Power brings visibility—public scrutiny—and other costs as well. Chapter 10 treats the downsides, the costs of being in a powerful position. Power tends to produce overconfidence and the idea that you can make your own rules, and these consequences of having power often cause people to behave in ways that cost them their power and their position. Chapter 11 explores how and why power is lost and what you might do to better maintain positions of influence once you have attained them.

Implicit in virtually all of the discussion in this book is the idea that you are creating your own personal path to power. Many people wonder about the connection between such material and organizational effectiveness, the topic of chapter 12. Chapter 13, the last chapter, provides examples of people who have implemented the principles of this book with some measure of success. Its goal is to convince you that you can actually acquire power—not by becoming a new individual but by doing some things slightly more strategically and differently. Just like the principle of compound interest, becoming somewhat more effective in every situation can, over time, leave you in a very different, and much better, place.

1

It Takes More Than Performance

IN 2004, the Miami-Dade County, Florida, school board hired former New York schools chancellor Rudy Crew as superintendent to help improve a typical urban school district struggling with both budget and failing schools problems. While Crew was in charge, the district was a finalist for the Broad Prize for Urban Education in 2006, 2007, and 2008, improved its bond rating, achieved improvements in student academic performance, and built thousands of classrooms to ease overcrowding.[1] Recognizing this performance, in the spring of 2008, the American Association of School Administrators named Rudy Crew the National Superintendent of the Year, bolstering his reputation as an innovative school administrator. His reward? By September 2008, less than six months after being named the best school leader in the country, Crew was negotiating his severance package with a school board that had voted to get rid of him.

If you think it's just in the domain of public education where success fails to guarantee job security, think again. At the Veterans Health Administration, Ken Kizer, appointed by Bill Clinton in

1994, inherited an antiquated, inefficient health-care system. The VA faced changes in its client population, the competitive health-care environment, and modalities for delivering care.[2] In just five years, Kizer instituted an electronic medical record system, made structural changes to enhance efficiency and quality of care—with 20,000 fewer employees, the VHA went from serving 2.9 to 3.5 million veterans—changed the culture to be more receptive to change, and according to a cover story in *BusinessWeek*, laid the foundation for making the VHA the purveyor of "the best medical care in the U.S."[3] In 1999, facing stiff Congressional opposition to his reappointment, Kizer relinquished his post. Balancing politics and medical care turned out to be difficult—"in particular, the closure of VHA hospitals in certain key Congressional districts had created acrimony in Congress."[4]

And it's not just in the public sector where there is a weak link between job performance and career outcomes. The world of business offers numerous cases, too. Although few may remember, Jamie Dimon, the now-celebrated CEO of financial powerhouse JP Morgan Chase, left Citibank when his onetime mentor and boss, Sandy Weill, turned on him. Arthur Blank and Bernard Marcus founded the large and successful home improvement company Home Depot after they were fired in the late 1970s from Handy Dan Home Improvement Centers by a boss who didn't like them. John Scully forced Apple cofounder and technology visionary Steve Jobs out of the company in the 1980s. And that's just a small sample from a very long list.

And it's not just at the highest levels or just in the United States where performance doesn't guarantee success. A marketing executive in India asked her CEO to formally recommend her for a list of "high potential leaders" in the organization, which would be accompanied by getting paid more than 30 percent higher than peers at the same level and becoming eligible for assignments more likely to advance her career. This request came just after she had been instrumental in turning around a distressed brand, had been nominated for an internal marketing award, and after she won an external advertising award at the Indian equivalent of the Cannes film festival. Her request was refused, past outstanding performance notwithstanding.

Not only doesn't good performance guarantee you will maintain a position of power, poor performance doesn't mean you will necessarily lose your job. Michael Jeffery maintained his position as CEO of LECG Corporation, a global expert services and consulting firm, for three years even though the company was almost never profitable during his tenure and in just the two years prior to the announcement he was voluntarily stepping down, the stock price declined 80 percent, much more than did competitors'. His prior relationship with the non-executive chairman of the company and his ability to "manage" the board and blame the company's problems on his predecessor (who had actually built the company) ensured his survival—for a while. Or consider the CEO of a medical device company who has presided over nearly a decade of flat stock price, a growth in sales that did not translate into a corresponding growth in profits, and turnover in the senior executive ranks that left the company with no inside successor. Notwithstanding this weak job performance, his salary has increased rapidly and his job is secure—because of his close relationship with the non-executive board chairman and with a majority of the board of directors. The lesson from cases of people both keeping and losing their jobs is that as long as you keep your boss or bosses happy, performance really does not matter that much and, by contrast, if you upset them, performance won't save you.

One of the biggest mistakes people make is thinking that good performance—job accomplishments—is sufficient to acquire power and avoid organizational difficulties. Consequently, people leave too much to chance and fail to effectively manage their careers. If you are going to create a path to power, you need to lose the idea that performance by itself is enough. And once you understand *why* this is the case, you can even profit from the insight.

THE WEAK LINK BETWEEN PERFORMANCE AND JOB OUTCOMES

There is a lot of systematic evidence on the connections between job performance and career outcomes. You need to know the facts if you are going to intelligently plot a strategy to acquire power. The data shows that performance doesn't matter that much for what happens to most people in most organizations. That includes the effect of your accomplishments on those ubiquitous performance evaluations and even on your job tenure and promotion prospects.

More than 20 years ago social psychologist David Schoorman studied the performance appraisal ratings obtained by 354 clerical employees working in a public sector organization.[5] Employees were categorized by their supervisors' involvement in their hiring. In some cases, managers "inherited" employees—they were there when the manager took on the supervisory role. In other cases, the boss participated in the hiring decision and favored the job candidate now being evaluated. In still other instances, the supervisor participated in the hiring or promotion decision but he or she was overruled by others involved in the final choice. In this latter case, managers found themselves supervising an employee they had not favored hiring. The simple but important question Schoorman asked was: how does a supervisor's mere involvement in the hiring process affect the performance evaluations subsequently given to subordinates?

As you might guess, supervisors who were actively involved in hiring people whom they favored rated those subordinates more highly on performance appraisals than they did those employees they inherited or the ones they did not initially support. In fact, whether or not the supervisor had been actively engaged in the selection process had an effect on people's performance evaluations even when objective measures of job performance were statistically controlled. Supervisors evaluated people hired over their opposition more negatively either than those whom they had favored in the hiring or those they had inherited. David Schoorman's study shows the effects of behavioral commitment—once someone has made a positive or negative judgment about a potential job candidate, that judgment colors subsequent performance appraisals. What this research means is that job performance matters less for your evaluation than your supervisor's commitment to and relationship with you.

Extensive research on promotions in organizations, with advancement measured either by changes in position, increases in salary, or both, also reveals the modest contribution of job performance in accounting for the variation in what happens to people. In 1980, economists James Medoff and Katherine Abraham observed that salaries in companies were more strongly related to age and organizational tenure than they were to job performance.[6] Ensuing research has confirmed and extended their findings, both in the United States and elsewhere. For instance, a study using data from Dutch aircraft manufacturer Fokker reported that white-collar workers who received performance ratings of "very good" were only 12 percent more likely to be promoted than colleagues rated "good."[7] Meanwhile, many studies have documented the influence of numerous factors, ranging from educational credentials to race and gender, on careers, with performance often having a statistically significant but substantively small effect on advancement. For instance, a study of more than 200 employees from a variety of companies found that managers considered job tenure, educational credentials, overtime work, and absence as well as job performance in determining internal mobility for employees.[8] A study of federal civil service employee's, an excellent setting because of the extensive measures captured in the database, noted that performance ratings were weakly tied to actual productivity and that people with more educational credentials were more likely to be promoted even if they weren't the best employees.[9]

Not only may outstanding job performance not guarantee you a promotion, it can even hurt. Consider the case of Phil. A talented young executive working in a large financial institution, Phil had the uncanny ability to bring complex information technology implementation projects in on or ahead of schedule and under budget. His boss, a very senior executive in the bank, profited mightily from Phil's performance. He was willing to reward Phil financially. But when Phil asked his boss about broadening his experience by moving to other jobs in the bank, the answer was immediate: "I'm not going to let you go because you are too good in the job you are doing for me." And while Phil's boss was quite willing to expand Phil's scope of responsibility for IT implementation in his division, he was completely unwilling to do anything that would bring Phil to the attention of others and thereby risk losing him.

A slightly different variant of this same story comes from "Glenda." A Scottish manufacturing executive with an extraordinary ability to bond with front-line employees, Glenda had worked for her employer for more than a decade, moving around the world to accomplish almost miraculous turnarounds in troubled plants. Her job evaluations were great and she received performance bonuses and regular raises for her work. But there were no promotions in Glenda's recent past with her employer nor, she told me, in her future.

Glenda figured out the problem: the senior executives in her company saw her as extremely effective in her *current* position. But they did not want to lose her abilities in that role, and they did not see her as senior executive material—as a great candidate for much more senior jobs in the company. Thus, great performance may leave you trapped because a boss does not want to lose your abilities and also because your competence in your current role does not ensure that others will see you as a candidate for much more senior jobs.

Doing great doesn't guarantee you a promotion or a raise, and it may not even be that important for keeping your job. Most studies of job tenure examine CEOs, because CEOs are highly visible and that's the position for which there is the best data. Performance does affect job tenure and its obverse, getting fired, but again the effects are small. According to one study, CEOs who presided over three straight years of poor performance and led their firms into bankruptcy only faced a 50 percent chance of losing their jobs.[10] Whether or not poor performance led to dismissal depended on the CEO's power. Executives who had power because of their own ownership position, because other ownership interests were dispersed, or because there were more inside board members—executives who reported to the chief executive—were more likely to retain power even in the face of bad business results. A study of the top five executive positions in almost 450 companies found the sensitivity of turnover to company performance was even smaller for those jobs than it was for CEOs. Turnover in senior executive ranks was affected by CEO turnover, particularly when an outsider came in. That's because CEOs like to put loyalists in senior positions—regardless of what past incumbents have accomplished.[11]

So great job performance by itself is insufficient and may not even be necessary for getting and holding positions of power. You need to be noticed, influence the dimensions used to measure your accomplishments, and mostly make sure you are effective at managing those in power—which requires the ability to enhance the ego of those above you.

GET NOTICED

People in power are busy with their own agendas and jobs. Such people, including those higher up in your own organization, probably aren't paying that much attention to you and what you are doing. You should not assume that your boss knows or notices what you are accomplishing and has perfect information about your activities. Therefore, your first responsibility is to ensure that those at higher levels in your company know what you are accomplishing. And the best way to ensure they know what you are achieving is to tell them.

The importance of standing out contradicts much conventional wisdom. There is a common saying that I first heard in Japan but since have heard in Western Europe as well: the nail that sticks up gets hammered down. Many people believe this statement and as a consequence seek to fit in and not do anything to stand out too much. This rule may make sense in some places and at some times, but as general career advice, it stinks.

For you to attain a position of power, those in power have to choose you for a senior role. If you blend into the woodwork, no one will care about you, even if you are doing a great job. As one former student commented:

> I am the guy you notice when he is gone, but necessarily while he is there. I call this phenomenon becoming "the foundation guy." The foundation is necessary for the house and all goes to hell without it, but it is buried underground and works just fine

about 95 percent of the time. It usually goes unnoticed. Quiet work, or heads-down work, which is efficient and effective—but never flashy—usually fails to get noticed. You can make a great career as a middle manager doing quiet work, but can you gain a lot of power? The answer is most definitely, "no."

In advertising, one of the most prominent measures of effectiveness is ad recall—not taste, logic, or artistry—simply, do you remember the ad and the product? The same holds true for you and your path to power. That's because of the importance of what is called "the mere exposure effect." As originally described by the late social psychologist Robert Zajonc, the effect refers to the fact that people, other things being equal, prefer and choose what is familiar to them—what they have seen or experienced before. Research shows that repeated exposure increases positive affect and reduces negative feelings,[12] that people prefer the familiar because this preference reduces uncertainty,[13] and that the effect of exposure on liking and decision making is a robust phenomenon that occurs in different cultures and in a variety of different domains of choice.[14]

The simple fact is that people like what they remember—and that includes you! In order for your great performance to be appreciated, it needs to be visible. But beyond visibility, the mere exposure research teaches us that familiarity produces preference. Simply put, in many cases, being memorable equals getting picked.

An Italian executive who has worked in numerous large multinational corporations and has risen quickly through the ranks is an outspoken and provocative individual. Consequently, he sometimes irritates people. But as another manager told me, "decades from now I will remember him, while I will have forgotten most of his contemporaries." It is obvious whom that manager would choose to fill a position—the memorable Italian leader. You can't select what you can't recall.

DEFINE THE DIMENSIONS OF PERFORMANCE

Tina Brown served as editor of *Vanity Fair* and *The New Yorker* before founding *Talk* magazine and more recently starting the popular website The Daily Beast. A great editor and arbiter of popular culture who was able to garner tremendous amounts of publicity, Brown increased *Vanity Fair*'s circulation fourfold to almost one million during her eight-year tenure. At *The New Yorker*, newsstand sales increased 145 percent and the magazine won almost two dozen major awards.[15] The year before *Talk* folded in 2002, ad revenues grew 6 percent even as the overall economy languished. But Brown apparently never earned a profit at any of these magazines, partly because increasing circulation, timeliness, and "buzz" can only be achieved at considerable expense.

Tina Brown's performance as a magazine editor depends on what criteria you choose to evaluate her work. She presided over great growth in advertising revenue and circulation. She garnered press attention for herself and the magazines. But there was no economic profit. That might not have mattered to S. I. Newhouse, the billionaire whose Advance Publications owned *The New Yorker* and *Vanity Fair*. The absence of profit apparently mattered more to the Hearst Corporation, co-owner of *Talk*.

No one is going to perform equally well on all the dimensions of their work. What you can do is consistently emphasize those aspects on which you do well. When Matt Lauer of the *Today* television show interviewed Tina Brown right after *Talk* folded, he pressed her to admit that she had a flawed business model. Her constant refrain—that the magazine had great content and that advertising was growing even in the midst of the recession.

Chris was the CEO of a human capital software company selling a hosted service focused on selecting hourly employees. His venture-funded company operated in an increasingly competitive market and some rivals offered similar products at much lower pricing. One way to compete would have been to offer an increasing range of services to manage employees over the life cycle from hiring through career development to retirement. But Chris's company had an inferior technology platform and Chris was no technologist, so he could not lead a technology enhancement effort.

To lock in customers to make the company more salable, Chris and his management team offered reduced pricing for customers who renewed their contracts in advance of expiration. In his presentation to the board, Chris maintained that this strategy was a great way to grow the amount of deferred revenue on the books, ensure customer continuity, and make the company more valuable by preempting competitive threats. The presentation diverted the board's attention away from *why* reduced prices were required to lock in business.

It was a board member who provided data showing Chris's company was losing market share to competitors. But Chris had defined performance criteria in a way that made him look good. After the company was sold at a multiple of revenue about one-third that of competitors, with Chris nonetheless pocketing about $4 million, the new buyer lost customers—defections had been delayed but not prevented.

There are limits to what you can do to affect the criteria used to judge your work. But you *can* highlight those dimensions of job performance that favor you—and work against your competition.

REMEMBER WHAT MATTERS TO YOUR BOSS

When Rudy Crew ran Miami's schools, the district budget was about $4.5 billion and the school system employed more than 55,000 people. Crew may have thought his job was to improve school performance, but with vast resources at stake, some school board members were interested in who was getting the contracts and the jobs. Fraught with divisions along racial and class lines, the school board apparently cared a lot about the ethnic composition of the senior staff. As one person, providing public comment at the school board meeting that began Crew's dismissal, stated, if Rudy Crew's last name had been "Cruz," perhaps he would have kept his job, given the large Latino population in Miami. And, of course, school board members cared about their egos, and Crew was not nearly deferential enough to earn some members' endearment.

One of the reasons that performance matters less than people expect is that performance has many dimensions. Furthermore, what matters to your boss may not be the same things that you think are important. Jamie Dimon lost his job at Citigroup when he got into a tussle with Sandy Weill's daughter, who also worked for the company. Weill cared about his family, not just about the financial results of Citigroup.

Many people believe that they know what their bosses care about. But unless they are mind readers, that's probably a risky assumption. It is much more effective for you to *ask* those in power, on a regular basis, what aspects of the job they think are the most crucial and how they see what you ought to be doing. Asking for help and advice also creates a relationship with those in power that can be quite useful, and asking for assistance, in a way that still conveys your competence and command of the situation, is an effective way of flattering those with power over you. Having asked what matters to those with power over you, act on what they tell you.

MAKE OTHERS FEEL BETTER ABOUT *THEMSELVES*

You can almost always tell at least one aspect of your job performance that will be crucial: do you, in how you conduct yourself, what you talk about, and what you accomplish, make those in power feel better about themselves? The surest way to keep your position and to build a power base is to help those with more power enhance their positive feelings about themselves.

Most people, not just those who are somewhat insecure, like to feel good about themselves. They are motivated to self-enhance—to seek out positive information and avoid negative feedback—even though, objectively, people may learn more from mistakes and learning what they have done wrong. People overestimate their abilities and accomplishments—a phenomenon called the above average effect—with way more than half of surveyed respondents reporting they are above average on positive attributes such as intelligence, sense of humor, driving ability, appearance, negotiating ability—pretty much anything and everything.[16] And because people like themselves, people prefer others who are similar, because what is more self-enhancing than to choose someone who reminds you of—you! A large literature documents the importance of similarity in predicting interpersonal attraction.[17] For instance, people are more likely to marry others whose first or last names resemble their own and, in experiments, are more attracted to people whose arbitrary experimental code numbers were similar to the participants' actual birthdays. And because people like those who are similar to them, they also favor their own groups and disfavor competitive groups—

an effect called ingroup bias and outgroup derogation[18]—and also prefer people from their own social categories, for instance, of similar race and socioeconomic background.

One sure way to make your boss feel worse is to criticize that individual, and this criticism is going to be particularly sensitive if it concerns an issue that the boss feels is important and where there is some inherent insecurity. A talented manager working at a large credit card organization in the valuation and decision infrastructure group—a department that creates predictive models of customer payment as well as modeling customer acquisition and retention—was seeking accreditation as a credit officer. The chief credit officer in the company was a big fan of hers. But then "Melinda" talked to him when she was angry about one of his subordinates' bad behavior at a meeting. She told the chief credit officer that his subordinate's bad behavior reflected on his own leadership style, which sometimes entailed screaming at people himself. Because leadership was one of his areas of personal insecurity, he reacted badly to the criticism. He then held up Melinda's accreditation for a while—just to show her who was boss and in a form of revenge.

"Brent" was a reporter for the Associated Press, covering stories all over the world, literally putting his life on the line to be where the news was happening. Even though he covered one of the biggest stories of 2006, North Korea's underground nuclear test, he received a poor performance evaluation that year. The evaluation commented on Brent's contentious relationships with editors, who he felt were adversely affecting the news product—a feeling he shared with his bosses.

The lesson: worry about the relationship you have with your boss at least as much as you worry about your job performance. If your boss makes a mistake, see if someone else other than you will point it out. And if you do highlight some error or problem, do so in a way that does not in any way implicate the individual's own self-concept or competence—for instance, by blaming the error on others or on the situation. The last thing you want to do is be known as someone who makes your boss insecure or have a difficult relationship with those in power.

One of the best ways to make those in power feel better about themselves is to flatter them. The research literature shows how effective flattery is as a strategy to gain influence.[19] Flattery works because we naturally come to like people who flatter us and make us feel good about ourselves and our accomplishments, and being likable helps build influence. Flattery also works because it engages the norm of reciprocity—if you compliment someone, that person owes you something in return just as surely as if you had bought the individual dinner or given a gift—because a compliment is a form of gift. And flattery is effective because it is consistent with the self-enhancement motive that exists in most people.

The late Jack Valenti, for some 38 years head of the Motion Picture Association of America and prior to that an aide to President Lyndon Johnson, understood both the power of flattery and how to do it. In advice written to Johnson in 1965, Valenti noted, "What I am suggesting is that the President fasten down support for his cause by resorting to an unchanging human emotion—the need to feel wanted and admired."[20] Valenti himself flattered Johnson by showing him loyalty and consistently agreeing with him. In a speech to the American Advertising Federation Convention in June 1965, Valenti said, "I sleep each night a little better, a little more confidently because Lyndon Johnson is my President."[21] Valenti also flattered the studio heads for whom he worked for more than 30 years. In fact, he understood and used the power of flattery almost continuously. When I wrote him a note after he visited my class, he sent back a handwritten message on the note complimenting me on my thank-you.

In his autobiography, written when he was in his eighties and published after his death, there is no dishing of dirt or unflattering portraits of anyone mentioned.[22] A practice of flattering the other, begun decades earlier as Jack Valenti began his path to power, persisted even to the end of his life. And although the autobiography did not win reviewer plaudits because of its generally genial tone and a consequent absence of nitty-gritty details of the important events he had witnessed, no one who read the book would think ill of Valenti because of anything he had written about them.

Most people underestimate the effectiveness of flattery and therefore underutilize it. If someone flatters you, you essentially have two ways of reacting. You can think that the person was insincere and trying to butter you up. But believing that causes you to feel negatively about the person whom you perceive as insincere and not even particularly subtle about it. More importantly, thinking that the compliment is just a strategic way of building influence with you also leads to negative self-feelings—what must others think of you to try such a transparent and false method of influence? Alternatively, you can think that the compliments are sincere and that the flatterer is a wonderful judge of people—a perspective that leaves you feeling good about the person for his or her interpersonal perception skill and great about yourself, as the recipient of such a positive judgment delivered by such a credible source. There is simply no question that the desire to believe that flattery is at once sincere and accurate will, in most instances, leave us susceptible to being flattered and, as a consequence, under the influence of the flatterer. So, don't underestimate—or underutilize—the strategy of flattery. University of California–Berkeley professor Jennifer Chatman, in an unpublished study, sought to see if there was some point beyond which flattery became ineffective. She believed that the effectiveness of flattery might have an inverted U-shaped relationship, with flattery being increasingly effective up to some point but beyond that becoming ineffective as the flatterer became seen as insincere and a "suck up." As she told me, there might be a point at which flattery became ineffective, but she couldn't find it in her data.

This chapter has emphasized managing up—both the importance of doing so and some ways of being successful at the task. That's because your relationship with those in power is critical to your own success. Best-selling author and marketing guru Keith Ferrazzi says that, contrary to what most people think, they are not responsible for their own careers. As he noted, your driving ambition and even your great performance are not going to be sufficient to assure success in a typical hierarchical organization. The people responsible for your success are those above you, with the power to either promote you or to block your rise up the organization chart. And there are always people above you, regardless of your position. Therefore, your job is to ensure that those influential others have a strong desire to make you successful. That may entail doing a good job. But it may also entail ensuring that those in power notice the good work that you do, remember you, and think well of you because you make them feel good about themselves. It is performance, coupled with political skill, that will help you rise through the ranks. Performance by itself is seldom sufficient, and in some instances, may not even be necessary.

2

The Personal Qualities That Bring Influence

Ron Meyer, the president and chief operating officer of Universal Studios since 1995, is the longest serving head of a major motion picture company. A powerful figure in the film industry, Meyer also provides an example of a life transformed. Ron Meyer dropped out of high school when he was 15 and a couple of years later joined the U.S. Marines. After leaving the Marines he got a job at a talent agency as a chauffeur, a position that permitted him to learn a lot about the entertainment business as he listened to the conversations of clients. After working as an agent for the William Morris Agency, Meyer and some friends founded the Creative Artists Agency, a position that helped establish him as a power broker in Hollywood.[1]

Meyer, like many successful people, profoundly changed over the course of his life. He developed qualities that permitted him to obtain and hold on to influence. If you are going to do likewise, you need to successfully surmount three obstacles. First, you must come to believe that personal change is possible; otherwise, you won't even try to develop the attributes that bring power—you will just accept that you are who you are rather than embarking on a sometimes difficult path of personal growth and development. Second, you need to see yourself and your strengths and weaknesses as objectively as possible. This is difficult because in our desire to self-enhance—to think good things about ourselves—we avoid negative information and overemphasize any positive feedback we receive.[2] And third, you need to understand the most important qualities for building a power base so you can focus your inevitably limited time and attention on developing those.

CHANGE IS ALWAYS POSSIBLE

People often think that whatever qualities are needed for building a path to power, either you have them or you don't, at least by the time you are an adult. But the biographies of Ron Meyer and scores of other figures in political and business life belie that idea. Willie Brown, the longest-serving speaker in the history of the California Assembly, two-time mayor of San Francisco, and one of the most powerful and effective figures in American politics, lost his first election for the Assembly and also lost the contest the first time he tried to become speaker. Over time, Brown developed more patience and empathy with others and honed his ability to forge interpersonal relationships.[3] Just as people learn to play musical instruments, speak foreign languages, and play sports like golf or soccer, they can learn what personal attributes provide influence and they can cultivate those qualities. It may be easier when you are younger, but it is never too late.

John, a business school student, was uncertain whether or how he could become more effective in acquiring power. In a class on power, he saw the material as something to be used later in life, when he was "higher in the food chain," as he put it. Nonetheless, John decided to run a small personal experiment as he looked for a job, to see if he could act differently and what the results would be.

John understood he needed to project confidence and self-assurance, even though his personal history and family background did not always leave him feeling as if he "belonged." Girding himself for the arrival of on-campus recruiters, John dressed in a stylish fashion to stand out while still fitting in and projected himself forcefully during his interviews while still being respectful of the other person. "I would stand and approach the interviewer as they approached me, making eye contact, shaking their hand before they shook mine, sitting in a slightly dominant position through the course of the interview," he said. "All of this was done to convey that I had some level of power in the room."

John received seven job offers from his seven interviews. And he attributed his success to the way he had presented himself, in part because a number of those offering him jobs commented on how he stood out from his peers through his behavior.

You can change, too. Choreographer Twyla Tharp, the winner of two Emmy Awards and a Tony, in talking about creativity, made a comment that also rings true for developing power and political skill:

> Obviously, people are born with specific talents. . . . But I don't like using genetics as an excuse. . . . Get over yourself. The best creativity is the result of habit and hard work.[4]

Of course people have personalities and individual attributes that come from some combination of genetics and upbringing. But strategically changing individual attributes to become more personally effective is both possible and desirable. When one man I interviewed, Paul, questioned his ability to develop and use the qualities that produce power, I asked him this:

PFEFFER: Did you learn to ski?

PAUL: Sure.

PFEFFER: Was skiing a natural act?

PAUL: No.

PFEFFER: You learned to ski, and you just admitted that the skills involved in skiing weren't natural. If you learned those skills, you can also develop the qualities that will make you more powerful.

DO AN OBJECTIVE SELF-ASSESSMENT

If you are going to develop yourself, you need to begin with an honest assessment of where your developmental needs are the greatest—where you have the biggest opportunity for improvement. Such an assessment poses a big motivational challenge. In the first place, because we like to think well of ourselves, we overestimate our own abilities and performance. We avoid people who are critical of us and our work and frequently try to downplay any negative information about ourselves. We tell ourselves that our past success shows evidence of our talents, so we can just keep doing what we have always done. Marshall Goldsmith recognized the challenge of overcoming defensiveness about our abilities and behaviors in his best-selling book based on his many years of work as an executive coach.[5] If, as you progress through your career, you need to develop *new* ways of thinking and acting, and such development requires effort, you must be sufficiently motivated to expend the effort. But to admit you need to develop new behaviors and skills seems to require admitting you are not as perfect as you would like to believe.

Goldsmith, in his work with high-level executives, who mostly have huge egos, has tried to develop coaching techniques that mitigate the natural human tendency to first avoid and then reject any information about our deficiencies. For instance, instead of giving people feedback about what they have done right and wrong in the past, he focuses on "feedforward," which emphasizes what people need to do to get ready for the subsequent positions and career challenges they will confront. The idea is this: when people focus on what they need to get to the next stage of their careers, they are less defensive. This is very clever: focusing on what you need to change to accomplish future personal goals can be much more uplifting than going back and reviewing past setbacks or considering areas of weakness. I don't care what you do or how you do it, but just as improving the décor of a house when you stage it for sale requires a walk-through in which you and others assess what needs to be changed, enhancing your own skills requires the same sort of evaluation of your own areas for improvement.

Here's a suggestion. After considering the personal qualities described later in this chapter, do a self-assessment exercise. Grade yourself on a scale of 1 ("I don't have this quality at all") to 5 ("I have a lot of this quality and can readily use it") on each of the attributes. Better yet, have others grade you as well. And then, either by yourself or with a friend, develop a specific action plan for building those qualities where you scored the lowest. Regularly review your progress, and make sure you are continuing to develop those personal qualities that help build power.

And recognize a second challenge in your self-assessment. Even if you are willing to do the emotionally tough work of being clinically objective about your strengths and weaknesses, you may not have the requisite expertise to know how or what to improve. Simply put, knowing what you're doing wrong requires already having some level of knowledge and skill—and if you had the knowledge and skill to recognize your mistakes, you probably wouldn't be making them in the first place!

I get asked for various kinds of help all the time—questions about the business literature, requests to meet and provide career advice or to assist people facing political difficulties inside their companies. I am sure many people receive such requests, often out of the blue and frequently over the Internet because there is so little anonymity these days. In most instances, the reason the person is having a particular problem is evident in how the request is made: no attempt to provide any sort of evidence of similarity or social connection; no understanding of the other's perspective as the recipient of such a request; no explanation as to how I, as the target, was selected. And if the question is school- or project-related, there is often no familiarity with or mastery of the subject matter. Later in this book we will meet Ray, an effective, book-smart human resources executive and leadership trainer who lost his job to organizational politics. Talking to Ray convinced me that although he was tremendously knowledgeable about designing leadership training, and a hard worker with great values, he understood little about the political dynamics inside companies—and because of that, he did not know what he did not know.

This situation is not unusual. Cornell social psychologists Justin Kruger and David Dunning did pathbreaking research about a decade ago showing that people without the requisite knowledge to perform a task successfully also lacked the information and understanding required to *know* they were deficient, and in what ways.[6] For instance, people who scored in the 12th percentile on tests of grammar and logic thought they were in the 62nd percentile. Not only did they overestimate their own performance; they also had difficulty assessing what they had answered correctly and where they had made mistakes, and they could not accurately recognize the relative competence of others.

Fortunately, there is a simple solution to this problem: get advice from others who are more skilled than you and will tell you the truth about yourself. Unfortunately, asking for this sort of help sometimes feels like weakness and people are reluctant to admit what they do not know—that self-enhancement thing again. Ironically, therefore, those who admit ignorance are more likely to improve—in all domains, including understanding power dynamics inside companies—than those who either don't know their deficiencies or are afraid to admit them to others. As Confucius said, "Real knowledge is to know the extent of one's own ignorance." And to be able to improve requires sharing this information with others who can help remedy the lack of knowledge.[7]

As for the third obstacle, it is possible to both identify what personal skills and qualities produce power and then work to develop them. Here I highlight seven of the most important qualities you need to traverse a path to power.

SEVEN IMPORTANT PERSONAL QUALITIES THAT BUILD POWER

Although there is a growing research literature on power in organizations, there is less systematic evidence than I might like on the personal attributes that produce power. In part that's because such research is inherently difficult. Asking about the qualities of people already in power can confound whether the qualities *created* the influence or whether they were a *consequence* of holding power. What research there is,[8] plus my own analysis of scores of political and business biographies and observing literally hundreds of leaders in all walks of life, leads me to emphasize two fundamental personal dimensions and seven qualities that are both logically and empirically associated with producing personal power.

The two fundamental dimensions that distinguish people who rise to great heights and accomplish amazing things are *will*, the drive to take on big challenges, and *skill*, the capabilities required to turn ambition into accomplishment. The three personal qualities embodied in will are ambition, energy, and focus. The four skills useful in acquiring power are self-knowledge and a reflective mindset, confidence and the ability to project self-assurance, the ability to read others and empathize with their point of view, and a capacity to tolerate conflict. After describing each attribute, I will discuss a quality often associated with power but one that I think is, beyond some level, highly overrated—intelligence.

Ambition

Success requires effort and hard work as well as persistence. To expend that effort, to make necessary sacrifices, requires some driving ambition. The late Richard Daley, former mayor of Chicago and considered one of the 10 best mayors in American history, did not run for that office until he was 53 years old. "Daley realized early in life that he desired power, and he was willing to wait patiently for the opportunity to exercise it. He spent three decades toiling quietly at the routine jobs of urban machine politics."[9] Doris Kearns Goodwin's Pulitzer Prize–winning biography of Abraham Lincoln emphasized Lincoln's driving ambition as one of the most important qualities that produced his success in political life. Lincoln's drive enabled him to overcome an impoverished background, early political setbacks, and personal slights.[10]

And what is true in politics is also true in business. Jill Barad, who rose to become CEO of toy company Mattel, possessed unquenchable ambition. She often wore a bumblebee pin. "The bee is an oddity of nature. It shouldn't be able to fly, but it does. Every time I see that bee out of the corner of my eye, I am reminded to keep pushing for the impossible."[11]

Organizational life can be irritating and frustrating and can divert people's effort and attention. Ambition—a focus on achieving influence—can help people overcome the temptation to give up or to give in to the irritations. As Melinda, a vice president in a large credit card organization, told me, the relentless focus on a goal permits her to put up with the annoying, stupid, frustrating situations she encounters—to, in her words, not get hung up with the imperfect in the moment. Her desire for career success helps her control her emotions and continue to work to achieve her objectives. And Melinda's efforts to stay focused on the outcomes she is seeking and not get hung up on the people and their idiosyncrasies have been an important factor in her rapid career progress in the credit card company where she works.

Energy

Laura Esserman, director of the Carol Franc Buck Breast Care Center at the University of California–San Francisco, and a person who has led remarkable changes in medical practice both locally and nationally from a position of little formal power, got her MBA degree while practicing medicine full-time and having her first child. As she once said to me, "You don't change the world by first taking a nap." The late Frank Stanton, president of CBS and a huge influence in the news and broadcasting world, worked prodigious hours including on the weekend and typically got five hours of sleep a night.[12] Rudy Crew, the school system leader, is an insomniac, often up at three in the morning. Crew was typically the first person to arrive in the New York City chancellor's office, where he made the coffee.[13] I know of almost no powerful people who do not have boundless energy.

That's because energy does three things that help build influence. First, energy, like many emotional states such as anger or happiness, is contagious.[14] Therefore, energy inspires more effort on the part of others. As a young congressional secretary working for Representative Richard Kleberg in the early 1930s, future U.S. president Lyndon Johnson worked his two aides mercilessly. But because he worked alongside them with just as much effort, they didn't complain.[15] Your hard work signals that the job is important; people pick up on that signal, or its opposite. And people are more willing to expend effort if you are, too.

Second, energy and the long hours it permits provide an advantage in getting things accomplished. Research on genius or talent—exceptional accomplishment achieved in a wide range of fields—consistently finds that "laborious preparation" plays an important role. Social psychologist Dean Keith Simonton has spent more than a quarter century studying the determinants of genius. He writes, "individual differences in performance in a wide diversity of talent domains can be largely attributed to the number of hours devoted to the direct acquisition of the necessary knowledge and skill. . . . Some investigators have even suggested that the notion of talent or innate genius may be pure myth."[16] Obviously, having the energy that permits you to put in long hours of hard work helps you to master subject matter more quickly.

Third, people often promote those with energy because of the importance of being able to work hard and also because expending great energy signals a high degree of organizational commitment and, presumably, loyalty. As Melinda, the credit card executive, commented, if there are two people and one is willing and able to work 16 hours and one just 8, it is clear who will be chosen for a promotion opportunity.

People can develop more energy and get by on less sleep. Laura Esserman credits her surgical training and having to go long hours without sleep during her internship and residency with helping build her endurance. This suggests that there is a practice or training effect in developing energy. Kent Thiry, the CEO of kidney dialysis company DaVita, and someone known to do backward somersaults at employee meetings, has his personal assistant schedule exercise time for him—a lifestyle influence on energy that implies that even people who have demanding jobs and travel a lot can eat and exercise in ways that enhance their capacity for hard work. And you are more likely to have energy if you are committed to what you are doing, so in that sense, energy goes along with ambition.

Focus

Put some dried grass out in the sun and nothing happens, even on the hottest day. Put the dried grass under a magnifying glass and the grass catches on fire. The sun's rays, focused, are much more powerful than they are without focus. The same is true for people seeking power.

There are several dimensions to focus. One is specialization in a particular industry or company, providing depth of understanding and a more substantial web of focused relationships. From an early age, Bruce Cozadd knew he was interested in the drug industry. His bachelor's degree from Yale was in science. After he received his MBA, he took a job with ALZA, a pharmaceutical company, rapidly rising to become the chief financial officer and then executive vice president and chief operating officer. After Johnson and Johnson purchased ALZA, Cozadd consulted for several pharmaceutical companies before founding Jazz Pharmaceuticals. He serves on the boards of two other companies—both in biotechnology. Unlike many of his peers, Cozadd stuck with one company, ALZA, for the first 10 years after business school and has remained in the same industry throughout his career. He argued that this focus has provided him with more detailed knowledge of the industry, its technology and management issues, and also a denser network of contacts within the industry than if he had a more diffuse background.

Melinda has worked for the same credit card company since 2002. She noted that one advantage of staying in one place is that you get to know more people in a single organization, and this deeper knowledge permits you to better exercise power because of the stronger personal relationships you form and your more detailed knowledge of the people you are seeking to influence. Although there is a lot of talk recently about increased career mobility, it remains the case that it is often easier to acquire positions of influence as an insider. A recent profile of CEOs of S&P 500 companies found that the median tenure with their company was 15 years.[17]

A second dimension of focus is concentration on a limited set of activities or functional skills. If, as much research suggests, genius requires a large number of hours to achieve outstanding levels of competence, it is true, by definition, that you can acquire those hours in less elapsed time if you focus your attention more narrowly.

A third aspect to focus is to concentrate on those activities within your particular job or position that are the most critical—that have the most impact on getting work done and on others' perceptions of you and your effectiveness. Vernon, a rapidly rising executive at Barclays Bank, has impressed his peers with his laserlike focus on the things that matter most to the company, whether it is some presentation to a senior-level executive or an information technology project. Vernon argues that this focus on the 5 to 10 percent of all the possible job duties that actually have the most leverage allows him to manage his time more effectively and also permits him to allocate the resources of his team for greatest effect.

Focus turns out to be surprisingly rare. People are often unwilling or unable to commit themselves to a specific company, industry, or job function. Particularly talented people often have many interests and many opportunities and can't choose among them. Moreover, they often feel that diversification in their work roles provides some protection against making the wrong choice. That may all be true, but the evidence suggests that you are more likely to acquire power by narrowing your focus and applying your energies, like the sun's rays, to a limited range of activities in a small number of domains.

Self-Knowledge

A few years ago while conducting some executive training inside Fireman's Fund, a $12 billion insurance company owned by the German financial services conglomerate Allianz, I met Joe Beneducci, who was chief operating officer at the time. In 2007, when he was 39 years old, *Insurance and Technology* magazine named him one of the tech-savvy CEOs of the year. When I inquired about how he had reached such a high level at such a young age, Joe assured me that it was not his educational background—he had done well in his studies but had not gone to an elite school. Instead, he attributed his success to extensive reading—he read at least one nonfiction book a week—and to his practice of structured self-reflection. After every significant meeting or interaction, he would make notes in a small notebook. He would write down what had gone well and what hadn't, what people had said and done, and the outcome of the meeting. That notebook captured his thoughts about what had transpired so that he could make future interactions more effective; and the discipline of writing fostered reflection and also imprinted the insights more forcefully into his consciousness.

Dr. Modesto "Mitch" Maidique, a Cuban American who served as the president of Florida International University for 23 years and previously ran two companies and served as a partner in the investment banking firm Hambrecht and Quist, has had a distinguished career in both the profit and nonprofit world. When I asked him what leadership habits he thought made him effective, his response was immediate: making notes about decisions, meetings, and other interactions and reflecting on what he had done well or poorly so that he could improve his skills.

There is no learning and personal development without reflection. Andy Hargadon, a business school professor at University of California–Davis, has noted that many people who think they have 20 years of experience really don't—they just have one year of experience repeated 20 times. Structured reflection takes time. It also requires the discipline to concentrate, make notes, and think about what you are doing. But it is very useful in building a path to power.

Confidence

Two decades ago, I watched Dr. Frances K. Conley, the first female full professor of neurosurgery, in action. On one occasion she met with her surgical fellows and then with a patient with a malignant brain tumor. Even today, treatments for cancerous brain tumors aren't often successful, and some 20 years ago, the treatment options were even more limited. With her trainees, Dr. Conley exhibited uncertainty about what to do and asked for their thoughts. But when she walked into the patient's room, she became a different person.

Without denying the seriousness of the situation or glossing over the prognosis, Dr. Conley spoke confidently about what she recommended as a course of treatment. When I later asked her about her changed demeanor, Dr. Conley replied that there is some placebo effect as well as an effect of attitude and spirit on the course of disease; therefore, she did not want the patient to give up or become depressed. Had she expressed self-doubt, the patient might have left to seek treatment elsewhere, from people or facilities less qualified to provide state-of-the-art care.

Formal job titles and positions can provide influence and power. But in many situations, you will be working with peers or with outsiders who may not know your formal status. And in any case, observers are going to try and figure out if they should take you seriously or not. Consequently, you need to seize control of the situation. In making decisions about how much power and deference to accord others, people are naturally going to look to the other's behavior for cues. Because power is likely to cause people to behave in a more confident fashion, observers will associate confident behavior with actually having power. Coming across as confident and knowledgeable helps you build influence.

Amanda was a middle-aged, talented executive sent by her large, successful consumer products company to get a master's degree in management. The very fact that the company sent her and paid her salary and her tuition during the one-year program signaled they had great expectations. The question was, could she leverage the opportunity? In the spring, Amanda began thinking about her organizational reentry. She drafted an e-mail she was going to send to her company sponsors, but fortunately decided to run it by a friend, a woman executive from another company. That friend strengthened the tone of the message, making it clear that Amanda aspired to the senior executive ranks and was looking for a career path that would get her there and stating much more explicitly the type of position she expected on her return. Although she was initially reluctant to send what she viewed as a presumptuous message, Amanda did forward it and was pleasantly surprised by the response. Her company colleagues liked her confident approach and her expressions of ambitious career aspirations. And why not? That's how senior executives behave, and Amanda had shown she was just like them.

Showing confidence seems often to be a particular issue for women, who are socialized to be deferential and less assertive. But that behavior causes problems. Research by social psychologist Brenda Major shows that women work longer and harder for the same amount of money, award themselves lower salaries, and have lower career-entry and peak-earnings expectations than men.[18] One implication of this research is that because women don't think they are worth as much, they are disadvantaged in salary negotiations, which is one reason why there are persistent male-female earnings differentials.

The consequences of not being confident and assertive apply to everyone, not just to women, and not just in salary determination. If you aren't confident about what you deserve and what you want, you will be reluctant to ask or to push, and therefore you will be less successful in obtaining money or influence compared to those who are bolder than you.

Empathy with Others

Training in negotiation often includes advice to negotiate over "interests" rather than "positions." Through a process of mutual concessions, both parties may end up better off, but in order to succeed at such an approach, you need to understand where the other is coming from. This ability to put yourself in another's place is also useful for acquiring power. One of the sources of Lyndon Johnson's success as Senate majority leader was his assiduous attention to the details of his 99 colleagues, knowing which ones wanted a private office, who were the drunks, who were the womanizers, who wanted to go on a particular trip—all the mundane details that permitted him to accurately predict how people would vote and figure out what to give each senator to gain his or her support.

University of Texas psychologist William Ickes has studied empathic understanding. He notes:

> Empathetically accurate perceivers are those who are consistently good at "reading" other people's thoughts and feelings. All else being equal, they are likely to be the most tactful advisors, the most diplomatic officials, the most effective negotiators, the most electable politicians, the most productive salespersons, the most successful teachers, and the most insightful therapists.[19]

What sometimes gets in the way of putting ourselves in the shoes of others is too much focus on the end goal and our own objectives and not enough concern for recruiting others to our side—or at least curtailing the likelihood of their opposition. When Laura Esserman was pushing for changes at the breast care center at UCSF, she also agreed to raise funds for a mammography van to provide access to these diagnostic services in the poorer sections of San Francisco. Meanwhile, the department of surgery, where she held her primary appointment, was running a deficit, and the department chair wondered why a radiology service was being supported out of surgery; the medical center's chief financial officer was worried about the bond ratings for the debt required to build a new medical school campus in the Mission Bay section of San Francisco; and many administrators were concerned about treating more Medicaid patients, given the inadequate reimbursement rates, in the event that the mobile diagnostic unit turned up lots of poor women with breast cancer.

Initially focused on saving lives, providing treatment to disadvantaged women, and "doing the right thing," Esserman ignored the others' concerns. But then one day she realized that mammography was not even a diagnostic modality she was interested in pushing and that she was diverting her efforts into an enterprise that only provoked opposition. So she called her department chair and said, "I understand your point of view, I agree, and I will take care of this." Within two weeks she closed the service down, and that simple act gained her support from people whose help she needed. It also conveyed an important lesson: far from diverting you from accomplishing your objectives, putting yourself in the other's place is one of the best ways to advance your own agenda.

Capacity to Tolerate Conflict

There are lots of books and quite a bit of empirical research on the detrimental effects of workplace bullying—the screaming, ranting, profanity, and carrying on that sometimes occur in workplaces—on both the people who are the targets and the organizations in which they work.[20] So why does such behavior persist? Because it is often extremely effective for the perpetrator. Because most people are conflict-averse, they avoid difficult situations and difficult people, frequently acceding to requests or changing their positions rather than paying the emotional price of standing up for themselves and their views. If you can handle difficult conflict- and stress-filled situations effectively, you have an advantage over most people.

Rahm Emanuel, President Obama's chief of staff and formerly a very successful member of the House of Representatives from Illinois who ran the Democratic Congressional Campaign Committee, is known for his temper. "Emanuel seems to employ his volcanic moments for effect, intimidating opponents . . . but never quite losing himself in the midst of battle," observes Ryan Lizza.[21] Former New York City mayor Rudolph Giuliani, recognized for accomplishing a lot while in office, was someone who never shrank from a fight: "Mr. Giuliani was a pugilist in a city of political brawlers," noted *New York Times* writers Michael Powell and Russ Buetnner. "But far more than his predecessors, historians and politicians say, his toughness edged toward ruthlessness and became a defining aspect of his mayoralty."[22]

Some people mistakenly believe that this willingness to engage in conflict is a source of power only in Western cultures, with their higher tolerance for individualistic behavior and more open, less circumspect style of interaction. But I don't see much evidence for this view. In Singapore, a country that runs campaigns promoting courteous behavior, former long-serving prime minister Lee Kuan Yew, the father of the country, has been described as someone who was "often rude and contemptuous."[23] Lee came to power by taking on the British, who governed the country, and has shown no reluctance to back down from fights with political opponents over the ensuing years. Katsuji Kawamata, who went to work at Nissan in 1947 after a failing career at the Industrial Bank of Japan, eventually rose to become head of this large auto company even though he had no experience in the industry. His path to power in this typical Japanese organization entailed unexpected displays of toughness. As described in David Halberstam's book *The Reckoning*, Kawamata's rude and coarse behavior had a purpose: "It was . . . a power play. 'What he was telling us—and we did not realize it at first—was that what interested us did not have to interest him,' one of them [a Nissan manager] said years later, 'but what interested him had to interest us.' "[24]

INTELLIGENCE

As we have already seen, job performance is not strongly correlated with the ability to acquire power. But what of intelligence? There is probably no human trait that has been studied as much.

The research shows that intelligence is the single best predictor of job performance.[25] However, intelligence is often overrated as an attribute that will help people obtain power. That's because intelligence seldom accounts for much more than 20 percent of the variation in work performance in any event, and the relationship between performance and attaining power is equally weak.

Explaining career success has been the holy grail for researchers and practitioners—pursued by, among others, test developers and colleges and graduate schools that would like to find more valid ways of screening applicants. However, the goal remains elusive and the importance of general mental ability in understanding who actually gets ahead is small. A meta-analysis—a statistical summary of existing research—examining 85 data sets from a variety of countries concluded that the correlation between intelligence and income was .2, and although this was statistically significant, it meant that only about 4 percent of the variation in income was explained by variation in intelligence.[26]

Many studies of the predictors of career success, focusing on both the general population and specific subpopulations such as business school graduates, have found that mental aptitude correlates somewhat with grades in school but has virtually no ability to explain who rises to the top. That's because academic performance is a weak predictor of career success measures such as income.[27] To take just one recent example, Justice Sonia Sotomayor scored poorly on the scholastic aptitude tests that measure general academic ability and was admitted to Princeton on the basis of affirmative action. Nonetheless, she graduated from Princeton with academic honors and then reached the highest levels of the law, finally being appointed to the Supreme Court of the United States.[28] The inability of measures of intelligence to account for much variation in who gets ahead has led to the idea of multiple intelligences and efforts to develop indicators of constructs such as emotional intelligence that might be more useful in accounting for various career success measures.[29]

Furthermore, intelligence, particularly beyond a certain level, may lead to behaviors that make acquiring or holding on to influence less likely. People who are exceptionally smart think they can do everything on their own and do it better than everyone else. Consequently, they may fail to bring others along with them, leaving their potential allies in the dark about their plans and thinking. Being recognized as exceptionally smart can cause overconfidence and even arrogance, which, as we will see in more detail later, can lead to the loss of power. And smart people may think that because of their great intelligence they can afford to be less sensitive to others' needs and feelings. Many of the people who seem to me to have the most difficulty putting themselves in the other's place are people who are so smart they can't understand why the others don't get it. Lastly, intelligence can be intimidating. And although intimidation can work for a while, it is not a strategy that brings much enduring loyalty.

Many books about fiascoes—smart people making poor decisions—make this very point in their titles: *The Best and the Brightest*, Halberstam's study of Vietnam, for instance, or *The Smartest Guys in the Room*, McLean and Elkind's book about Enron. The late Robert McNamara, secretary of defense during the Vietnam War and a person invariably described as brilliant, told documentary producer Errol Morris in *The Fog of War* that the big mistake was not seeing things from the perspective of the North Vietnamese.[30] Enron's collapse resulted in part because some people thought they were so smart they denigrated anyone who doubted their approach, and no alternative viewpoints could survive inside the company. So while intelligence helps in building a reputation and in job performance, it often holds the seeds of people's downfall in creating overconfidence and insensitivity.

Once you set out to develop the attributes that can bring you influence, your next task is to figure out where best to deploy them. That is the subject of the next chapter.

3

Choosing Where to Start

WHERE YOU begin your career affects your rate of progress as well as how far you go. At two University of California campuses, the speed with which professors moved up a civil service–type salary ladder reflected the power of their academic department—those in more powerful departments moved up the salary scale more quickly.[1] A study of 338 managers who began their career in a 3,500-employee public utility found that the power of the unit where people began their careers affected the rate of salary growth, with people starting in more powerful units moving up more rapidly.[2] That study also found that managers who began their careers in higher-powered departments, such as operations, distribution, and customer service, were more likely to remain in high-power units as they changed jobs. Prior to its breakup by the government, the road to the CEO position at AT&T was through the Illinois Bell subsidiary. If you wanted to be CEO at Pacific Gas and Electric, the legal department was the best place to build your career. The shift in power from engineers to lawyers was visible over time: in 1950, only 3 of the company's most senior positions were occupied by attorneys; by 1980, the comparable number was 18.[3] For many years, finance was the route to the top at General Motors.[4] At the University of Illinois, where I began my academic career, senior university positions were often filled with people from the physics department.

At Wells Fargo, prior to the merger with Norwest, senior leaders came disproportionately out of the management sciences department. This list included Clyde Ostler, who during his 30-year career was the chief financial officer, head of retail banking, and head of Internet banking; Robert Joss, who rose to become vice chairman of Wells Fargo before going on to be CEO at Westpac Bank in Australia and then dean of Stanford Graduate School of Business; Frank Newman, who also served as CFO at Wells Fargo before going on to run Bankers Trust; and Rod Jacobs, who served as CFO and later as president of Wells Fargo. As the management sciences group provided analysis for many of the bank's most critical decisions, people in that department had exposure to the bank's most senior leaders. At the young age of 23, Ostler did analyses for Wells Fargo's investment committee, whose members included the top six decision makers. Committee members were also part of the bank's management committee, so Ostler was soon working with that group and sitting in at their meetings. At a very early point in his career, Clyde Ostler had an excellent position within the bank's communication network, with access to both critical information and key people.

We intuitively know that not all career platforms are equal in value as a path to power, and research supports that intuition. But people often err in choosing where to start building their power base. The most common mistake is to locate in the department dealing with the organization's current core activity, skill, or product—the unit that is the most powerful at the moment. This turns out to not always be a good idea because the organization's most central work is where you are going to encounter the most talented competition and also the most well-established career paths and processes. Moreover, what is the most important function or product today may not be in the future. So if you want to move up quickly, go to underexploited niches where you can develop leverage with less resistance and build a power base in activities that are going to be more important in the near future than they are today. The following two examples illustrate this idea in action.

UNEXPECTED PATHS TO POWER

You might think that knowing something about cars would be a good way to rise to the top of an automobile company, or that having a background in software would be important for having a successful career in one of the world's largest software firms. But you'd be wrong in both cases. And in understanding why, you can gain some important insights into where to launch your career.

By 2009, Zia Yusuf was executive vice president of the Global Ecosystems and Partner Group for SAP, the $15 billion company headquartered in Germany that competes fiercely with Oracle in the enterprise resource planning and database software market. One of the top executives in the multinational company where he had worked for just nine years, the 41-year-old Yusuf headed a group that was responsible for SAP's partner relations, online communities, and customer outreach. But Yusuf did not seem to have a background that would augur for career success in a high-tech, engineering-dominated company.[5]

Zia Yusuf was born in Pakistan and educated at Macalester College in Minnesota, where he earned a bachelor's degree in economics and international studies. With an interest in international development, he went to work for a firm doing development economics consulting and obtained a master's degree from the Georgetown University School of Foreign Service. Yusuf then joined the World Bank, where he did quite well, becoming a permanent staff member. However, the bank did not permit Yusuf to move to its private-sector arm, the International Financial Corporation, so on the advice of his wife, Yusuf decided to go back to business school to strengthen his private-sector credentials and get a second master's degree. He obtained his MBA from Harvard in 1998 and went to work for Goldman Sachs, a position that leveraged his banking and economics background and was a common destination for HBS grads. Yusuf did well at Goldman and was particularly skilled at managing client relationships, but he did not enjoy the banking work.

The late 1990s was the height of the dot-com boom and a time of great excitement about Silicon Valley; many of Yusuf's HBS classmates and Goldman Sachs associates were going west to pursue their careers. One of his colleagues from Harvard was a board assistant to Hasso Plattner, one of the cofounders of SAP. Yusuf, who had never even heard of SAP let alone knew what it did, flew to the Bay Area to talk to Plattner about a position in the company's Palo Alto office. At the time, he thought this was a good way to transition to the area—SAP would pay for the move and he could get a better feeling of the Silicon Valley culture and opportunities at close range.

Yusuf's first real job at SAP was as chief operating officer of the SAP Markets group, a separate legal entity wholly owned by SAP that had been established to build an electronic marketplace—an exchange that brought buyers and sellers together and made money by taking a small fee on each transaction. Other companies such as Commerce One were also pursuing this business model, which ultimately turned out not to be successful. Although the unit in SAP did develop some important software components used in other SAP product offerings, the 600-person operation was disbanded.

When SAP Markets closed down, Yusuf got the assignment to build an internal strategy consulting capability. Hiring talented people both from outside and from other units inside SAP, Yusuf built a department that had its hand in almost every high-level decision that required data collection and analysis—issues such as how to redo the human resources department, pricing questions, and organizational structure and design choices. The department, called the corporate consulting team (CCT), became the point of contact for managing any outside consultants SAP used. When Hasso Plattner became interested in user-centered design and design thinking, it was natural for Yusuf and his group to take the lead in making connections with IDEO, the award-winning product design firm, and with other outside resources that could help SAP build its user-centered design capability.

After four years as head of the CCT, a unit with offices in Germany and Palo Alto, Yusuf took on the job of consolidating and developing an ecosystem activity for the company, reporting to Leo Apotheker, who later became CEO. With favorable publicity for this activity in *BusinessWeek*,[6] and with increasing revenues and products coming from partners and the developer and customer community that fell within the ecosystems domain, Yusuf had already accomplished quite a bit. Moreover, because of his visibility to customers, partners, and competitors, Yusuf was in the sights of executive search firms to fill a CEO role in a high-tech company, and many thought that would be his next move.

Zia Yusuf had gone from being a banker to a senior leadership role in a large software company and a possible chief executive in a high-tech company in less than a decade—with no degree in engineering and never even having run an engineering or sales organization. In late 2009, Yusuf announced he was leaving SAP—as he told me, to find a COO or CEO role in a smaller company. His resignation prompted calls from the most senior SAP executives, including Plattner and Apotheker, who assured him that if he stayed, he would soon be on the executive board, one of the top seven people in the company.

Zia Yusuf's successful career had followed the trail developed decades earlier at the Ford Motor Company—leveraging an analytical staff position into a power base. Right after World War II, a small group of highly trained, very smart young men who had worked together in the Pentagon providing analytical support for the war effort moved as a team to one company where they felt they could have a substantial and immediate impact. The company they chose, Ford Motor, was led by a young and inexperienced Henry Ford II and was a mess, with rampant internal corruption, union troubles, and lax to nonexistent financial controls.[7]

The so-called Whiz Kids gravitated to the finance, accounting, and control functions. Their analytical bent was not well suited to the backslapping, hard-drinking world of sales and was particularly out of place in the tumult and grime of the factories. Plus, none of them knew anything much about manufacturing or, for that matter, cars. While Tex Thornton, their informal leader, left for Hughes Aircraft and later founded Litton Industries, others, including Robert McNamara and Arjay Miller, eventually rose to the top of the company and influenced a whole generation of management in many large corporations. People from Ford, protégés of the finance group, eventually held senior positions at Xerox, International Harvester, and other leading companies.

The career success of the Whiz Kids at Ford, and particularly McNamara, who became the first non–Ford family member to be named president of the company, depended on several factors. First, they had advanced degrees and elite credentials from leading universities. Henry Ford II, who had not finished college and was facing the very difficult task of turning around a faltering Ford Motor Company, was impressed with the Whiz Kids' pedigree. Second, the analytical orientation and the numbers the group produced provided at least the appearance of rationality and certainty to a troubled company. Third, the finance people talked the language of Wall Street and the financial markets, which, even in the 1950s, with Ford becoming a public company, seemed important. Ed Lundy, vice president of finance and a McNamara ally, would speak authoritatively on what would happen to the stock price if a certain decision were made and that argument would invariably carry the day. Fourth, the finance people were conservative when it came to spending money, and the money they weren't spending was Ford money. Cutting out waste and internal corruption, McNamara and his colleagues increased profits, and with this initial success, Henry Ford II became increasingly risk-averse.

But perhaps the most important source of the finance group's success was their centrality in consequential decisions. Was money needed to modernize plants or invest in new product development? Finance was not only involved in such decisions, but its criteria and data were the most important considerations. Finance had staff people ensconced in every plant, gathering information and seeing what was going on, and to ensure loyalty to finance, those people were regularly rotated back to headquarters, where, they were told, their careers would be made. Finance moved talented people into other areas of the company to extend its influence and came to control the agendas and the flow of information throughout the company. Vice president of finance Ed Lundy and his group even gained control over the performance evaluation process and the ratings that determined salary progress and promotions. Not surprisingly, finance people and those loyal to the finance in-group did better: "The company's personnel charts were marked with green tape to designate employees who were outstanding. An exceptional number of Lundy's people, because they were smart but also because they were doing each other's personnel reports, were graded outstanding."[8] And because finance produced numbers, not cars, it was largely immune to criticism. Finance people didn't have to make or sell anything—just keep Henry Ford II happy and their opponents on the defensive.

WHAT MAKES SOME DEPARTMENTS MORE POWERFUL THAN OTHERS

The Whiz Kids and the finance function at Ford illustrate one source of departmental power—unit cohesion. At Ford's finance function, there were socialization rituals—running the overhead projector at meetings, preparing briefing books, gathering articles and information—that served the same function as training in the military for the company's young, up-and-coming executives: imparting some specific skills and knowledge but more importantly building common bonds of communication and trust that come through shared experiences. Speaking with one voice, being able to act together in a coordinated fashion, is an important source of departmental power and effectiveness.[9] That's why the military evaluates leaders in part on the cohesion of their units and why coaches of team sports work so hard to build unity of action and purpose.

Another source of departmental power is the ability to provide critical resources, such as money or skills, or the ability to solve critical organizational problems, both topics the subject of literally decades of research.[10] Naturally, as competitive exigencies change, creating different pressing issues and changing the sources of money, so, too, does the locus of power. Berkeley sociologist Neil

Fligstein's historical study of the backgrounds of large company chief executives nicely illustrates this process at work.[11] Around the beginning of the 1900s, entrepreneurs held the CEO positions. Then manufacturing and production became the most common backgrounds for corporate leaders: with the emergence of the large-scale industrial enterprise and national markets, solving production and engineering issues were the most critical tasks companies faced. Starting in the 1920s and into the 1930s, CEOs tended to come from marketing and sales, as selling products and services, rather than producing them, became a more important challenge. And finally, beginning in the 1960s and then increasingly in the 1970s and 1980s, CEOs came out of finance. This change reflected the growing power of the capital markets, the consensus that shareholder value was the most important measure of organizational success, and the need for companies to build strong relationships with the financial community.

Both Zia Yusuf at SAP and the finance function at Ford benefited from being ahead of the changes confronting the two companies. When Yusuf arrived at SAP, the big issue facing the company wasn't how to design and build software: the company, filled with talented engineers and software designers, had already done that. The problem was that most of the large corporations that were target customers had already purchased enterprise resource planning (ERP) systems either from SAP or from a competitor. Therefore, in order to continue to grow, SAP needed to design products that could be purchased and readily used by small and midsized enterprises—and that required a new strategy and marketing approach. The CCT, the company's first corporate-wide strategy unit, was able to provide strategic focus and data necessary for the change.

Yet another avenue for growth was to build or sell applications that could turn the enormous amounts of raw data sitting in these ERP systems into business intelligence and solutions to specific business problems. Consequently, SAP needed application developers who, much like companies did with Apple's iPhone, would build and sell tailored applications that would use SAP's platform—hence, the importance of the ecosystems unit that Yusuf developed and ran. And as the ERP marketplace became more competitive, pricing and marketing strategy and user-centered design were all becoming much more critical. All of these changes made Yusuf's skills and the departments and connections he built more important. Describing his interactions with some of his SAP colleagues about his group's and his own role and their importance to the company, Yusuf said, "You know about software design and development—good, two points for you. How are we going to sell and make money off this software? All right, two points for me." Indeed, Hasso Plattner had recognized the changing skill sets needed inside SAP, which is why he had encouraged the company to bring in people with different, broader backgrounds.

Similarly, when the Whiz Kids arrived at Ford, they found a young CEO and a company that was out of control. The most critical problem was imposing financial discipline on this sprawling enterprise. Although it is hard to remember now, in the 1940s, after World War II, people would buy any car that was built; even into the 1950s and 1960s, the big three U.S. automakers owned the market. Design and engineering weren't that critical when innovation was mostly about the size of tail fins, and although the industry was always cyclical, sales skills were not that critical, either. As the Whiz Kids arrived, finance and business education were both about to take off on a sustained period of expansion, and to be an analytically skilled, highly educated person in finance at Ford was to be almost in the center of this emerging universe. Without for a moment denying the considerable skills of Yusuf and the finance folks at Ford, both also benefited mightily from being at the right place at the right time. In Yusuf's case, this entailed an element of luck, but Halberstam's description of the move of the Whiz Kids to Ford Motor shows a good amount of strategic thinking about which company would provide the group the best opportunity.[12]

DIAGNOSING DEPARTMENTAL POWER

It is always useful to be able to diagnose the political landscape, whether for plotting your next career move or for understanding who you need to influence to get something done. UK professor Andrew Pettigrew, studying power dynamics in a decision to purchase a computer, noted the importance of understanding power distributions for influencing the decision process.[13] Carnegie-Mellon professor David Krackhardt's analysis of power in a small entrepreneurial company found that the people within the firm with the most accurate perception of the power distribution and networks of influence had more power.[14] Skill at diagnosing power distributions is useful.

A single measure or a single indicator of anything invariably has measurement error. That's why a good doctor will take more than one reading of your blood pressure and, in diagnosing an illness, typically uses multiple tests and considers many symptoms. The same is true for diagnosing departmental power. Any single indicator may be misleading—but if many such indicators provide a consistent answer, then your confidence should be greater. Over the years, I have found the following to be reasonably good clues to which departments have the most power.

RELATIVE PAY

Both starting salaries and the pay of more senior positions in departments connote relative power. In the public utility study mentioned earlier, the starting salary was about 6 percent higher for people beginning their careers in the departments with higher power. Although that appears to be a small difference, this was a company that hired new managers into a relatively standardized training and initial career rotation program, so *any* difference would be unexpected. Some years ago, a study of salaries of the most senior executives (now called "C level," as in "chief") in different countries revealed that in Germany, the head of research and development was the best paid; in Japan, it was research and development and human resources; while in the United States, it was finance. These relative pay levels speak to the power of the different departments and show how that departmental power varies across countries.[15]

PHYSICAL LOCATION AND FACILITIES

Being physically close to those in power both signals power and provides power through increased access. Some years ago, a student group obtained floor plans for the Pacific Gas and Electric Company's headquarters building over many years. The company provides electricity and natural gas to much of northern California and portions of Nevada. Over time, the engineering department moved down in the building as the lawyers and finance folks moved up. Finally, engineering went to a satellite facility miles away from headquarters in San Francisco. This was occurring as the proportion of lawyers and finance types in senior management was increasing.

The importance of office location leads to an often-expensive shifting and redoing of offices as political fortunes wax and wane. This is particularly true in highly politicized places such as the White House. As John Dean, counsel to President Nixon, commented,

"Success and failure could be seen in the size, décor, and location of offices. Anyone who moved to a smaller office was on the way down. If a carpenter, cabinetmaker or wallpaper hanger was busy in someone's office, this was a sure sign he was on the rise."[16] I once visited the office of a friend who had taken over as head of training for a large bank. His office looked out on some air-conditioning units in a run-down building several blocks from corporate headquarters. When I arrived he said, "Let me tell you about the role of training in this bank." He didn't have to. The office, unfortunately, told it all. He soon left for other opportunities as he discovered that training really didn't matter at that time at that bank.

POSITIONS—ON COMMITTEES AND IN SENIOR MANAGEMENT

One way of seeing the power of finance is to look at the salary of the head of that function. But another would be to look at who, besides the CEO, is the insider most likely to serve on a company's board of directors. In many instances, particularly as boards have replaced insiders with outsiders, finance is the only internal management function represented on the board. That signals its relative power.

So, too, does the background of the senior-level team, particularly the CEO and the COO. One way to sense the shift in power going on at SAP would be to look at Zia Yusuf's success. But another would be to note that the most recent appointee as CEO, Leo Apotheker, came out of a sales background—the first nontechnologist to lead the company. The changing environment of health care has produced a shift in the power structure of hospitals: they used to be run by doctors; now they are more likely to be part of a large chain run by people with business and administrative experience. Neil Fligstein's study of CEO backgrounds, discussed earlier in this chapter, is interesting and important because it reflects the shifting power positions of different business functions over time. And it is not just positions, but also the composition of powerful committees—such as the executive committee—that can tell you the power of various departments. Paying attention to what departments are represented in powerful positions provides an important clue as to where the power lies.

THE TRADE-OFF: A STRONG POWER BASE VERSUS LESS COMPETITION

You face a dilemma. Being in a powerful department provides advantages for your income and your career. But for that very reason, lots of talented people want to go to the most powerful units. The Ford finance department in the 1960s, clearly the road to senior positions not only at Ford but at other companies that recruited from that department, could take the best of the best graduates of the leading business schools—which was great for the department and its ability to maintain its power but not so great for those individuals facing heightened competition. Early entrants into the corporate consulting team at SAP, not just Zia Yusuf, benefited from being valued pioneers of an important, new (for the company) business unit with tremendous visibility at the executive board level. Many people moved from the CCT to other important roles within SAP—something that was intended from the beginning, since one of the department's defined objectives was to be an entry point for talented people from different academic disciplines. But after a while, what was novel became routine, and it is far from clear that those entering SAP today would benefit as much from beginning their careers in the CCT.

This type of trade-off—pioneering a new path and the risk that entails versus entering an established domain but facing greater competition—occurs at the business level as well. When Apple introduced the first personal computer in the late 1970s, there was no competition, but, as Steve Jobs frequently noted, the product was often dismissed by those who thought it was too small to do serious computing. Now the legitimacy of the small computer product category is unquestioned, but current entrants confront a highly competitive market with very strong players.

Your answer to this dilemma depends on the extent to which you are an organizational entrepreneur and risk taker. It also depends on whether you are satisfied being carried along by a powerful tide or you want to get ahead of the wave or create your own pond where you can stand out.

Ann Moore became chairman and CEO of Time, Inc., in 2002 and has been frequently listed by *Fortune* as one of the 50 most powerful women in business. Moore graduated from Harvard Business School in the late 1970s, but instead of following her classmates into consulting or investment banking, she chose her lowest-paying job offer to join Time's finance department. After spending one year in the more typical MBA role of financial analyst, Moore sought a central role within the magazine group. She moved to *Sports Illustrated*. At the time, the cable division, which included HBO, looked like where the action was going to be, as magazines were perceived as a dying entity. Moore started a sports magazine for children and later moved to *People*, where she was named president of the magazine in 1993 and increased *People*'s performance from an already high level. Moore's career success came from her standout performance in a "dying" unit, and from being a woman in a man's sports magazine, which helped provide her visibility. By taking a different path, she helped her prospects for career success.

Entering the Ford finance function, the University of Illinois physics department, the cable division at Time, or the consulting unit at SAP even relatively late in the game would, as long as the department remained powerful, assure you of a good career both in terms of position and money. But if you want to break out of the pack, other things being equal, you would be better off in a different department with more new opportunity. Witness Yusuf's move to the ecosystem unit and the additional career success that has provided, and even more recently, his move out of SAP to pursue new opportunities.

What I have detailed is the risk-return trade-off faced in countless business arenas. As such, there is no right or simple answer. But whatever your choice, you would be well served to try to understand not just what today's powerful departments are, but where you think the power is going. And that forecasting skill is possible, although not assured or easy, by paying attention to the unfolding dynamics of the particular business and its environment.

Cisco, the designer and manufacturer of networking equipment, was founded by computer scientists from Stanford. The power inside the company originally resided with engineers and those with the technical expertise necessary to develop and manufacture the company's first products. But by 1994, the year Mike Volpi graduated from business school and turned down offers from McKinsey, Bain, and Microsoft to join Cisco in its business development function, it was becoming clear that Cisco could not and would not invent all of the technologies necessary to maintain its market leadership position. John Morgridge, then running the company, had already made the first large acquisition, purchasing Crescendo Communications in 1993. Soon, Cisco was busy making acquisitions—acquiring some 70 companies between 1993 and 2000. The companies that Volpi and his business development team brought into the fold contributed 40 percent of Cisco's revenues by 2001.

At Cisco, as in many companies, acquisitions fell under the

purview of business development. Volpi moved to further enhance the business development unit's power by building the skills inside that unit that could diminish its reliance on external advisers, such as investment bankers. Mike Volpi and his colleagues gained considerable power at Cisco in a short period of time. By the early 2000s, Volpi was among the four most senior executives at the company even though he was relatively young and inexperienced with technology. There were other executives, some with banking or consulting backgrounds, who joined the business development group early on in its rise to power and participated in its success. Seizing that opportunity required understanding the company's need to acquire technology externally and to take seriously its initial steps down the path to becoming a serial acquirer of existing businesses. Joining Cisco's business development unit in 1994 when it had two people, as Mike Volpi did, put him in a rapidly expanding strategic business function with enormous visibility to senior management and the board of directors that ultimately discussed and approved all acquisitions. Joining much later provided comparatively fewer career advantages.

In this chapter, we have seen how and why power varies across departments, with implications for developing your power base. In the next chapter, we consider how, once you decide where you want to be, you can get the job or opportunity that you want.

4

Getting In: Standing Out and Breaking Some Rules

WHEN KEITH FERRAZZI, now a best-selling author, marketing maven, and star of the lecture circuit, graduated from Harvard Business School in 1992, he had offers from two consulting companies, McKinsey and Deloitte. Pat Loconto, the former head of Deloitte Consulting, recalled that before accepting the offer, Ferrazzi insisted on seeing the "head guys," as Ferrazzi called them. Loconto met Keith at an Italian restaurant in New York City, and "after we had a few drinks at this restaurant, Keith said he would accept the offer on one condition—he and I would have dinner once a year at the same restaurant. . . . So I promised to have dinner with him once a year, and that's how we recruited him. That was one of his techniques. That way, he was guaranteed access to the top."[1]

Not many people would have the audacity to ask to speak with the head of the firm where they were being hired, and even fewer would ask that individual to have dinner with them once a year.

They would be afraid of being turned down, of seeming arrogant or audacious, of creating waves, and plus, that's not how things are done in the typical recruiting scenario. In chapter 3 we saw that it's important to know where you want to go—the department you want to be in and the path to power you see for yourself. It's even more important to be able to get what you want. As the Ferrazzi story and research discussed in this chapter show, launching or relaunching your career requires that you develop both the ability and the willingness to ask for things and that you learn to stand out. People often don't ask for what they want and are afraid of standing out too much because they worry that others may resent or dislike their behavior, seeing them as self-promoting. You need to get over the idea that you need to be liked by everybody and that likability is important in creating a path to power, and you need to be willing to put yourself forward. If you don't, who will?

The late Reginald Lewis was a successful African American corporate lawyer and founder of a buyout firm, TLC Group. TLC bought the McCall Pattern Company in the early 1980s and, under Lewis's turnaround efforts, returned investors 90 times their money. TLC later bought Beatrice Foods, creating the first black-owned company with revenues of over $1 billion and making Lewis one of the wealthiest people in the United States. But back in 1965, Lewis wasn't someone with a prominent place in African American business history. He didn't have an international law program at Harvard and an African American history museum in Maryland named after him.[2] He was just a young man from a tough Baltimore neighborhood who was graduating from Virginia State University and had set his sights on going to Harvard Law School. During that summer he was in a Rockefeller Foundation–funded program at Harvard Law School for high-potential college students designed to interest them in careers in the law and help them prepare for the application process. There was just one problem—one of the rules of the program was that no one who participated could even be considered for admission to Harvard Law School. Moreover, Lewis had not taken the Law School Aptitude Test, or even applied to Harvard Law, and he wanted to start the program that fall.

Even as he was doing well in the summer program by expending enormous effort and standing out in the mock court trial to such an extent that 30 years later professors still talked about his performance, Lewis met with a Harvard Law professor and then with the dean of admissions. With these faculty members he pressed his case by forcefully arguing "the myriad ways an association between Reginald Lewis and the law school would be mutually beneficial."[3] At the end of the summer, Reggie Lewis matriculated at Harvard Law School, becoming the only person in the history of the school who was admitted before he filled out an application.

Both Reginald Lewis and Keith Ferrazzi understood that the worst that could happen from asking for something would be getting turned down. And if they were turned down, so what? They would not be any worse off than if they had not asked in the first place. If they didn't ask or if they were refused, they would not receive what they sought, but at least with asking, there was some hope. Some people do believe that worse things could occur: that their bold behavior could offend those exposed to it and they could develop a "bad reputation." Probably not, and the risk of standing out is well worth taking, as we are about to see.

ASKING WORKS

Asking often works. After reading the Keith Ferrazzi case, one student in my class decided to ask the head of the London-based consulting firm recruiting him to have a meal together once a year. The head of the firm not only agreed but suggested a lunch once a month and also volunteered to be this former student's mentor. Another individual, Logan, was working at Deloitte Consulting while the firm was being reorganized. Logan, a talented person with a good reputation in the Atlanta office, would be getting a boss who didn't know him. The new boss was coming to town to meet with everyone for 30 minutes as part of a get-acquainted visit. Logan called the guy and commented that since he had to have lunch anyway, why not have lunch together? The new boss agreed and Logan used the opportunity to start forging a positive, personal relationship with his new boss.

Asking Works, but People Find It Uncomfortable

Asking for help is something people often avoid. First of all, it's inconsistent with the American emphasis on self-reliance. Second, people are afraid of rejection because of what getting turned down might do to their self-esteem. Third, requests for help are based on their likelihood of being granted: why ask for something like a meeting or dinner once a year if you are *certain* the answer is going to be no? The problem is that people underestimate the chances of others offering help. That's because those contemplating making a request of another tend to focus on the costs others will incur complying with their request, and don't emphasize sufficiently the costs of saying no. Rejecting an appeal for help violates an implicit and socially desirable norm of being "benevolent." Would you rather be known as generous or stingy? In addition, turning down a request made in person is awkward. We are taught from childhood to be generous, so we are inclined to grant the requests of others almost automatically. Furthermore, saying yes to a request for assistance reinforces the grantor's position of power. To offer mentoring or to open doors for another not only causes someone to depend on you and reciprocate the favor, perhaps by becoming a loyal supporter in the future; it also signifies that you can do something for someone else and that you therefore have power.

Business school professor Frank Flynn and a former doctoral student, Vanessa Lake, studied how much people underestimate others' compliance with requests for assistance in a series of studies that illustrate how uncomfortable asking for help can be. In one study, participants were asked to estimate how many strangers they would need to approach in order to get 5 people to fill out a short questionnaire. The average estimate was about 20 people. When the participants actually tried to get people to fill out the short questionnaire, they only needed to approach about 10 people on average to get 5 to comply with the request. Asking for some small help from strangers was apparently so uncomfortable that about one in five of the study participants did not complete the task. This dropout rate is much higher than typical in experiments where almost everyone finishes once they agree to participate.

In another study, people estimated they would need to approach 10 strangers to let them borrow their cell phone to make a short call—the actual number approached to reach the target of 3 acceptances was 6.2. And people also overestimated the number of strangers they would need to approach to get someone to walk them to the Columbia University gymnasium about three blocks away. They thought it would take 7 asks, but it took just 2.3 on average. Once again, asking people to walk with the participant to show them the gym was apparently very uncomfortable, as more than 25 percent of the participants did not complete the task after agreeing to do so. The Flynn and Lake research demonstrates that people are pretty bad at predicting the behavior of others. It is hard for us to take the other's perspective and see the world from his or her point of view. Their research also shows that asking people for small favors makes the requesters very uncomfortable.[4]

Asking Is Flattering

One reason why asking works is that we are flattered to be asked for advice or help—few things are more self-affirming and ego-enhancing than to have others, particularly talented others, seek our aid. When Barack Obama arrived in the U.S. Senate, he built relationships by asking for help. He asked about one-third of the senators for advice and forged mentoring relationships with Tom Daschle, the party's former Senate leader who had just lost his reelection bid, as well as with Ted Kennedy and Republican senator Richard Lugar. As an article about Obama in the *New York Times* noted, "His role as a good student earned him the affection of some fellow lawmakers."[5] If you make your request as flattering as possible, compliance is even more likely.

Ishan Gupta is a young man on the move. He cofounded Appin Knowledge Solutions, a technology training institution in India. I met him when he was in business school, which he attended after he lost a power struggle at Appin. He was still in his twenties and about to graduate into the difficult labor market in the recession of 2009 with multiple offers. Gupta had done a great job building networks and branding himself as an up-and-coming talent, particularly in India, and he did it by writing a book on entrepreneurship.[6] Although India has a number of large and successful high-tech companies, such as Infosys and Wipro, there is not yet much of a culture of entrepreneurship.

Gupta's book is interesting not so much for its content as for who it includes as chapter authors and endorsers. The foreword is by Sabeer Bhatia, the founder of Hotmail, the free e-mail service purchased by Microsoft in 1998 for a price rumored to be in the hundreds of millions of dollars. On the back cover is a picture of Gupta and his coauthor on either side of Dr. A. P. J. Abdul Kalam, who also wrote an endorsement that appears on the front cover—Kalam was the president of India at the time of the book's publication. Inside are 18 very, very short chapters by leading Indian entrepreneurs, all of whom now know Ishan Gupta and are at least committed enough to him to have written something for his book. He told me that of all the people he approached to write a piece for the book, only four or five turned him down, even though he knew none of them personally when he first approached them.

Gupta's strategy for getting these people's help was simple: determine who he wanted to be involved in the project and then ask them in a way that enhanced their feelings of self-esteem. Of course, once some prominent people agreed, those who were approached later were flattered to be asked to join such a distinguished group. Gupta focused his pitch on how important the subject of entrepreneurship was to India's economic development, how successful the people he approached had been in building businesses, how much wisdom and advice they could share, and how much help they could provide to others. He told them that he was a fellow entrepreneur and a graduate of the Indian Institute of Technology like many of them, that he appreciated how they had risked striking out on their own, and how unusual and courageous it was to start a business at that time in Indian society. Gupta then paid them the ultimate compliment, noting that no one would take a book by someone like him seriously and he might miss important insights, but with their help, it would be a better and more widely read book. Gupta also lowered the cost of agreeing to his request by asking the prominent and busy people he approached to write just a page or two, a few hundred words, with some key advice. People love to give advice as it signals how wise they are, and Gupta packaged the request brilliantly.

Gupta had cleverly noted that he was a fellow entrepreneur and an IIT engineer—albeit one with much less success than the people he was approaching. This strategy works because research shows that people are more likely to accede to requests from others with whom they share even the most casual of connections. Participants in an experiment who believed that they shared a birthday with another person were almost twice as likely to agree to a request to read an eight-page English essay by that person and provide a one-page critique the following day. In a second study, people who believed they shared the same first name as the requester donated twice as much money when asked to give to the Cystic Fibrosis Foundation.[7]

If you are approaching someone to ask for something—help finding a job, a chapter for a book like Gupta's, advice on some matter of consequence—presumably you have selected the person you are asking because of their qualifications and experience. Show that you understand their importance and how wise they are in how you frame the request. Research summarized by social psychologist Robert Cialdini in his best-selling book, *Influence*, illustrates how effective flattery can be in getting others on our side. Asking for help is inherently flattering, and can be made even more so if we do it correctly, emphasizing the importance and accomplishments of those we ask and also reminding them of what we share in common.

DON'T BE AFRAID TO STAND OUT AND BREAK THE RULES

There is lots of competition inside organizations—for jobs, for promotions, for power. Your success depends not only on your own work but also on your ability to get those in a position to help your career, like your boss, to want to make you successful and help you in your climb. For someone to hire you or promote you they must notice you. You need to do some things to stand out. And to do that, you need to get over the idea that "the nail that stands up gets hammered down" and similar aphorisms I hear over and over again as well as a natural reluctance to toot your own horn. In other words, you need to build your personal brand and promote yourself, and not be too shy in the process.

When President Barack Obama selected Hillary Clinton to be secretary of state, she was a U.S. senator from New York and Governor David Patterson had to appoint her successor in the senate. Initially, virtually everyone thought they knew who was going to be selected—Caroline Kennedy, the daughter of the assassinated former president John F. Kennedy and a longtime New Yorker who had been actively involved in the New York City schools and in a variety of public-service activities such as serving on nonprofit boards. Kennedy had tried to live as normal a life as possible up until that time and was unprepared for the limelight and the scrutiny that came with it. She was also surprisingly unprepared for the rough-and-tumble competition for the job and reluctant to engage in the campaigning—self-promotion—required to secure it. Although there are many reasons Kennedy eventually decided to take her name out of consideration for the post, Lawrence O'Donnell, a political analyst for the television network MSNBC and a personal friend of Kennedy's, commented: "Most of us have modesty impulses—you don't want to brag—and you have to learn to defy these basic human impulses and say, 'I'm the greatest, and here is why you need me for this job,' and do it without any hesitation or any doubt."[8]

Many people believe that they can stand out and be bold once they become successful and earn the right to do things differently.

But once you are successful and powerful, you don't need to stand out or worry about the competition. It's early in your career when you are seeking initial positions that differentiating yourself from the competition is most important.

When Henry Kissinger, the Nobel Prize–winning secretary of state and national security adviser, joined the Harvard undergraduate class of 1950 as a sophomore in 1947, he was surrounded by talented peers. As Walter Isaacson described in his biography, Kissinger sought the sponsorship of William Elliott, a pillar of the Government Department. On the basis of his grades, Kissinger was entitled to have a senior faculty member as his tutor, but Elliott brushed him off as he did many others, giving him 25 books to read and telling him not to return until he had completed a difficult essay assignment. Kissinger read the books, completed the essay, and got Elliott to take him under his wing. Elliott's sponsorship proved important in his academic career. Later, Kissinger wrote an undergraduate honors thesis of some 383 pages, resulting in a rule that specified that, in the future, no undergraduate thesis could be more than 100 pages and informally known as the "Kissinger rule." Once in the doctoral program in the Government Department, Kissinger carried himself as if he were a senior faculty member. He made appointments as if his time were very precious, and invariably arrived fifteen minutes late. Although such behavior and his apparent arrogance did not endear him to his fellow students, he built a reputation for his brilliance in part on the basis of his intellectual capacity but also on the basis of behavior that differentiated Kissinger from his colleagues.[9]

But does this strategy of standing out work in cultures that are not as focused on the individual and as brash as the United States? Absolutely. In Japan, where I first heard the aphorism about the nail being hammered down, Akio Morita, the cofounder of Sony Corporation, defied convention as an eldest son by not going into the family's sake business, broke from the mold as a father by sending his children out of Japan for some of their education, offended many of his business colleagues in Japan and elsewhere by writing a book highly critical of American business practices, led Sony to become the first Japanese company to list on the New York Stock Exchange, and built products that were smaller and more portable than those of his competitors.[10] Soichiro Honda, founder of the Japanese automobile company that bears his name, was famous for his antics, which included hurling tools at workers who did inferior work and skydiving even when he was in his seventies.

From another Japanese, Kiich Hasegawa, who built the consulting company Proudfoot into one of the larger consulting companies in Japan, I learned the wisdom of standing out, even in, or possibly particularly in, places where it is "not done." Proudfoot put on unconventional marketing events, such as a lavish reception with a beautiful female Japanese violinist. Hasegawa often employed a brash style, speaking frankly to customers and even potential customers about their organization's problems. When I asked him about his unusual approach, he described his marketing strategy as almost seducing people to come to you and your company to see what you are about. One way of doing that was by doing things differently, which intrigued others and piqued their interest. He argued that he and Proudfoot had been successful precisely because they did things differently from the expected Japanese way of doing things.

In advertising, the concept of standing out to become memorable is called "brand recall," which is an important measure of advertising effectiveness. What works for products can work for you too—you need to be interesting and memorable and able to stand out in ways that cause others to want to know you and get close to you.

This advice, and much other advice in this book, although based on solid research findings, seems to defy conventional wisdom and break the rules of how you are supposed to behave. Of course it breaks the rules! As Malcolm Gladwell has insightfully noted, the rules tend to favor—big surprise—the people who make the rules, who tend to be the people who are already winning and in power. Gladwell described research that shows how playing by the rules—following conventional wisdom—in arenas ranging from sports to war favors the already more powerful, while doing things differently and following an unconventional strategy permits even heavily outresourced underdogs to triumph. In every war in the last 200 years conducted between unequally matched opponents, the stronger party won about 72 percent of the time. However, when the underdogs understood their weakness and used a different strategy to minimize its effects, they won some 64 percent of the time, cutting the dominant party's likelihood of victory in half. As Gladwell noted, "When underdogs choose not to play by Goliath's rules, they win."[11] So, if you have all the power you want or need, by all means not only follow the rules but encourage everyone else to do so too. But if you are still traversing your path to power, take all this conventional wisdom and "rule-following" stuff with a big grain of salt.

LIKABILITY IS OVERRATED

People are sometimes afraid to ask for things and to pursue strategies that cause them to stand out because they are concerned they won't come across as likable. Research generally shows that people are more likely to do things for others whom they like, and that likability is an important basis of interpersonal influence,[12] but there are two important caveats. First, most of the studies examined situations of relatively equal power where compliance with a request for assistance was largely discretionary. Second, as Machiavelli pointed out 500 years ago in his treatise *The Prince*, although it is desirable to be both loved and feared, if you have to pick only one, pick fear if you want to get and keep power.

Machiavelli's advice anticipated research in social psychology about how we perceive others. That research found that the two virtually universal dimensions used to assess people are warmth and competence.[13] Here's the rub: to appear competent, it is helpful to seem a little tough, or even mean. Harvard Business School professor Teresa Amabile studied how participants reacted to excerpts from actual reviews of books. Amabile found that negative reviewers were perceived as more intelligent, competent, and expert than positive reviewers, even when independent experts judged the negative reviews to be of no higher quality.[14] The title of her paper, "Brilliant but Cruel," says it all. Other research has confirmed her findings: nice people are perceived as warm, but niceness frequently comes across as weakness or even a lack of intelligence.[15]

Condoleezza Rice served as national security adviser under President George W. Bush. Before joining the government, Rice was provost at Stanford under President Gerhard Casper; there she was known for being someone you did not want to cross. As Jacob Heilbrunn wrote, "Rice slashed the budget and challenged proponents of affirmative action . . . earning the enmity of many students and much of the faculty for her blunt style. Rice's credo, as she told one protégé, was that 'people may oppose you, but when they realize you can hurt them, they'll join your side.' "[16]

Likability Can Create Power, but Power Almost Certainly Creates Likability

Condoleezza Rice is right: people will join your side if you have power and are willing to use it, not just because they are afraid of your hurting them but also because they want to be close to your power and success. There is lots of evidence that people like to be associated with successful institutions and people—to bask in the reflected glory of the powerful.

Some years ago, social psychologist Robert Cialdini and some colleagues did a wonderful study of this effect. Cialdini taught at Arizona State University, which has a first-class but not dominating football team. In a typical season ASU will win some but not all of its football games. This created a great opportunity for the ASU researchers to ask: If the team won the game the previous Saturday, would more students wear clothes with school insignia the following Monday? Their study found that a higher proportion of people wore visible items of clothing with the school colors, letters, name, or other insignia following a victory than following a defeat. They also found that people were more likely to use the inclusive pronoun "we" to refer to a group following that group's success rather than failure.[17]

What this research implies is that people's support for you will depend as much on whether or not you seem to be "winning" as on your charm or ability. When writer Gary Weiss profiled Timothy Geithner, who was then the up-and-coming president of the New York Federal Reserve, "some of the nation's most prominent figures in government and finance—former Federal Reserve chairmen Paul Volcker and Alan Greenspan, as well as John Thain, then CEO of Merrill Lynch, and former New York Fed chief Gerald Corrigan—were only too happy to share fond anecdotes about this youthful public official." But things changed in the fall of 2008, when Geithner became Obama's secretary of the Treasury and ran into trouble as the financial meltdown unfolded: "When I approached them [these same prominent figures] again for this article, to get a word of defense of their beleaguered friend, the reaction was far different."[18]

What's Likability Got to Do with Anything?

At a conference in Florida where I was giving a presentation, I sat next to a Harvard Business School graduate from the class of 1992 at dinner. I asked if he knew Keith Ferrazzi, who had graduated that same year. The answer was, "Of course." He wasn't a close personal friend of Keith's and noted that Ferrazzi was not necessarily very popular with his HBS classmates. My next question, had he hired Ferrazzi to do marketing consulting for his company in the online publishing space? The answer: "Certainly. What's liking got to do with hiring someone to help you build your business? The question is, 'Can they be helpful to you?' "

This instrumental view of personal relationships is not uncommon and indeed may be necessary for organizational survival. During Clarence Thomas's well-publicized Supreme Court nomination hearings, Anita Hill came forward with accusations of sexual harassment. The question frequently asked of her was: if she was so uncomfortable and Thomas had actually behaved inappropriately toward her, why had she continued to have anything to do with him? In *Strange Justice*, Jane Mayer and Jill Abramson provided a possible answer: "Hill chose to stay in touch with Thomas because it was good for her career. Thomas was one of the most powerful people—and probably the most powerful African-American—in her field. . . . Whether Hill liked it or not, she and Thomas were professionally linked, and it was up to her to either put a good face on it or allow it to be a festering problem."[19]

Research shows that attitudes follow behavior—that if we act in a certain way, over time our attitudes follow. For example, if we act friendly toward an adversary whose help we need, we will come to feel more friendly as well. There are many theoretical mechanisms that account for this effect. One holds that people infer their own attitudes from their behavior—or as Michigan professor Karl Weick put it, "I know what I think when I see what I say." Another is Leon Festinger's theory of cognitive dissonance, which argues that people seek to avoid inconsistency, and one way of accomplishing that is to adjust their attitudes to be consistent with their behaviors.[20] What this implies is that if we interact with powerful people because we need them to do some task or to help us in our career, over time we will come to like them more or at least forgive their rough edges. And in choosing who we will associate with, usefulness to our career and job loom as important criteria.

People Forget and Forgive

The principle of hedonism underlies many theories of individual behavior, ranging from economics to psychology—we seek pleasure and avoid pain. This is as true for our memories and our interpersonal relationships as it is for any other aspect of our lives. Therefore, over time we will forget the specifics of painful interactions just as women tell me they forget the pain of childbirth, and although we can remember the fact that we had pain from a surgery, the intensity and specificity of that memory soon fades. We also forgive the slights and wounds inflicted by others, and are particularly likely to forgive people if we are in contact with them. And we are more likely to remain in contact if they are powerful. Over time, even the most contentious adversaries can become close friends.

In the 1920s, Robert Moses, New York City's master builder and urban planner, was beginning his career as Long Island parks commissioner. He seized some land called the Taylor estate using a constitutionally questionable process. Kingsland Macy, a stockbroker and a member of a corporation that had an interest in the estate, opposed Moses and fought him in court, believing that no one's home was safe if Moses's power was not curtailed. A few years later, Macy's financial resources were exhausted by the struggle and he finally gave in. Macy subsequently went into politics and for decades ruled the Suffolk County Republican organization with an iron hand. The two formerly bitter adversaries became close friends:

> And when after Macy had fought his way to power, Robert Moses, needing his help, made overtures of friendship, Macy accepted them. Although the strength of their personalities often made them clash, the two one-time "amateurs in politics" were for more than thirty years the closest of political allies, allies so close, in fact, that when, in 1962, cancer-ravaged King Macy knew he was about to die, Moses was the only person outside his immediate family whom he wanted to see.[21]

Standing out helps you get the jobs and power you may seek. Asking for what you need and being less concerned about what others are thinking about you can help in launching your path to power. But acquiring and wielding power requires the resources to reward your friends and punish your enemies, the information and access that can foster your rise in the organization. So let's explore how to acquire resources, even if you seemingly have nothing.

5

Making Something out of Nothing: Creating Resources

IN VIRTUALLY all organizational domains, controlling access to money and jobs brings power. In government, Jesse Unruh, a former Democratic political boss and treasurer of California, called money the mother's milk of politics. Former two-term San Francisco mayor Willie Brown, whose 16 years as speaker and virtual ruler of the California Assembly prior to becoming mayor marked him as an extremely effective politician, began his campaign for the legislative leadership post by raising a lot of money. And since he was from a "safe" district, he gave that money to his legislative colleagues to help them win their political contests. Brown understood an important principle: having resources is an important source of power only if you use those resources strategically to help others whose support you need, in the process gaining their favor. In contrast to Brown, the Assembly speaker at the time, Leo McCarthy, irritated his Democratic colleagues to the point of revolt by holding a $500,000 fundraiser in Los Angeles featuring Ted Kennedy and then using 100 percent of the money for his nascent efforts to run for statewide office.[1] He was soon out of his job, replaced by Willie Brown.

Investigative journalists have long adhered to the maxim "Follow the money" as they uncover power structures in governments and communities. And for good reason: research shows a correlation between campaign contributions and public officials' voting behavior, partly because legislators reward their supporters and partly because political action committees choose to direct their funding toward legislators with compatible voting records.[2] What's true in government and community power is just as true for understanding power dynamics inside profit and nonprofit organizations—the people and the subunits that control resources possess an important source of power, as I briefly discussed in chapter 3. You can see this dynamic play out over time in financial institutions, where the power of investment bankers waned as more profits came from the firms' trading activities—that is, until trading got the companies into financial trouble. Then power migrated back to those responsible for more traditional, stable, and less risky sources of revenue and earnings.

There are numerous examples of the connection between resources and indicators of power in the corporate world. As one example, research on executive compensation consistently shows a connection between the size of the firm and CEO pay, an effect much larger than the relationship between pay and performance. One meta-analysis of chief executive compensation found that firm size accounted for more than 40 percent of the variation in pay while performance accounted for less than 5 percent.[3] The positive association between firm size—the amount of resources controlled by the CEO—and pay results in efforts to expand the size of the pot regardless of the financial consequences. Such behavior includes merging with other companies to create a larger entity, even though studies consistently show that the vast majority of mergers destroy shareholder value. The relationship between organizational size and pay extends down into the employee ranks and holds for other organizations such as universities and other nonprofits as well.

Resources are great because once you have them, maintaining power becomes a self-reinforcing process. CEOs of larger companies with more resources can afford to hire high-priced compensation consultants who, big surprise, recommend pay policies that favor the CEOs who hired them. People with money or with control over organizational money get appointed to various for-profit and nonprofit boards where they are in contact with others who have business and investment ideas and social and political influence. That access gives them even more money and resource control as they obtain information and opportunities to get involved with other organizations in powerful roles and meet additional important people. Or they get asked to serve on advisory committees or they become members of elite organizations like the Council on Foreign Relations or the World Economic Forum where they are privy to information and relationships that further build their power and reputation. Furthermore, the best, most talented people want to work with those with the most power and resources, so those with access to important resources have advantages in hiring precisely the sorts of smart, hard-working individuals who can further their success. It's an old but accurate and important story: power and resources beget more power and resources. Your task is to figure out how to break into the circle.

There are two simple but important implications of resources as a source of power. The first is that in choosing among jobs, choose positions that have greater direct resource control of more budget or staff. That generally means preferring line to staff positions, since line positions typically control more staff hiring and more budgetary authority. At first glance, the examples of Zia Yusuf at SAP and the finance function at Ford Motor Company would seem to belie this advice. But finance at Ford controlled the process for allocating capital to the plants and for new product development, and it also controlled the performance evaluation process that determined people's salaries and promotions. And the strategy group at SAP was involved in many if not most major strategic decisions at the company, which, along with the imprimatur of analytical neutrality, gave that group substantial influence over consequential organizational choices. Moreover, Yusuf moved from the strategy group to the ecosystem group and described his position to me referencing the amount of revenues it was responsible for bringing in.

Most headhunters will tell you that when they seek candidates for senior general management positions, including the CEO job, they look to people who have had responsibility running operations, and the larger the division or operation the potential candidate has run, the better, other things being equal. Job analyses such as the Hay system used to determine salary ranges consider the number of direct and indirect reports you have, as well as the amount of budget you can spend without higher-level authorization, as measures of your responsibility and consequently the economic value of your job. Getting control of resources is an important step on your path to power.

The second straightforward implication is that your power comes in large measure from the position you hold and the resources and other things you control as a consequence of holding that position. It is easy for people, motivated by self-enhancement, to believe that the deference and flattery of others is due to their inherent intelligence, experience, and charm. This may be the case, but not often. When you retire or otherwise leave a position in which you once had control over substantial amounts of resources, people will pay you much less heed and give you less attention.

I had lunch with a very senior managing partner at a venture capital firm as she was stepping down from the firm to spend more time with her family following a long and successful career in that company. She commented that once she announced her retirement, not only did her colleagues behave differently toward her, no longer inviting her to meetings and seeking her advice as often, but her time was less in demand by colleagues in the high-technology and venture capital communities more generally. Her wisdom and experience hadn't changed—the only difference was her soon-to-be-diminished control over investment resources and positions in the venture capital firm. The loss of personal importance and power that occurs when you leave a position with substantial resource control is why, as Jeffrey Sonnenfeld documented in his book *The Hero's Farewell*, many CEOs who have enjoyed a lot of fawning attention because of their position have great trouble stepping down from that role.[4]

"But," you may say, "I'm just starting out," or "I'm mired in some midlevel job," or "I'm involved in a serious competition for promotion to a position of more influence. If I had control over lots of jobs and budget, I wouldn't need to read about how to get power—I would already have it!" True enough. But there are numerous examples of people who have made something out of almost nothing. They understood that building a power base is a process of accumulating leverage and resource control little by little over time. It's important to be able to see or even create opportunities that others may miss—and even more important to have the patience and persistence to follow through on those opportunities.

CREATING SOMETHING OUT OF ALMOST NOTHING

It would be nice to be Sergey Brin or Larry Page, cofounders of Google, or Bill Gates of Microsoft. As they move through venues like the World Economic Forum, they are surrounded not just by security staff but by people who want to meet them and get close to them and the organizations they lead. But you can begin from where you are. In fact, one of the big mistakes I see people make is to think that they can't build a resource base from their current position—they need to be higher up. Getting to higher-level positions is easier and more likely if you build a power base, and it is never impossible or too soon or too late to begin.

A resource is anything people want or need—money, a job, information, social support and friendship, help in doing their job. There are always opportunities to provide these things to others whose support you want. Helping people out in almost any fashion engages the norm of reciprocity—the powerful, almost universal behavioral principle that favors must be repaid. But people do not precisely calculate how much value they have received from another and therefore what they owe in return. Instead, helping others generates a more generalized obligation to return the favor, and as a consequence, doing even small things can produce a comparatively large payoff.

Provide Attention and Support

Sometimes building a relationship so that others will help you requires nothing more than being polite and listening. One of the most amazing things about Willie Brown's rise to power in the California Assembly was that he originally got the job because of the support of numerous conservative Republican legislators who were elected after a tax-cutting initiative and swept into power with President Ronald Reagan. Brown received this support even though he was best known for promoting legislation to relax the penalties for possessing small amounts of marijuana and decriminalizing homosexual activity. The source of the bond: when conservative Republican legislators got together for lunch, they talked about how Brown, at the time the chairman of a powerful committee, treated them fairly, gave them a chance to speak, listened to their points, and occasionally even agreed with them.[5] Being nice to people is effective because people find it difficult to fight with those who are being polite and courteous.

Small things can matter a lot—attending birthday parties, funerals, going to lunch with people whose help you want, visiting them or their family members when they are ill. Senator Ted Kennedy was an unabashed liberal who worked diligently during his 47 years in the U.S. Senate to promote bills and causes he believed in. His ability to get things done and the number of friends he had even among conservative Republicans came from his skill and assiduousness at being friendly, listening, and spending time with others at events that were important to them. So here's some simple and practical advice: most people like to talk about themselves—give them the opportunity to do so. Being a good listener and asking questions about others is a simple but effective way to use a resource everyone has—time and attention—to build power. And here's some more advice: if you don't have much power, you probably have time. Use that time to befriend others and go to events that are important to them.

Do Small but Important Tasks

People appreciate help with doing some aspect of their job, and they particularly appreciate assistance with tasks that they find boring or mundane—precisely the kinds of tasks great for beginning to build a power base. When Frank Stanton, later to become president of CBS and a major figure in the broadcasting industry, arrived at the company in October 1935 as a 27-year-old PhD from Ohio State University, he joined a research department of two people. Although he didn't have control over many resources, he didn't have a lot of competition, either. Seven years later, Stanton was named a vice president of CBS in charge of a research department that had grown to 100 people; he was also in charge of advertising, sales promotion, public relations, building construction, operations and maintenance, and overseeing the seven company-owned radio stations.[6]

Sally Bedell Smith described Stanton's rise to power in her book on William Paley and CBS. His strategy? Making himself indispensable by working as hard as he could to find as much information as possible about any and every topic of possible interest to senior CBS management—such as who listened to various radio programs and why, who owned buildings where CBS wanted office space, demographic information on various media markets, essentially any data that might be useful. In many instances, these data were sitting around at CBS waiting to be compiled or came through surveys that anyone could have done—but no one had bothered to compile the data, do the survey, or check public records to see who owned a particular building that CBS might want to buy or lease for one of its radio stations. And Stanton was not above using artifice to impress his superiors. He noted, "Every time management would ask me a question, if I didn't know it, I would fake it to a certain extent, and then run like hell down the back stairs and get the *World Almanac*. . . . At that time I had more information than I think most agencies had on Madison Avenue, because I kept this thing on my desk."[7]

Taking on small tasks can provide you with power because people are often lazy or uninterested in seemingly small, unimportant activities. Therefore, if you take the initiative to do a relatively minor task and do it extremely well, it's unlikely that anyone is going to challenge you for the opportunity. Meanwhile, these apparently minor tasks can become important sources of power.

Michael was graduating from business school in a year and had already taken a job with a hedge fund. The arrangement was that he would work full-time over the summer, be in touch with the firm during the last year of his studies, and then go to work full-time upon graduation. Michael was one of six people who worked at the hedge fund that summer, and he had a big disadvantage compared to the other five: they had completed their degrees and would be staying on when the summer ended. Michael saw the managing partner's attention naturally shift to the new full-time employees. Once back in school, he decided to nevertheless try and build a power base at the fund. First, he visited the office regularly, informally meeting people. This helped him overcome the "out of sight, out of mind" phenomenon and use the mere exposure effect to his advantage. Then he took charge of recruiting junior analysts. In professional service firms, recruiting analysts—junior people who will probably return to school in a couple of years to get another degree and who do much of the grunt work—is mostly viewed as a necessary evil. The hiring process takes time and thus diverts people from their "real" jobs—and the people hired are going to be just cycling through the firm anyway.

When Michael got a "broadcast to everyone" e-mail from the head of the firm about organizing a day of interviews for finalists for the analyst positions, he immediately responded that since he was in school, he had more free time than the full-time employees and would happily take responsibility for coordinating the day. He proceeded to organize the recruiting logistics, including coordinating travel schedules, developing interview schedules with the partners, and organizing a private dinner where he sat himself at the center of the table. This initiative got Michael at the hub of all the recruiting communications, caused him to be much more in touch with senior partners, including the head of the firm, and built his reputation as someone who was willing to help out even when he didn't have to (because he was still a student). All of the analysts who were hired knew him as the point person for analyst recruiting, and associated him with their employment success. Thus, even before joining the firm full-time, Michael had burnished his reputation and recruited allies.

When Karen joined a large Internet services company with a number of well-known consumer brands, her background was in investment banking and venture capital. She needed to build a power base in an organization that was much more technology- and marketing-oriented than where she had previously worked. Avoiding her boss's advice to not waste her time on "small" projects, that's precisely what she did in an effort to learn about all of the company's businesses. She organized summits and invited important outside companies that her firm's businesses wanted to get to know to come and make presentations. She also invited prominent outside people who would be of interest to managers throughout the company. Through these activities, she got to know many outside businesses and the people in them. She also made contacts inside her own organization as she solicited ideas about what would be interesting to the brands inside her company.

Build a Resource Base Inside and Outside Your Organization

When I first met Dan more than 20 years ago, he was the head of labor relations for a private university. But he had big ambitions—he wanted to become a university president. Although he had a PhD and had published some articles on higher education, a position in labor relations or even human resources was clearly not an obvious launching pad for a senior academic administrative post. Dan knew he needed to move out of labor relations into other administrative roles such as provost if he wanted to fulfill his dreams. The question was how to leverage his current role to acquire the resources that would be useful to building his power base.

Like most people with professional jobs, he was a member of a job-related professional association, the College and University Personnel Association (CUPA). That association, like most, had an annual meeting with speakers and exhibitors. Dan volunteered to work on those activities, and over time he rose up the association's ranks, first becoming vice president of research, responsible for the association's programs, and later becoming president. In his leadership roles, he met companies selling pension and other human resource products to colleges and universities, invited people whose support he wanted to speak at the meetings (and paid them), and met scores of senior people in academic administration. Eventually he did become provost and is currently a system-wide vice president of research at a large state university. His path to a college presidency now seems assured because he understood how to find and use resources.

Ivan joined a management consulting company as a junior consultant, one of many in this large and prestigious firm. Ivan knew that the firm wanted to get involved in more public-sector and public-policy work. He volunteered to put on a series of seminars for the office, a task that required extra effort since he still had to do his regular consulting. Doing something that the firm valued, he prevailed upon the partners who ran the office to give him a budget to invite people of interest who could help the firm build both contacts and connections in the public sector. Ivan was then in a position to use those resources to cultivate relationships with powerful outside people, who were both flattered to be invited to address such a prestigious firm and grateful for the payments they received.

Leverage Your Association with a Prestigious Institution

If you're in a place that has status, you can use that status to your advantage. The Sloan program at Stanford is a one-year master's management program—sort of an MBA for midcareer executives who attend full-time. Some people are sponsored by their employers, and while sponsorship means that your company has invested a lot in your development, it also means you are away for a year and out of the action. Jim, an operations executive from a large computer manufacturer, used the opportunity presented by the prestige of the program to get the highest performance evaluation from his boss, an "exceptional" rating reserved for just 15 percent of all employees, even though he was not even working at his employer's during the year as he was in school.

In addition to staying in contact with his boss under the guise of sharing his learning, he knew that his boss, let's call him Ken, wanted to have the opportunity to teach a class at a business school. Fortunately, a case on the allocation of overhead costs that used Jim's and Ken's company as the subject was taught in a managerial accounting class. Jim had the perfect opportunity to create resources—to link Ken, who wanted to teach a class in a business school, with the accounting professor, who would be grateful to have someone from the company appear in the class when the company was discussed.

Jim did a great job of convincing Ken that even though he would ask on his behalf and work hard to make the visit happen, there was no guarantee that the professor would want him to help with the class. Jim joked that if he could get Ken a role as a guest speaker in the accounting class, Ken should help Jim get a job working directly for the company's CEO when his time at school was over. Ken replied, "Absolutely." The class came to pass and Jim got his excellent performance rating from a grateful Ken.

There are literally scores of examples like these—instances where people were able to create resources almost out of thin air, and some are quite amazing. In 1971 Klaus Schwab was a 32-year-old Swiss university graduate with doctoral degrees in economics and engineering. He might have followed the conventional academic route of doing research and publishing as a career strategy. Instead, he saw an opportunity to organize a meeting, the European Business Forum, made up of European business leaders concerned with the growing American economic success. Out of that modest beginning came the World Economic Forum, an organization with a staff of more than 100 running meetings all over the world, with Schwab at the head. Its budget is over $100 million per year, his wife and son are on the board and involved in the foundation, and because of his leadership of the forum, Schwab has received six honorary doctoral degrees and a number of lucrative positions on corporate boards of directors.[8] Although journalists, academics, and nonprofit leaders get in free, companies pay dearly—membership in the World Economic Forum costs $39,000, and there is a charge of $20,000 to attend the large annual meeting in Davos, where there are panel discussions by prominent people from the worlds of government, business, and the arts as well as lots of private meetings and dinners. Schwab recognized that global business and political leaders needed a forum to exchange ideas and do business in one convenient place, the media needed access to these people, and everyone needed ideas about the changing economy and social issues. As a former managing director of the WEF commented, "Contacts ultimately mean contracts."[9]

Power accrues to people who control resources that others cannot access. As the examples of the World Economic Forum and, on a less grand scale, Karen's summits at the Internet company illustrate, there are often natural monopolies created by those who move first. The World Economic Forum is a great venue bringing influential people together, but they don't want or need many such places or meetings because they have limited time. Once Karen started her summits, or Ivan began his public–sector, public-policy lectures at the consulting firm, there was no need for others to do so and almost no possibility that a competing effort would get much traction. So, doing what these examples illustrate often works if you are first off the mark. And taking initiative to create resources by finding speakers, organizing meetings, making connections, and creating venues where people can readily meet others, learn interesting things, and do business brings appreciation for your efforts, even as you create the resources to help you on your path to power.

Bringing people together entails your taking on a brokerage role and becoming central in social networks. Networking skills are important and the networks you create are an important resource for creating influence, as we will see in the next chapter.

6

Building Efficient and Effective Social Networks

IN THE 1980S, Heidi Roizen was the CEO of the spreadsheet software company T/Maker and president of the Software Publishers Association. After her company was purchased in the 1990s, Roizen became vice president of worldwide software developer relations at Apple Computer. After leaving Apple, she became a partner at the venture capital firms Softbank and, later, Mobius, serving on boards of high-tech companies and making investment decisions about which companies and technologies to back financially. Nothing unusual about this career in software and high technology, except maybe for the level of success—that is, until you realize that Roizen's bachelor's degree was in creative writing and her master's was in business, not computer science, engineering, or mathematics. Roizen's success was built on her intelligence and business competence combined with her ability to build strategic social relationships—to network—both inside and outside her employers. Her first job following her undergraduate years was editing the company newsletter at Tandem Computer. That was a great starting position as her job required her to interact with people throughout the company, including those at senior levels, who came to know her and appreciate her talents.

The subject of a Harvard Business School case study, Roizen is often used as an example of someone who succeeded on the basis of her networking abilities.[1] Students are often perplexed and even upset that a person could hold senior positions in important software organizations and even lead the major industry group without a technical background. Holding aside Roizen's considerable substantive business skills, people miss the point: some jobs are mostly about networking and *everyone* can benefit from developing more efficient and effective social networks and honing networking skills.

A DEFINITION OF NETWORKING AND NETWORKING SKILLS

If we're going to talk about networking, we better define it and, in that process, describe the behaviors that you might consider doing more frequently. Two German professors, Hans-Georg Wolff and Klaus Moser, offer a good definition of networking: "Behaviors that are aimed at building, maintaining, and using informal relationships that possess the (potential) benefit of facilitating work-related activities of individuals by voluntarily gaining access to resources and maximizing . . . advantages."[2] Their study of more than 200 people in Germany developed some scales of networking behaviors that demonstrate what actions are required. These included:

1. Building internal contacts (e.g., "I use company events to make new contacts.")

2. Maintaining internal contacts (e.g., "I catch up with colleagues from other departments about what they are working on.")
3. Using internal contacts (e.g., "I use my contacts with colleagues in other departments in order to get confidential advice in business matters.")
4. Building external contacts (e.g., "I accept invitations to official functions or festivities out of professional interest.")
5. Maintaining external contacts (e.g., "I ask others to give my regards to business acquaintances outside of our company.")
6. Using external contacts (e.g., "I exchange professional tips and hints with acquaintances from other organizations.")[3]

The networking behaviors they describe entail making some incremental effort to build, maintain, and use social ties with people. The people targeted are not necessarily in your sights if you are focused just on your immediate job and company.

NETWORKING JOBS

Many of the positions Roizen has held, including manager of software developer relations at Apple and venture capitalist, are, at their core, jobs that entail bringing together different parties who would otherwise not be in contact. Venture capital involves bridging the gap between people and institutions who have money to invest and entrepreneurs with business ideas who need capital. The role of the venture capitalist also entails helping start-ups find talent and occasionally business partners to assist in distribution or product development, and an extensive set of contacts is obviously helpful in these tasks. Roizen's job at Apple linked the software development community to a computer company that relied on these developers to build products that improved the usefulness and therefore the marketability of its machines.

In general, jobs high in networking content require bridging separate organizations, brokering deals, and relationship building to influence decision making. When in 1966 Jack Valenti left his position as a White House aide to become head of the Motion Picture Association of America, he could provide political access to the movie studios that needed help staving off censorship and dealing with foreign governments on commercial issues, including the repatriation of funds. At the same time, he could provide an entrée to Hollywood and its enormous fundraising potential for the Democratic Party and Valenti's patron, Lyndon Johnson. When Valenti finally stepped down, he was replaced by the former Kansas congressman and Clinton's agriculture secretary Dan Glickman, another Democratic politician with strong Washington establishment connections.

The Pharmaceutical Research and Manufacturers of America is closer to the Republican Party. PhRMA represents U.S. drug companies, which face numerous political problems ranging from staving off the importation of medicines from Canada to maintaining the right to continue direct-to-consumer advertising of prescription drugs, Consequently, in 2005 it appointed as its head Billy Tauzin from Louisiana, who had served in the House of Representatives from 1980, including serving in the Republican leadership and as chairman of the Energy and Commerce Committee, which has some responsibility for overseeing the drug industry. Tauzin had already been helpful to the drug industry as one of the leaders passing the expansion of Medicare to cover drug costs during the Bush administration.

Networking skills are not just important in the public sector or in brokering transactions across organizational boundaries. Inside companies, the job of project or product manager entails getting disparate groups to cooperate in making information technology projects work and in managing consumer products successfully. There are many leadership tasks where the essence of the work is bringing people and organizational units with different competencies and perspectives together to complete a task or consummate a transaction.

THE ABILITY TO NETWORK IS IMPORTANT IN MOST JOBS

Although your social network—sometimes referred to as social capital—is more or less important depending on the specifics of your job, the evidence shows that networking is important for people's careers, period. Many studies show that networking is positively related to obtaining good performance evaluations, objective measures of career success such as salary and organizational level, and subjective attitudes assessing career satisfaction.[4] There is a problem with many of these studies in that networking and success are measured at the same time, so it is not clear what is causing what. For instance, it may be that successful people have more social contacts not because the networking produced their success but because others want to be in touch with them to obtain the benefits of their status. Thus, the study by the German academics Wolff and Moser is particularly informative because of its longitudinal design. They measured networking behavior in October 2001 and then did follow-up surveys late in 2002 and 2003 with more than 200 employees in Germany. Their measures of career success were total compensation and a career satisfaction scale. Networking affected career satisfaction, concurrent salary, and salary growth over time, with the two most important networking behaviors being "maintaining external contacts" and "building internal contacts."[5]

Another longitudinal investigation considered the effect of being competent at networking on career advancement. This study, by Italian business school professor Arnaldo Camuffo and some colleagues, sought to assess the effect of MBA education by looking at what happened to people who graduated from a part-time MBA program in Venice. Competencies were assessed by the students themselves, their classroom peers, and objective observers using structured interviews. Competencies did affect career advancement as measured by both salary progress and promotions. The study showed that networking was the second most important competency, following only the use of technology in importance in explaining how well these managers did. This study plus research in Germany and Australia shows that networking is important in business contexts outside of the United States, too.

We have previously discussed at least one mechanism that makes networking important for career success—salience. You can't select what you can't remember, and that includes professional advisers, candidates for leadership positions, or job applicants. The effect of mere exposure on preference and choice is important and well demonstrated. Networking brings you into contact with more people and keeps you in contact with them, thereby increasing the chances that when they need advice, want to find an investment partner, or are thinking of a candidate for some position, they will remember you. Thus, effective networking creates a virtuous cycle. Networking makes you more visible; this visibility increases your power and status; and your heightened power and status then make building and maintaining social contacts easier.

NETWORK SKILLS CAN BE TAUGHT AND LEARNED

Although people have different levels of social skill and different preferences for how they spend their time, there is some evidence that people can learn how to diagnose network structures and become more effective in developing their social capital, with positive effects on their career. University of Chicago professor Ronald Burt worked with the Raytheon Company to develop an executive education program, called the Business Leadership Program, with a strong network component. Raytheon, a large electronics and defense contracting company, faced the challenge of "how to coordinate across the organization silos of its acquired companies and its many product programs."[6] BLP was offered to directors and vice presidents to enhance their ability to get things done across internal organizational boundaries.

Evaluation of training is inherently difficult, because in the real world, people are not randomly selected to attend (expensive) executive development activities. Because more senior and more highly rated and capable people are those typically chosen to participate, the fact that such people typically do better along numerous dimensions is not surprising, nor does it reflect the effects of the program. To deal with this issue, the researchers estimated an equation predicting who would be chosen to attend sessions of the BLP. They then constructed a control group of people predicted to be eligible to attend the program but who had not yet attended, either because of scheduling constraints or because the program had not yet included all of its intended beneficiaries. They also could compare the results of people attending the program to those who didn't attend and who wouldn't be predicted to be eligible to attend.

The people who attended the program and learned how to diagnose and use networks received 35 percent higher scores on their performance evaluations than did the control group. Program attendees had a 43 percent higher likelihood of being promoted subsequently. And people who attended this executive training experience were 42 percent less likely to leave the organization. These results and others that show favorable evaluations of the program and an enhanced ability to diagnose networks provide a demonstration that skills in building social capital can be increased.

SPEND SUFFICIENT TIME

If networking is so helpful for people's job performance and career success, the obvious question is, why do some people devote insufficient time and attention to the activity? One answer is the effort required. Another possibility is that some people find the activity distasteful because they believe it is insincere to build relationships with people for instrumental purposes. And a third answer is that people undervalue the importance of social relationships and overvalue other aspects of job performance in thinking about what produces career success. The evidence shows that networking is important in affecting career progress, and you need to get over qualms about engaging in strategic behavior to advance your career—and that includes who you are in touch with.

Networking actually does not take that much time and effort. It mostly takes thought and planning. Keith Ferrazzi's book title *Never Eat Alone* makes the point. People are going to eat and exercise anyway—why not use that time to expand your network of contacts? When Ferrazzi turned 40, he didn't have one birthday party; he had seven, in seven different cities around the United States, hosted by seven different friends. A birthday celebration became a wonderful opportunity to renew existing social ties and build new ones. Heidi Roizen does what many people do—sends out a holiday letter with some pictures and stories about her family. The difference—she gets about 700 copies printed and mailed. When she took the original in to be reproduced and told the vendor how many she wanted, the response was, "Lady, no one has that many friends." But Roizen recognizes that an occasional note, for instance, at the holidays, or an occasional e-mail or lunch or short phone call keeps you in front of and salient to a set of people who can be helpful to you or may call on you for help.

Ignacio, an Argentinean who graduated from a prestigious U.S. business school, did what many such graduates do—he went to work for the office of a large, high-status management consulting company back in his home country. But he did one thing that distinguished him from many of his colleagues in the firm or, for that matter, in the country: in June 2007, he set up an "MBA en USA" network and website in Argentina with the goal of increasing the number of Argentinean applicants and students in top U.S. schools—the institutions that supply guaranteed financing for those admitted to the program. In two years, he has recruited almost 400 members, with a 10-person board of directors; made presentations in three universities; and become *the* reference person for Argentineans pursuing U.S. business education opportunities. When he began this network, it consisted of one person, himself. Because he had neither great credentials nor high status, he involved others with high status, including those from his consulting firm and alumni of leading U.S. business schools living and working in Argentina, in his presentations and efforts. The results: Ignacio has become known in his office as a great speaker who is good at coaching others; he has substantially enhanced his visibility and built many more connections not just in Argentina but with the leading consulting firms in the United States; and he is at the center of an expanding network of companies, universities, students, and alumni. Not bad, for a very part-time and inexpensive initiative.

Because networking does entail some effort, you ought to be strategic about your networking activities. Make a list of people you want or need to meet and organizations where some personal connection might be helpful. Work your way down that list, figuring out ways to build social relationships with a wider and more diverse set of individuals. A person I know wanted to build a career in biotech even though he did not have a scientific background or any experience in the industry. He targeted people to meet, asking others to introduce him when possible, followed up after meetings with thank-yous, and provided information and contacts to the people he had met so they would receive value from interacting with him. In a short time, proceeding from a position of little formal power, he developed a large and influential network of contacts in the industry that helped him launch his career in biotechnology.

Another barrier that seems to stand in the way of networking is that people naturally fall into habits, and one habit is interacting with the same set of people all the time. You get comfortable with them, you come to trust them, and it is easier and more pleasant to interact with people you already know than to build relationships with strangers. So go out of your way to meet new people. Katie works at an executive recruiting company. Executive recruiting assignments come, in part, from the human resources department. To build a network of HR managers and to meet more people to help her in her job, Katie organized short seminars in which participants would read and listen to and then discuss ideas from thought leaders in managing people. Her very first meeting was a big success, with lots of participants, a lively discussion, and the creation of an ongoing forum that will be very useful for Katie in her current job and in building relationships useful to her future career. Once again, not that much work. All that was required was some initiative and being willing to reach out to strangers—to get out of one's comfort zone.

NETWORK WITH THE RIGHT PEOPLE

Not everyone is going to be equally useful to you and you should account for that fact in how you spend your networking time. In the early 1970s, sociologist Mark Granovetter conducted a classic study in Boston about how people find jobs.[7] Two of his findings are scarcely surprising. Granovetter found that social ties were important in the job-finding process and the more one used social ties, as contrasted with less personal mechanisms such as formal applications, the better the job the individual found. He also found that the process used to fill jobs differed by job type: managerial jobs were more likely to be found through personal contacts rather than through more formal means such as responding to newspaper advertisements or making a formal application, whereas lower-level or even well-paid but technical jobs tended to rely on more formal means of hiring. What was surprising was the type of social ties that mattered in the job-finding process: weak ties.[8] Strong ties are typically with family, friends, and close associates at work and involve frequent interaction. Weak ties are with casual acquaintances, people you hardly know and with whom you have fairly infrequent interactions.

The intuition behind the idea that weak ties are frequently more useful than stronger ones is that the people you are closest to, your close friends and family, are more likely to travel in the same circles, be close to each other also, and therefore provide redundant information. Weak ties, by contrast, are more likely to link you to new people, organizations, and information, providing new information and contacts. For weak ties to be useful, however, two things must be true: casual acquaintances must be *able* to link you into diverse networks and they must be *willing* to do so. Frank Flynn's research on asking, reviewed earlier, shows that people are likely to comply with small requests, even from perfect strangers. Asking someone if she knows about a job opening or about the particulars of a company or job will almost always produce information even if the relationship is fairly weak and casual. Providing any information lets the provider feel good about herself and is consistent with social norms of benevolence.

Consequently, an optimal networking strategy is to know a lot of different people from different circles, have multiple organizational affiliations in a variety of different industries and sectors that are geographically dispersed, but not necessarily to know the people well or to develop close ties with them. This advice does not imply that the relationships aren't genuine, just that the social ties are not so close that it becomes difficult, because of time constraints, to build as large and diverse a set of contacts. This advice is not inconsistent with the advice in chapter 2 to focus your efforts. You *are* focusing your efforts on building social ties that can be helpful—it's just that such ties should be as many and as diverse as possible and useful for your obtaining power.

It's also the case that both organizations and people are known by the company they keep—so it behooves you to associate with high-status people. This simple fact has interesting consequences, for it means that you cannot readily move down the status food chain to take advantage of opportunities if you don't want to risk losing your own status. Joel Podolny, a sociologist who was former dean of the business school at Yale and currently heads Apple University, asked an interesting question about investment banks: because high-status investment banks have cost advantages deriving from their status (as just one example, they can raise money at lower cost than lower-status and presumably riskier banks), why don't they dominate the market for both equity and debt securities, over time taking away most of the business from their lower-status competitors? His answer, from an empirical study of the investment banking industry, is that higher-status banks are constrained from "moving down" and capturing more of the market because in doing so, they would have to associate with lower-status securities issuers and, as a result, lose at least some of their status advantage.[9]

One way to acquire status is to start an organization that is so compelling in its mission that high-status people join the project and you build both status and a network of important relationships. That's what Philippe did in Mexico. Mexico is a highly stratified society and many of the people who do manual and unskilled labor have little education. Because of these educational deficits, people cannot get better jobs and are consigned to a life of poverty. Philippe started a foundation to educate unskilled workers, mostly in the construction industry, which is a large employer of unskilled and semiskilled labor. The social importance of such an activity attracted the most prestigious professor from his engineering school and a board that consisted of some of the top social entrepreneurs in Mexico. Because the foundation's work focused mostly on construction workers, Philippe got access to the best people in the real estate industry, and these social contacts have opened numerous real estate career opportunities as well as built a large and influential network of people from both the private sector and the government. As Philippe explained, he was both doing good and doing well.

The fact that status hierarchies are stable means not only that it is difficult to move up but also that it is difficult to move down. Once you have achieved power and status through the network of your relationships, you will be able to maintain your influence without expending as much time and effort.

You can monetize your high-status network. I have a friend who is a well-known executive coach. A while ago he was asked to submit a proposal to coach a certain CEO. His price: $250,000. The CEO told my friend that he had received a proposal from another coach for $25,000. My colleague replied that he knew and had trained the person supplying the lower-priced bid, and he thought the quality of this other coach's work was exceptional. Why should the CEO choose him, at 10 times the price? Because, the executive coach noted, he was having dinner with the CEOs of several large, prominent companies (whom he named). Could the other coach provide such access and a similar sort of experience? He got the business. People like to bask in reflected glory and associate with high-status others. Versions of this story in different contexts happen every day.

CREATE A STRONG STRUCTURAL POSITION

Power and influence come not just from the extensiveness of your network and the status of its members, but also from your structural position within that network. Centrality matters. Research shows that centrality within both advice and friendship networks produces many benefits, including access to information, positive performance ratings, and higher pay.[10] One study at a newspaper publishing company found that "being in a position to control communications within the department is particularly important to being promoted."[11] These results contradict the idea from human capital economics that it is only individual human capital—education, years of experience, and intelligence—that matters for people's careers, as well as the commonly held belief that job performance determines career outcomes. Network position matters a great deal for your influence and career trajectory.

If virtually all information and communication flows through you, you will have more power. One source of your power will be your control over the flow of information, and another is that people attribute power to individuals who are central. You can assess your centrality by asking what proportion of others in your work, for instance, nominate you as someone they go to for advice or help with their own work. Another way of assessing centrality is to ask what proportion of all communication links flow through you.

If you are sensitive to the importance of centrality, you can do things and make choices that increase your structural centrality. When Henry Kissinger became President Nixon's national security adviser, he made sure that communication about foreign policy issues flowed only through him. He appointed a staff of young, talented, nonpartisan foreign policy analysts to work with him. This move gave Kissinger a good image with the press because it appeared that he was just interested in obtaining talent. But because the Nixon loyalists were uncomfortable interacting with people so different from themselves, and the staffers were estranged from the Nixon people, Kissinger was at the center of the flow of information between the NSC staff and the White House.[12]

One way of building centrality is through physical location. A person I know took a job at a Silicon Valley venture capital firm as an analyst, a low-level position. When he started at the company, he had two options as to where to locate his desk: a large cubicle in the corner that was quiet but outside of the flow of traffic, or a small workstation outside the named partner's office, which had no walls and no privacy. Almost by chance he chose the location outside the partner's office. Because of his location, he knew what was going on in the firm and interacted with the numerous people coming by to see the partners. As he noted, "Within just a few months of starting, at the weekly Monday morning all-hands meeting, nearly every question began to be pointed in my direction. The net of it was that I was the first analyst in the firm's history to be invited for a position after graduation."

Centrality provides power within a network, but it is also important to have power through connections across diverse networks. Most people tend to associate with those similar to themselves—a tendency called homophily. Consequently, groups that might gain from interacting with other groups don't do so, because group members are more comfortable associating with the people in their own group. This natural tendency to associate with those close to us creates an opportunity for profiting by building brokerage relations—or, to use the terminology of University of Chicago business school professor Ronald Burt, by bridging the structural holes that exist between noninteracting groups.[13] The fundamental idea is deceptively simple: by connecting units that are tightly linked internally but socially isolated from each other, the person doing the connecting can profit by being the intermediary who facilitates interactions between the two groups.

Consider the case of Kenji, working in a large Japanese electric utility. Kenji, with an undergraduate degree in nuclear engineering and an MBA, speaks both English and Japanese. When he returned to his company following his postgraduate education, he went into international business development, where he worked building and acquiring power plants all over the world. Even though Kenji had a low job title and little seniority in a culture where seniority was valued, he was in a great position to broker relations between important departments—engineering and business development. He was the only MBA with a degree in nuclear engineering and the only nuclear engineer with a business degree. He told me, "Right now I am in a unique position, where critical information related to business development in the global nuclear power sector flows through me since I am the only one who is well connected to both the international division and the nuclear division." Because Kenji's English skills were better than many of his colleagues', he was invited to participate in telephone calls with some of the most senior people on international development projects to help with the translation. Because of his access to information from brokering relations between engineering and the international business development people and the insights he acquired from his participation in many calls about projects, senior managers began consulting Kenji on a number of important topics.

Although it is too soon to tell how things will work out for Kenji on his path to power, the research strongly suggests that occupying brokerage positions—filling structural holes—is advantageous for one's career. Social capital, measured by how many structural holes an individual bridges, positively affects promotions, salary, and organizational level attained. Other research discovered that social capital also increases an individual's returns to personal attributes such as education and experience—education and years of work have a greater effect on the salaries of individuals who are rich in social capital.

One other research finding is important for the building of social networks. People sometimes believe that if they are connected to someone *else* who occupies a good brokerage position, they can achieve almost as much benefit. However, Ron Burt found that this intuition was not accurate. People even one step removed from the person doing the brokerage enjoyed virtually no benefit.[14] To return to the Japanese electric utility example, while Kenji enjoys many benefits from his network position, someone who is connected to Kenji profits very little. You have to do the network "work" yourself if you want to accrue the benefits.

RECOGNIZE THE TRADE-OFFS

You can overdo any strategy, including networking. Bridging structural holes and being in the center of many social ties requires time. You should decide how much time to spend and your specific networking strategy based on the extent to which your job requires building social relationships for you to be successful—a topic already considered in this chapter—and the type of knowledge most useful in your job.

The research literature typically divides knowledge into two types: explicit, codified knowledge such as that represented in diagrams, formulas, or "recipes" for task performance; and implicit, tacit knowledge such as that possessed by good clinicians who understand not only the scientific basis of job performance but also know, based on their experience, when to do what. University of California–Berkeley professor Morten Hansen has studied what types of social networks are most useful given different types of product development efforts. When you need to access tacit knowledge, a smaller network of close ties is important because it takes close relationships to get people to spend the time to explain their tacit expertise. When the project requires locating explicit knowledge that can be readily transferred once you find it, a large network of weak ties provides greater benefit.

Hansen also distinguishes between product development efforts that entail doing very new things, where the type of information required was almost impossible to specify in advance, and product development projects using existing competencies and information that could mostly be anticipated. Hansen and his colleagues found that a network rich in weak ties was most useful for doing new things because a large network of weak ties permitted product development teams to explore broadly for information that was helpful. In contrast, when the product development effort leveraged well-established existing competencies, a smaller network got the product out the door more quickly.[15] Hansen's research empirically demonstrates what many people intuitively know: a large network of weak ties is good for innovation and locating information, while a small network of strong ties is better suited to exploiting existing knowledge and transferring tacit skills.

Both in the process of creating social ties and once you have created a network, your ability to create and leverage social ties depends in part on how others perceive you. And those perceptions depend in part on your ability to speak and act with power. That is the focus of chapter 7.

7

Acting and Speaking with Power

IN NOVEMBER 1986, U.S. Marine Corps Lt. Colonel Oliver North was fired by President Ronald Reagan from his position at the National Security Council for his involvement in the Iran-contra scandal. Iran-contra involved selling weapons, via intermediaries, to Iran and using the funds from these sales to finance the Nicaraguan resistance then trying to overthrow a left-leaning government. After testifying before Congress in the summer of 1987, North was indicted the following year on 16 felony counts, including accepting illegal gratuities, aiding and abetting the obstruction of a congressional inquiry, and destroying documents and evidence. Although he was convicted on three counts, his conviction was overturned on appeal on the basis that jurors had been influenced by the congressional hearings, during which he had been granted immunity for his testimony. During the nationally televised hearings, North admitted that he had shredded documents, lied to Congress, and violated, or at least come exceedingly close to violating, a law prohibiting giving aid to the Nicaraguan resistance.

But Oliver North knew how to act and speak with power. These abilities would produce an amazing effect on his reputation and his subsequent career. North defended himself and his actions by appealing to a higher purpose—protecting American interests, saving American lives, protecting important U.S. intelligence secrets, following the orders of his superiors, and doing what he was told to do as a good Marine lieutenant colonel—in short, being a good soldier. North wore his ribbon-decorated uniform to the hearings, even though he was seldom if ever in uniform at his job at the NSC. He took responsibility for what he did, saying that he was "not embarrassed" about his actions or about appearing to explain them. And he asserted that he had controlled what had occurred, frequently using phrases such as "I told" and "I caused." This phrasing demonstrated that he was not running away from what he had done. Observers watching people who don't deny or run away from their actions naturally presume that the perpetrators don't feel guilty or ashamed, so maybe no one should be too upset. This phrasing also communicated power, that North was in charge rather than a "victim" of circumstance.

Only seven years after this incident, using the celebrity and sympathy that his testimony created, Oliver North ran for the U.S. Senate from Virginia and lost by just 3 percent of the vote to the incumbent, Charles Robb. During that campaign, North raised some $16 million through direct-mail solicitations, making him the top recipient of direct-mail political funds in the United States that year. Today, North, author of several books, is a television commentator on Fox News and a well-paid speaker at both public and private organizations. And even at the time of the hearings, he enjoyed a positive image. The *Wall Street Journal* asked dozens of senior U.S. executives if they would hire Oliver North. "The majority said they would. . . . A poll of the general public reflected the bullishness on Col. North . . . 56 percent of those surveyed said they would hire Col. North; 35 percent said they wouldn't hire him and 9 percent weren't sure."[1]

Donald Kennedy, a biology professor and former commissioner of the Food and Drug Administration, served as president of Stanford University. Kennedy got caught up in a scandal over indirect costs in the early 1990s. Because it is impossible to associate all the costs of running any organization, for instance, the water and power, police and fire protection, and infrastructure such as libraries, with specific research projects, research grants have an overhead rate that reflects these costs. That rate is then charged to the government for all contracts. In the case of Stanford and other research universities, the claim was that unallowable charges, for instance, for lobbying, liquor, a yacht used by the sailing club, silverware and furniture for the president's house, and other items, had been included in the cost pools used for calculating the overhead rate.[2] After several years of investigation, litigation, and audits, the government found no basis for its claim. Stanford agreed to pay just $1.2 million to the government for overcharges for over 18,000 research grants covering the fiscal years from 1981 to 1992 that involved hundreds of millions of dollars in total funds.[3]

After the brouhaha broke, Kennedy, like North, appeared before a congressional investigating committee. Donald Kennedy's performance could not have been more different from North's. North appeared at the witness stand with just his attorney. Kennedy came with a team that included the head of government contracts from the accounting firm Arthur Andersen, the controller and assistant controller from the university, and the chairman of the board of trustees, James Gaither. This coterie of colleagues conveyed the image that Kennedy could not answer the questions on his own. Using long, convoluted sentences full of subordinate clauses, answering questions indirectly, admitting that he was "embarrassed," and looking extremely uncomfortable, Kennedy made a weak impression—he looked guilty. He left his position as Stanford president soon thereafter.

The differences between Oliver North's and Donald Kennedy's presentations may have had little to do with personality or individual style. Kennedy was not only a distinguished scientist but a successful and effective teacher; he had testified in front of Congress numerous times before, and many people watching his testimony who knew him say he seemed like a different person. He came to the hearings prepared, as did North. What differed was how they chose to present themselves, how they decided to act, and the impression they made. Kennedy wanted to express contrition; North chose to convey incredulity—how could he be questioned?—and some righteous anger. As we will see later in this chapter, expressing anger is usually much more effective than expressing sadness, guilt, or remorse in being seen as powerful.

We choose how we will act and talk, and those decisions are consequential for acquiring and holding on to power. Harriet Rubin was, for eleven years, the editor of a line of books called Currency devoted to understanding leadership. During that time she at once occupied a position of leadership and published leaders' autobiographies and books on leadership. Her experience suggested that the secret of leadership was the ability to play a role, to pretend, to be skilled in the theatrical arts.[4] Rubin is right. Differences in the ability to convey power through how we talk, appear, and act matter in our everyday interactions, from seeking a job to attempting to win a vital contract to presenting a company's growth prospects before investment analysts.

In May 2008 I received an e-mail from a director of career management services that reinforced the importance of how we "show up" in our interactions with others for our job prospects. He had received comments from a Sam's Club/Walmart interviewer who had seen some students and commented on their self-presentation:

> There were a couple of students who were very confident in their interviews but more than half seemed slightly uncomfortable. . . . The students who impressed me the most spoke articulately, looked me in the eyes, and could rattle off stories right away. The students who didn't impress me were the ones who stumbled over their words, looked away, and had trouble giving examples of some basic stories.

Although the research literature shows the interview is not a reliable or valid selection mechanism, it is almost universally used. And the impressions people make as they talk to others matter for their likelihood of getting a job offer or a promotion. It may not seem right that we are judged on our "appearance," on how we present ourselves and our ideas. But the world isn't always a just place. To come across effectively, we need to master how to convey power. We need to act, and speak, with power.

Atoosa Rubenstein began as a fashion assistant at *Cosmopolitan* in 1993 and in five years rose to the job of senior fashion editor. Rubenstein, at the instigation of Hearst Magazine president Cathleen Black, came up with the idea for *CosmoGIRL!* and in 1999, at the age of 26, Atoosa became editor-in-chief at the magazine, the youngest person to hold such a position in the more than 100-year history of the Hearst Corporation. Named by Columbia University in 2004 as one of its top 250 alumni of all time and recipient of much recognition, Rubenstein believes that her early success came from projecting an appropriate image.[5] As she told some people writing about her:

> I'm an actress. My chief trait in business is that I'm an actress. I'm not creative but I can really whip it out when I have to. I put on the costumes and play the roles that people need me to play. Bonnie [editor of *Cosmopolitan*] needed me to be very fash-

> ionable. I put on the hair, the clothes; I became exotic. Because of that, I went from being a background player to being on the pages of the magazine. . . . Cathie [Black, president of Hearst Magazines] started sending me to black tie events to represent *Cosmopolitan*.

ACTING WITH POWER

Peter Ueberroth, *Time* magazine's man of the year for his success running the 1984 Los Angeles Olympics and former commissioner of major-league baseball, has a favorite maxim: Authority is 20 percent given, 80 percent taken.[6] Words to live by. If you are going to take power, you need to project confidence, as the case of Oliver North and the Walmart job candidates illustrate. You need to project assurance even if—or maybe particularly if—you aren't sure what you're doing. Andy Grove, a cofounder and former CEO and chairman of the semiconductor company Intel, has appropriate modesty about his (or anyone's) ability to forecast the technological future. In reply to a question at a Silicon Valley forum about how to lead if you aren't sure where you or your company is going, Grove replied:

> Well, part of it is self-discipline and part of it is deception. And the deception becomes reality. Deception in the sense that you pump yourself up and put a better face on things than you start off feeling. But after a while, if you act confident, you become more confident. So the deception becomes less of a deception.[7]

Grove understood the importance of being able to put on a show. As Harriet Rubin noted, "Grove insisted that his brilliant but shy managers attend a seminar they called 'wolf school.' Attendees learned how to lean into a superior's face and shout out an idea or proposal. . . . If they didn't feel fierce, they had to pretend."[8]

Andy Grove understood three important principles about acting with power. First, after a while, what started out being an act becomes less so. Over time, you will become more like you are acting—self-assured, confident, and more strongly convinced of the truth of what you are saying. Attitudes follow behavior, as much research attests. Second, the emotions you express, such as confidence or happiness, influence those around you—emotions are contagious.[9] Walk down an airport corridor and smile, and watch people smile back; change your facial expression to a frown, and you will be met with frowns. A study of emotional contagion and its use in marketing found that when a person smiled, another individual exposed to the smile would be happier and also have a positive attitude toward a product—emotions not only jumped from person to person, but when someone was in a good mood because she had been exposed to someone who was happy, that mood spilled over to other things like items to be purchased.[10] Third, emotions and behaviors become self-reinforcing: if you smile and then others smile, you are more likely to feel happy and smile. This reflexive quality in human interaction means that a mood or feeling, once generated, is likely to be quite stable. Grove may have had to act confident and knowledgeable at first, but as others "caught" that feeling, it would be reflected back, making Grove himself more confident.

If acting is important as a leadership skill and for acquiring power, it is important to know how to perform. One principle is to act confident. There are others.

BE AWARE OF YOUR AUDIENCE

Gary Loveman, CEO of the casino company Harrah's Entertainment, understands that because many employees may see him only once in a year, he needs to be "on" when he is in front of them. Even in momentary interactions, Loveman must convey that employees work in a company led by caring, engaged people they can trust. Even if he is tired or feeling ill, in public appearances Loveman radiates energy and competitive intensity—and this competitive vitality has helped make Harrah's successful.

You are on stage more than you think, and not just as a senior leader. Morten Hansen, who used to teach at the French business school INSEAD before moving to UC Berkeley, told me that he was sitting in the classroom one day watching some group presentations for his class. He had just come back from a long trip. In addition to watching the groups present at the front of the room, many of the students had been watching him. They noticed that he seemed tired, which they interpreted as not being interested in what the students were doing—and the class let him know. After that experience, Hansen has been much more aware of being on display, even if he is not in front of an audience.

To look engaged in meetings and other interactions, to signal that you care about those around you, put away the BlackBerry, the laptop, the cell phone, and all the other technological gadgets that compete for your time and attention. When you read an e-mail while you are talking to someone or in a meeting, the message you send is clear: I have other things to do that are way more important than paying attention to you. Some people will tell you that in today's high-technology, attention-deficit-disordered world, people expect such displays of rudeness. People, having witnessed multitasking in their interactions, may expect inattention as the norm. So when you do what IESE business school professor Nuria Chinchilla does when meeting with someone—turn the cell phone off and put it away—the effect is powerful. When you do what the late Jack Valenti of the Motion Picture Association of America did—call people on the phone or go meet with them in person—you have much more influence and will be much more memorable—and powerful.

DISPLAY ANGER INSTEAD OF SADNESS OR REMORSE

Barack Obama's chief of staff, former Illinois congressman Rahm Emanuel, is known for his temper. In his *New Yorker* portrait of Emanuel, Ryan Lizza observes:

> Emanuel seems to employ his volcanic moments for effect, intimidating opponents . . . but never quite losing himself in the midst of battle. . . . Greenberg [an old friend] argues that Emanuel's antics have been integral to his success. "Understand that the caricature and the mythology have always been helpful," Greenberg said. "Sending the [dead] fish to the pollster that he thought had failed sent a message about how public he can be about his displeasure, and showed that he's willing to step beyond the normal bounds, that he's willing to be outrageous and he doesn't suffer fools."[11]

What works for Emanuel may work even better for you: you may not have a job with a lot of power; Emanuel does, and people know it. Sometimes you will work with peers and colleagues of about equal rank whom you want to influence. Sometimes your actual power will be ambiguous. In such situations, displaying anger is useful.

Research shows that people who express anger are seen "as dominant, strong, competent, and smart," although they are also, of course, seen as less nice and warm.[12] Social psychologist Larissa Tiedens has conducted research on the relationship between expressed emotions and perceptions of power. In three studies using vignettes as the stimuli, Tiedens and some colleagues explored people's expectations for emotional expressions by high- and low-status others.[13]

The researchers found that in negative situations, participants believed that high-status people would feel more angry than sad or guilty and that low-status people would feel sad or guilty instead of angry. A second experiment demonstrated that angry people were seen as high-status while sad and guilty people were viewed as low-status.

In another series of experimental studies, Tiedens showed that people actually conferred more status on people who expressed anger rather than sadness. One study had participants watch two video clips from former president Clinton's testimony in the Monica Lewinsky scandal. In one clip he appeared angry, and in the other he hung his head and averted his gaze, typical for someone expressing guilt and remorse. People who viewed the anger clip were significantly more pro-Clinton in their attitudes. They believed it showed he was a person in power compared to those who saw him acting sad. In a second study, to avoid any contamination by preexisting attitudes about Clinton, an anonymous actor played the role of a politician and delivered the identical speech on terrorism, in one instance acting as if he were angry and in the other as if he were sad. Study participants were more likely to say they would vote for the politician in the angry rather than the sad posture. They also thought the angry person would be a better political leader.

In a study Tiedens conducted at a software company, people rated their coworkers on how frequently these individuals exhibited a variety of emotions. People rated coworkers who expressed more anger as better potential role models—people from whom they could learn. In yet another study reported in the same paper, participants assigned a higher-status position and a higher salary to a job candidate who described himself as angry. He was perceived as more competent when expressing anger rather than sadness.[14]

If you express anger, not only do you receive more status and power and appear more competent but others are reluctant to cross you. After all, who wants to be the brunt of anger? No wonder "General George Patton tried to practice his scowl in front of his mirror." Consider what political commentator and former legislative aide Chris Matthews said about Senator Ed Muskie of Maine: "Why tangle with the guy? Why ruin your day? A bad temper is a very powerful political tool because most people don't like confrontation."[15]

Does this recommendation to display anger hold across gender and cultures, or is it a behavior that is particularly effective for American males? According to a survey of some 1,200 senior executives conducted by Catalyst, an organization aimed at helping women advance in the workplace, women who acted more assertively and displayed ambition were seen as too tough and unfeminine, although they were also seen as more competent.[16] Some experimental research supports the view that women may benefit less than men by acting angry. Social psychologists Victoria Brescoll and Eric Uhlmann conducted three studies examining the interaction between emotional expression and gender on the conferral of status. They found that both men and women conferred less status on angry female professionals than on angry male professionals, and angry women, regardless of their presumed rank, received less status when they expressed anger than when they did not.[17] Another set of studies supported the stereotype that men are expected to be more dominant and women more affiliative, so men are expected to show more anger than women.[18]

When I asked Larissa Tiedens about this issue, she told me that she has not found gender differences in any of the studies she and her colleagues have run, although they have looked for them. She also noted that when women get angry, they often don't express their anger the way men do. Women frequently show their anger in more "submissive" ways—such as folding their arms in front of their chest, raising the pitch of their voices, or even crying. Tiedens maintains that forceful displays of anger that put the other person on the defensive are effective for both women and men.

At the moment, the question of gender differences in the effectiveness of expressing anger remains open. But if you have to choose between being seen as likable and fitting in on the one hand or appearing competent albeit abrasive on the other, choose competence. Self-deprecating comments and humor work *only* if you have already established your competence. As the former Israeli prime minister Golda Meir said, "Don't be so humble; you're not that great."[19]

WATCH YOUR POSTURE AND GESTURES

There is evidence that taller people earn more and are more likely to occupy high power positions.[20] There is also ample evidence that physical attractiveness results in higher earnings.[21] You don't need to wear lifts in your shoes or get plastic surgery to act on these findings. You can do a lot with what you have. You can dress up, an act that conveys power and status—to look like you belong in the position to which you aspire. You can do things with your hair, the style of the clothes you wear, and colors to enhance your appearance. Get professional help in enhancing the influence you convey by how you look.

And beyond clothes and hairstyle, you can "move with power." When Bill English, actor, director, and cofounder of the San Francisco Playhouse, teaches people how to "act with power," he often critiques their posture. When people are nervous or uncomfortable, they often shrink in on themselves, caving in their chest, folding their arms around them, going into what are essentially defensive postures. Bad idea if you want to project power. Everyone can stand up straight rather than slouching, and can thrust their chest and pelvis forward rather than curling in on themselves. Moving forward and toward someone is a gesture that connotes power, as does standing closer to others, while turning your back or retreating signals the opposite.

Gestures can also connote power and decisiveness, or their opposite. Moving your hands in a circle or waving your arms diminishes how powerful you appear. Gestures should be short and forceful, not long and circular. Looking people directly in the eye connotes not only power but also honesty and directness, while looking down is a signal of diffidence. Looking away causes others to think you are dissembling.

USE MEMORY TO ACCESS THE DESIRED EMOTION

Sometimes you will be called upon to display emotions you don't feel—confidence when you are uncertain, anger when you are fearful, and compassion and empathy when you may be feeling impatience or disappointment. To display the emotion you need to show, go within yourself to a time and event when you *did* feel the emotion you need to project at that moment. Recalling that event will bring back the associated feelings, which you can then display. In that sense, acting is not inauthentic, displaying something you do not really feel. Rather, acting, including acting with power, entails tapping into your authentic feelings but just from a different time and place.

Many situations require that you display more than one emotion at a time. In taking on a new, powerful role, you will want to project confidence and the sense that you know what you are doing so that those around you will be inspired to follow your lead. But at the same time, you may want to convey humility and affiliation with those around you so that they will not see you as arrogant but will be motivated to offer their assistance. Displaying several sometimes conflicting emotions at once requires more skill and practice, but the fundamental principle remains the same: recall events or people who trigger each of the emotions you want to show, at the same time.

SET THE STAGE AND MANAGE THE CONTEXT

Performers do their thing "on stage," and the setting that you create for yourself has a lot to do with your ability to command respect. We are often inattentive to how a physical setting can help or hinder our aims.

Settings can convey power and status. A partner at a prominent San Francisco law firm told me, when I inquired about why the firm had spent so much on its lavish location and even more expensive interior furnishings, that people weren't going to pay high hourly rates for someone who worked at a cheap metal desk. The Oval Office of the president of the United States is particularly powerful in this regard, and many presidents have used its iconic status to influence others whose support they needed by bringing them into the historic setting, subtly reminding them of the pomp and importance of the presidency.

When Peter Ueberroth was baseball commissioner, he set about establishing his power over a set of wealthy, independent individuals who were, collectively, his boss. He helped build his influence by managing the physical context of the owners' meetings. Ueberroth doubled the number of meetings to four per year and insisted that the owners personally attend rather than sending a stand-in. He set the meetings in sites the owners were not familiar with. He used classroom-style, tiered meeting rooms, which focused the owners' attention on the front of the room and, because of the seating arrangement, subtly reminded the owners that Ueberroth was the "teacher" and they were "students" under his direction. Although Ueberroth obviously benefited from his reputation resulting from his success with the 1984 Los Angeles Olympics, the physical arrangements helped him establish and exercise his authority over the owners.[22]

TAKE YOUR TIME IN RESPONDING

One reason people don't come across as forcefully or effectively as they might is that they begin to speak while they are flustered or unsure of the situation. In training people to act with power, Bill English of the San Francisco Playhouse puts them in a scenario in which they have just taken over as CEO of a company, say, a pharmaceutical manufacturer, when the previous CEO has left under a cloud. The company had to recall a product because of safety issues. Employees are embarrassed and fearful for their jobs. English asks people to give a speech to the employees to instill confidence, motivate them, and get them to accept the protagonist as their leader.

The people who do best at this task are those who, even though they are in front of an audience and feel pressure to fill the dead air, collect their thoughts and themselves, pausing often for what seems like a long time before beginning to speak. They know what they are going to say, have thought consciously about how they are going to use the space and their movements to inspire confidence, and have gotten their nervousness under control so they can project influence. Obviously it is always desirable to be prepared to make an important presentation. But there will be times when a question or comment blindsides you or when you find yourself in a situation without preparation. Breathe and take time to collect yourself—you will be much more effective than if you just rush into the situation.

SPEAKING POWERFULLY

The language people use and how they construct presentations and arguments help determine their power. Great orators move masses—Martin Luther King Jr.'s famous "I Have a Dream" speech and the speeches of Barack Obama in his campaign for the presidency being two notable examples. But power gets created in private interactions and small meetings, not just on a huge stage. There are some well-established principles that can help you subtly obtain more influence as you speak with power.

INTERRUPTION

One source of power in every interaction is interruption. Those with power interrupt, those with less power get interrupted. In conversation, interrupting others, although not polite, can indicate power and be an effective power move, something noted by scholars in a field called conversation analysis. Men interrupt others more frequently than women, and doctors seldom listen to their patients for very long without interrupting. In each instance, patterns of conversation reinforce differences in power and status derived from other sources such as general social expectations and expert authority.

Watching the Oliver North and Donald Kennedy hearings illustrates this phenomenon. North on one occasion stops an interrogator's anticipated interruption by holding up his finger and saying, "Let me finish." He refuses to be interrupted and in several other instances talks over the lawyers and legislators questioning him. By contrast, at one point Donald Kennedy requests permission to continue speaking, asking, "Can I continue?" and thanks the congressman when permission is granted.

CONTEST THE PREMISES OF THE DISCUSSION

In analyzing the Watergate hearings, sociologists Harvey Molotch and Deidre Boden note that there are three faces of power. The first is the ability to win in direct contests: Whose point of view prevails? The second is more subtle: Who sets the agenda, and in the process determines whether a specific issue will even be discussed or debated at all? And the third form of power is more subtle still: Who determines the rules for interpersonal interactions through which agendas and outcomes are determined?[23]

For interaction to take place at all, we must share at least some common understandings or we could never proceed. Molotch and Boden discovered that one way in which someone in a dominant position can leverage that influence is to question and challenge the basic assumptions that underlie another person's account. This is also a strategy to obtain power in an interaction.

For example, John Dean, counsel to President Nixon, was the organizer of the cover-up that followed the Watergate break-in and the arrest of its perpetrators. In the hearings, he had the best opportunity to cast a damaging light on the president's involvement because he had firsthand knowledge of what Nixon had said and done. Republican senator Edward Gurney attempted to damage Dean's credibility by denying him access to such typical conversational conventions as assertion of motive or recollection of impressions, insisting instead that Dean stick to "the facts." Dean remarked that the president had expressed appreciation of what he'd been doing, which implicitly meant that the president had to know what he had been doing about the cover-up—after all, how can you thank someone if you don't know what you are thanking them for? Gurney challenged this interpretation, noting that there was never any explicit conversation about the cover-up particulars.

I have observed similar ploys used to gain power in business meetings. In most companies, the strategy and market dynamics are taken for granted. If someone challenges these assumptions—such as how the company is competing, how it is measuring success, what the strategy is, who the real competitors are now and in the future—this can be a very potent power play. The questions and challenges focus attention on the person bringing the seemingly commonsense issues to the fore and causes people to have to renegotiate things that were always implicitly assumed.

PERSUASIVE LANGUAGE

Language that influences is able to create powerful images and emotions that overwhelm reason.[24] Such language is evocative, specific, and filled with strong language and visual imagery. When Winston Churchill became prime minister of Britain in May 1940, he was 65 years old and had been out of power for 10 years. Churchill and Britain faced uncertain prospects and terrible travails in the war with Germany. His oratory helped build his power and image, rally the country, and turn the tide of the war:

> You ask, what is our policy? I will say: It is to wage war, by sea, land and air, with all our might and with all the strength that God can give us. . . . You ask, what is our aim? I can answer in one word: It is victory, victory at all costs, victory in spite of all the terror, victory, however long and hard the road may be, for without victory, there is no survival.[25]

Churchill understood the power of language, having once commented, "Words are the only things that last forever."[26] So did Oliver North. When North says during the Iran-contra hearings that he would have offered the Iranians a free trip to Disneyland if that would have gotten the hostages home, you can picture both Disneyland and the hostages. In contrast, Donald Kennedy's testimony about indirect costs was filled with an alphabet soup of references to the various agencies that audit contracts for the government and descriptions of MOUs (memoranda of understanding that set out contract provisions). The sense is that even if there were no technical violations of regulations, he was trying to cower in the protection of legal technicalities rather than confront commonsense understanding of what is right and wrong.

Sociologist and conversation analyst Max Atkinson has analyzed speeches and everyday talk to understand what creates persuasion and makes the speaker seem potent. In addition to noting the importance of terms that push emotional hot buttons—in the United States, phrases such as "socialist," "free market," "bureaucracy," and "national security"—persuasive language that produces support for you and your ideas is language that promotes identification and affiliation. Good examples of such language would be presidential candidate John McCain's use of phrases such as "my friends" and "we" during his campaign. Words suggesting common bonds cause the audience to believe that you share their views.

In addition to using words that evoke emotions and signal common interests and shared identity, Max Atkinson describes a number of conventions that make speech more persuasive and engaging. Here are five such linguistic techniques.

1. Use us-versus-them references. "It is widely known that the need to resist an external threat, whether real or imagined, has always been an extremely effective rallying cry when it comes to strengthening group solidarity."[27] When United Airlines entered the California market in 1994, Herb Kelleher, then CEO of Southwest Airlines, sent his employees a video describing United as a "war machine" aimed to strike at Southwest and imploring his people to stick together to provide great customer service all over the system. Steve Jobs, cofounder and CEO of Apple Computer, focused first on IBM as the enemy—for instance, in Apple's famous "1984" commercial—and later on Microsoft as he used a common threat to energize Apple's employees.

2. Pause for emphasis and invite approval or even applause through a slight delay. "A pause just before getting to completion and a slightly extended final segment of talk are both common features in the design of most types of claptrap [a rhetorical device designed to produce applause and approval]."[28]
3. Use a list of three items, or enumerations in general. "One of the main attractions of three-part lists is that they have an air of unity and completeness about them."[29] Lists make a speaker appear as if he or she has thought about the issue and the alternatives and considered all sides thoroughly.
4. Use contrastive pairs, comparing one thing to another and using passages that are similar in length and grammatical structure. The contrast is strategically chosen to make a point. During the heated debate over health-care reform in 2009, opponents of government involvement would pose the question: Do you want your health-care decisions being made by you and your doctor or by some government bureaucrat? Proponents would employ a different contrast: Do you want greedy insurance companies who drop people when they get sick and exclude preexisting conditions deciding on your care, or would you like to leave those decisions to you and your doctor? The use of contrast as a rhetorical device relies in part on the "us versus them" construct, but it also invites explicit comparison that is structured to be favorable to the ideas advocated by the speaker.
5. Avoid using a script or notes. If you speak without aids, the implication is that you have a mastery of the subject and are spontaneous. In addition, not using notes or a script permits the speaker to maintain eye contact with the audience. Jack Valenti of the MPAA testified often before Congress. He commented that many of those testifying used notes. He didn't, as he wanted the language to be vibrant and spontaneous and to illustrate

his mastery of the issues. As he put it, "If you can't speak five minutes without a note in front of you, about a subject you know cold, you're not working at your job."[30] The use of PowerPoint presentations is effective in executing this strategy, as the presumption is that the presentation is there for the audience rather than the speaker.

To Atkinson's list of speaking tips I would add one important suggestion: use humor to the extent possible and appropriate. As the novelist Salman Rushdie noted on a radio program, "If you make people laugh, you can tell them anything."[31] Humor is disarming and also helps create a bond between you and your audience through a shared joke. When Ronald Reagan ran for reelection in 1984 against Minnesota senator Walter Mondale, he was the oldest person who had ever run in a presidential election (John McCain in 2008 would be older when he ran). During one of the presidential debates, Reagan was asked if he thought age would be an issue in the campaign. Reagan replied, with a smile, that he would not make an issue out of his opponent's youth and inexperience. Everyone laughed as Reagan used humor to diffuse a potentially troublesome issue and transform a serious concern into a laughing matter.

Sentence structure is also important for making language persuasive. During the 2004 presidential election, University of Illinois professor Stanley Fish had his students examine some of the speeches of the two candidates, George W. Bush and John Kerry. The students perceived Bush to be more effective, regardless of their own political views. Bush would be begin with a simple declarative sentence, "Our strategy is succeeding." Bush would also use the repetition of sounds. As Fish noted, "There is of course no logical relationship between the repetition of a sound [as in alliteration] and the soundness of an argument, but if it is skillfully employed, repetition can enhance a logical point or even the illusion of one when none is present."[32] By contrast, Kerry would use more convoluted sentence structure and words that did not seem presidential (for instance, "stupid"). Kerry often presumed his audience had information he had yet to provide.

We often avoid situations in which we feel uncomfortable, but if we are going to get better at talking and acting with power, there is no substitute for experience. Seek out opportunities to make presentations for your company, give talks at clubs or professional groups, and find someone to observe you and provide feedback on what you are doing well and poorly.

Social ties and how you present yourself through language and demeanor are components of creating a reputation and an image. We will examine other aspects of creating a reputation, an important source of power, in the next chapter.

8

Building a Reputation: Perception Is Reality

TWO HIGHLY SUCCESSFUL, almost iconic American football coaches, who coached about the same number of games: one had an overall winning percentage of 76 percent; the other, 61 percent. Both won National Football League titles. One quit coaching while still in his early forties before the team's owner could fire him, while the other never left a coaching position, in either the professional or college ranks, involuntarily or under pressure. The coach who left, John Madden, had the higher winning percentage. The coach who was never forced out of any job, Bill Walsh, was nicknamed "The Genius." Few people or organizations are going to fire a "genius" and be known for doing so. The lesson? Accomplishment matters, but so, too, does your reputation. Therefore, one important strategy for not only creating a successful path to power but also maintaining your position once you have achieved it is to build your image and your reputation.[1]

Reputations matter, not just in professional football, but in all domains, including business. In an experimental study of the performance appraisals people received, those who were able to create a favorable impression received higher ratings than did people who actually performed better but did not do as good a job in managing the impressions they made on others.[2] Or take senior corporate leaders. In a world where outside CEO successions are increasingly common and boards of directors seek people who will be well received on Wall Street and by the business media, being perceived as a superstar can change the negotiating dynamic. Instead of competing for a job and selling yourself to the board and senior executives, if you have a stellar reputation, companies will be fighting to hire you. If you have a reputation that can move the stock price up by the very announcement of your hiring, companies will pay outrageous sums of money in their quest to obtain a "corporate savior."[3] The companies will do this even though the evidence shows that these outside hires frequently fail and even if your reputation for executive brilliance is more myth than reality.

Sometimes reputation adheres to individuals, but sometimes individuals get a good reputation by their association with high-status institutions. General Electric is considered to be a great training ground for senior leaders. Consequently, senior executives can leave General Electric for CEO jobs at other firms with big salaries and enormous financial market expectations. Harvard Business School professor Boris Groysberg and some colleagues studied 20 former GE executives who left the company for the top job at another firm between 1989 and 2001. In 17 of the 20 cases, the stock market's reaction to the hiring announcement was positive, with an average gain of $1.1 billion in market capitalization for the hiring firm on the day the move was announced. In some instances, the gains from the hiring announcement were enormous—when Home Depot hired Robert Nardelli, shareholder value jumped almost $10 billion.[4] Groysberg's research shows that leaders are not particularly portable and this outside hiring often does not work. But for the leader with the great reputation, no problem—when Nardelli left Home Depot under duress, he departed with a total package valued at a quarter of a billion dollars. His reputation apparently still intact, Nardelli moved on to run Chrysler even though he had no auto industry experience. Chrysler subsequently went into bankruptcy.

The fundamental principles for building the sort of reputation that will get you a high-power position are straightforward: make a good impression early, carefully delineate the elements of the image you want to create, use the media to help build your visibility and burnish your image, have others sing your praises so you can surmount the self-promotion dilemma, and strategically put out enough negative but not fatally damaging information about yourself that the people who hire and support you fully understand any weaknesses and make the choice anyway. The key to your success is in executing each of these steps well.

YOU GET ONLY ONE CHANCE TO MAKE A FIRST IMPRESSION

Social perception—how people form judgments of others, which is something we do continuously to successfully navigate the world—has been studied extensively. That research reveals several crucial facts relevant to your building a reputation that will help you create a power base.

First, people start forming impressions of you in the first few seconds or even milliseconds of contact. Impressions aren't just based on extensive information about you, your behavior, and what you can do as manifested in job performance, but also on initial readings of your facial expression, posture, voice, and appearance. One study found that judgments of people made in the first 11 milliseconds correlated highly with judgments made when there were no time constraints, suggesting that extremely brief exposure was all that was required for people to form a reasonably stable impression.[5] This result suggests that the material from chapter 7 on acting and speaking with power is really important, as how you first present yourself matters a great deal.

Second, and this may surprise you, these fast first impressions are remarkably accurate in predicting other more durable and important evaluations. Social psychologists Nalini Ambady and Robert Rosenthal did a meta-analysis of the accuracy of predictions in many domains in clinical and social psychology. They found that short slices of behavior—less than five minutes—yielded accurate predictions, for instance, about assessments of people's personality. Moreover, they found that predictions based on extremely small samples of behavior, less than half a minute, did not differ in their accuracy from impressions formed using longer, four- and five-minute snippets of behavior.[6] In one empirical study using college teacher ratings as the outcome to be explained, Ambady and Rosenthal noted that ratings based on a silent video clip of the instructor lasting less than half a minute significantly predicted the course evaluations given by students at the end of the quarter. In a second study, again using an extremely short video clip, of high school teachers, ratings of these short silent videos significantly predicted the ratings given to the teachers by their principals.[7]

Not only are reputations and first impressions formed quickly, but they are durable. Research has identified several processes that account for the persistence of initial reputations or, phrased differently, the importance of the order in which information is presented.

All three processes are plausible. We don't need to know which is operating to worry about making a good first impression.

One process, attention decrement, argues that because of fatigue or boredom, people don't pay as close attention to later information as they do to information that comes early, when they first form judgments. When you first meet people, you are going to be quite attentive to what they say and do as you seek to learn about them and sort and assign them to categories, including how helpful and powerful you think they are or could be. After a while, you will think you know them and stop paying as close attention to what they say and do. As you sit in a meeting, because you think you know what the other person is going to say, you stop paying attention to what they actually do say.

A second process entails cognitive discounting—once people have formed an impression of another, they disregard any information that is inconsistent with their initial ideas. This process is particularly likely when the decisions and judgments are consequential. Who wants to admit that we are wrong about something important, with the negative consequences such an admission has for our self-image? It is much easier to discount inconsistent information and seek data that buttresses our original assessments.

Third, people engage in behavior that helps make their initial impressions of others come true. One study of interviewers of job applicants examined the impressions interviewers formed on the basis of test scores and resumés. Then the actual job interviews were analyzed. When interviewers had formed an initially favorable impression of an applicant, they showed positive regard toward that person, engaged more in "selling" of the company, provided more information about the job and the company, and asked for less information from the candidate. Interviewers built more rapport with candidates they thought they would like.[8] Other research shows that when people believe they are interacting with a qualified, intelligent individual, they ask questions and provide opportunities for the other to demonstrate competence and intelligence. Behavioral dynamics tend to reinforce initial impressions and reputations, making those impressions become true even if they weren't originally.

And yet another process, biased assimilation, involves taking later information and reinterpreting it in ways consistent with our original beliefs and judgments.[9] When Charlie Varon, a comedian, playwright, and performance artist, was asked by the California Medical Association in 2001 to give a speech, they expected some comedy over lunch. But Varon, with the cooperation of his hosts, reinvented himself as Albin Avgher, PhD, and gave a talk about his theory of human communication using all sorts of made-up statistics and facts to an audience filled with physicians and attorneys. Until they were let in on the joke, the audience almost to a person believed Varon was who he was introduced as being—an expert on human genomics. The audience interpreted the fact that some of his talk made no sense as coming from their own inadequacies and absence of particular specific knowledge. Had Varon been introduced as the comedic impostor that he was, the talk and his expertise would have been interpreted very differently.[10]

Many behaviors are ambiguous—is someone eccentric and brilliant or just socially incompetent? How people interpret what they see depends on their expectations that precede their observations. We see what we expect to see, so entering a situation with a reputation for power or brilliance is, other things being equal, more likely to have you leave the setting, regardless of what you do, with your reputation for power or brilliance enhanced. Impressions and reputations endure, so building a favorable impression and reputation early is an important step in creating power.

There are two important implications of the durability and rapid creation of first impressions. First, if you find yourself in a place where you have an image problem and people don't think well of you, for whatever reason, it is often best to leave for greener pastures. This is tough advice to hear and heed—many people want to demonstrate how wonderful they are by working diligently to change others' minds and repair their image. But such efforts are seldom successful, for all the reasons just enumerated, and moreover, they take a lot of effort. Better to demonstrate your many positive qualities in a new setting where you don't have to overcome so much baggage.

Second, because impressions are formed quickly and are based on many things, such as similarity and "chemistry" over which you have far from perfect control, you should try to put yourself in as many different situations as possible—to play the law of large numbers. If you are a talented individual, over time and in many contexts, that talent will appear to those evaluating you. But in any single instance, the evaluative judgment that forms the basis for your reputation will be much more random. This advice is consistent with that offered on network building, where again the best practice is to widely disperse your network building efforts and build many weak ties. Don't get hung up on making a favorable impression in any single place, but instead find an environment in which you can build a great reputation and keep trying different environments until this effort succeeds.

CAREFULLY CONSIDER AND CONSTRUCT YOUR IMAGE

You need to think strategically about the dimensions or elements of the reputation you want to build and then conduct yourself accordingly. Ryan Lizza's account of the rise of Barack Obama in the tough world of Chicago and then Illinois politics illustrates how Obama, from the very beginning, worked to build a political identity that would be useful to him:

> Obama seems to have been meticulous about constructing a political identity for himself. He visited churches on the South Side, considered the politics and reputations of each one, and received advice from older pastors. . . . Though he admired Judson Miner, he was similarly cautious about joining his law firm. . . . Obama was writing "Dreams" at the moment that he was preparing for a life in politics, and he launched his book and his first political campaign simultaneously.[11]

For more than a decade, John Browne served as CEO of British Petroleum; under his aegis, BP bought Amoco and Arco as well as making numerous smaller acquisitions. Browne was named to the British House of Lords and was voted the country's most admired business leader numerous times.[12] But as the many executives I have spoken with over the years point out, Browne is not necessarily the most obvious leader: he is short, less than five feet six inches tall; soft-spoken and awkward in social settings, essentially an introvert; and an intellectual in an industry known for brash, bold leaders who take big chances. Browne's rise to power and his consolidation of his position was based in part on his ability to build an image that served him well.

Although Browne's reputation is multifaceted, three dimensions stand out: hard work and dedication, intelligence, and intimidation of others. Browne was at BP throughout his working life, spending over 30 years in the company. He moved around the world—his postings include Anchorage, Alaska, New York, Cleveland, and London, among others. He worked enormous hours. It is helpful to be seen as someone devoted to the company above all else.

Browne's intelligence is legendary. Trained in physics, Browne always emphasized first principles and asked inquisitive questions. His analytical training permitted him to do well in his jobs both in finance and in exploration. But what comes across is how he uses his intelligence and memory to build his reputation as being super smart, not unlike what Robert McNamara did at both Ford and the Department of Defense.

Browne turned his shyness into a virtue. He carefully controlled his schedule. As a result, those who were lucky enough to get a meeting with him understood that each encounter was very important and high stakes. Browne turned even the ability to interact with him into a source of power—he controlled the scarce resource of his time. And as he displayed his intellectual prowess during those meetings, Browne built a reputation for brilliance that served him well both inside and outside BP.

The specifics of a useful reputation will obviously vary depending on the context and your own personal strengths and weaknesses. What is important is that you think carefully about the dimensions of the reputation you want to build, and then do everything in your power, from how you spend your time to what organizations and people you associate with, to ensure that is the image that you project.

BUILD YOUR IMAGE IN THE MEDIA

When Marcelo, a Brazilian, was 23 years old, he was named controller of one of the largest real estate companies in that country. At the time, he had four years' experience as a financial analyst, and he was given the responsibility for running a department with 70 people doing finance, accounting, internal audit, and investor relations. Why he got the job is not nearly as interesting as what he did once he was in it. Marcelo knew that he was not particularly qualified for the position, that many on his team—whose help and hard work he needed—would wonder about him, and that peers in other organizations, who might also prove helpful, would also need to be won over.

Marcelo built a three-pronged strategy. The first part entailed doing a lot of hard work and, to the best of his ability, delivering good results. The second was to build networks both inside and outside of the company—relationships that could help him be successful. But Marcelo also recognized the importance of creating a positive external image that would attract allies and support. He began to carefully cultivate the media as a way of becoming "better than he actually was" in the eyes of the world and, by so doing, actually *be* better because of the effect of positive expectations and image on how he would be seen.

Marcelo understood that, particularly in today's world with media budgets cut and organizations facing financial stress, journalists need and very much appreciate help doing their jobs. So Marcelo began writing articles about finance and management and sending them off to relevant Brazilian publications that wanted interesting content. At first, of course, not all the publications accepted his contributions, but over time, he got some of his writings placed. One of his angles was to play on his young age and offer a different generational perspective on management issues. Once some of his articles had been published, he had more credibility, so it was easier to get still other articles published. Marcelo also volunteered to do interviews about his company with the media. Many of his colleagues felt that this was a waste of time and a distraction from their real jobs. Few wanted to be bothered with drafting press releases and handling media relations. Marcelo was soon doing these tasks not just for his department but for many others in the company, and as his skill and success at these tasks grew, others came to him for help.

Through these activities, he was able to connect with many important people in the media in Brazil and also gain considerable stature inside his company.

When at the age of 27, with no top management experience, he was given the job of chief financial officer to guide a turnaround, lead a 100-person team, and be the co-general manager of one of the company's business units, Marcelo had already learned the importance of the media. He continued writing articles, doing interviews, and building relationships. In 2007, Marcelo, not yet 30 years old, was featured in a leading Brazilian business magazine as one of ten young executives designated "CEOs of the Future," and was on the cover of another leading Brazilian magazine with an article on how to trade in the stock market. Who knows what will eventually happen to Marcelo, but the odds of his being named a CEO are certainly enhanced by being designated as such by a leading business publication.

The lessons from the Marcelo story are to be persistent and to spend time cultivating media people—not just press, radio, television, and the Internet, but also business writers and thinkers who can help you burnish your image. The best way to build relationships with media people is to be helpful and accessible.

When Nuria Chinchilla completed her doctoral thesis at IESE, the business school of the University of Navarra in Barcelona, and joined the IESE faculty, she became interested in the topic of women in the workplace and building family-friendly workplaces. Although this issue gained prominence over the years as more women joined the labor force in Spain and elsewhere, and work-family conflicts continued to grow, what's interesting is how Chinchilla built an international reputation for herself as a leading, maybe *the* leading, speaker, consultant, and writer on this topic. There were, after all, many other professionals and policy analysts working on this topic, but few have had the visibility or influence in multiple countries as had Chinchilla, who has influenced awards and regulations in more than a dozen countries all over the world.[13]

When Chinchilla organized the first meeting for women human resource managers in 2001, she invited reporters to attend and interview the women there. A full-page article resulted. She recruited a former journalist and writer, Consuelo Leon, to come to IESE for a doctorate and to work in Chinchilla's research center with her. Leon now provides help with writing and research and also tacit knowledge of the media landscape. And Nuria makes herself open to doing interviews with journalists and building relationships with them: "I am doing my interviews mostly by phone in the car, in my office, from home. Every time, every hour. I am managing my time and providing a good service to the person who wants to have an interview. So this is why the television and radios and newspapers are happy with me, and then they come back. And also, because they know that I have data and this is what they want."[14]

There is no doubt that it is easier to get media attention once you are in power. Once in a very senior leadership role, you can hire the ghost writers to help you get your favorable story out and you can put your company's marketing muscle behind such efforts, which makes magazines and book publishers much more interested in the project. And by so doing, you can take control of your image, burnishing the positive aspects and ignoring anything negative. So you can read automobile executive Lee Iacocca's autobiography, one of the first big selling stories by a corporate CEO,[15] but never learn about his disinterest in issues of auto safety or see much about his role in the design and marketing of the Ford Pinto, a car with a gas tank engineered in such a way that it would explode and catch fire if hit from behind.[16] You can read Al Dunlap's autobiography and never learn that this former CEO of Scott Paper and Sunbeam perpetrated massive accounting fraud.[17] As John Byrne wrote, Dunlap was lionized in the business press until his fall from grace, and his "celebrity was based less on achievement than his eager willingness to say and do the offensive and the outrageous" as a way of playing to the media.[18] Byrne should know about how to hurt or help a CEO build his image, as his book with General Electric's chief executive Jack Welch took someone known more for downsizing—remember the nickname "Neutron Jack"—and turned him into a business hero,[19] even though there is evidence that GE polluted the Hudson River, engaged in massive price fixing, and never was quite as financially successful as it appeared.[20]

As the cases of Marcelo and Nuria Chinchilla illustrate, it is possible and desirable to have a media image–building strategy even at the beginning of your career. Consider getting public relations help early on. Reach out to the media and academics who write cases and articles, and write your own articles or blogs that enhance your visibility.

Marketing expert Keith Ferrazzi recommends writing articles because it helps you clarify your thinking. It does that, but writing can also be a way to build visibility and create an image, helping you find a good job. Karen, whom we discussed in chapter 5, worked at a venture capital company in San Francisco in the early days of blogging. Inevitably, there were discussions in the firm about whether someone should write a blog. What was the company's public relations strategy? People were busy with their deals and their board commitments. Karen loved writing and so she began a blog. It was successful, and soon she was being asked to be an occasional guest columnist on other blogs. One day she was approached by a headhunter about moving to a new, senior role in strategy at a large Internet company in another city. As Karen told me, when people are going to meet you, they Google you, and in her case, they could read her musings, which gave her credibility. Her future boss had only a 15-minute interview with her. He told her that they had read her blog, could see how she thought, felt there was a great fit, so basically she had been hired through her blog and because of her writing.

OVERCOME THE SELF-PROMOTION DILEMMA

As you burnish you image, you need to be cognizant of the self-promotion dilemma and figure out some ways around it. The dilemma is this: on the one hand, research shows that when people don't advocate for themselves and claim competence, particularly in settings such as job interviews or pushing for a promotion when they would be expected to do so, others believe they must be either incompetent or unskilled in handling such situations, a perception that works to their disadvantage.[21] On the other hand, self-promoting behavior, although expected in many instances, also creates difficulties. When you tout your own abilities and accomplishments, you face two problems: you are not going to be as believable as presumably more objective outsiders; and research shows that people who engage in blatant self-promotion are perceived as arrogant and self-aggrandizing, which causes others not to like them.[22] Although likability is not essential for obtaining power, there is no point in putting others off if there is a way to avoid it.

There is a solution to this dilemma: get others, even those you employ such as agents, public relations people, executive recruiters, and colleagues, to tout your abilities. In a series of experiments, I and some colleagues investigated what happened when a person claimed competence for himself compared to when another made the identical statements on his behalf.[23] Not surprisingly, when another made statements about how great an author was, for instance, that person was perceived as more likable than if he made the same statements on his own behalf. The author was also perceived as more competent when another stated his abilities than when he did so himself. And people were more willing to offer extra help to others who were not seen as arrogant or self-aggrandizing, who had an intermediary speak on their behalf rather than promoting themselves. In one of the experimental studies, we used a video scenario in which an actor, playing the role of an agent, made statements supporting the value of his client and that person's work while the client sat by his side in the picture. Even though participants in the study reported that the agent was under the control of the client and was acting on his behest, they nevertheless rated the client more highly than in situations where the client made the identical statements for himself. What these studies show is that even though people understand the financially intertwined interests of people hired to act on your behalf, and even though they know that agents or intermediaries are under your control, they will still rate you more highly and offer more help than if you acted on your own.

Those who speak on your behalf also have their statements judged as more credible than when you make the same claims yourself. And the very fact that you were able to get, for instance, a reputable public relations firm or a great agent to work for you signals your capability and adds luster to your reputation. The advice from this research and the observations that stimulated it: don't be cheap—hire people to represent and tout you. It can work to your advantage in several ways.

THE UPSIDE OF SOME NEGATIVE INFORMATION

Larry Summers, Treasury secretary under Bill Clinton, president of Harvard University, and the head of President Barak Obama's

National Economic Council, is often described as prickly, outspoken, and not very sensitive. Ryan Lizza's description of Summers in the Obama White House is typical:

> Summers is a brilliant yet heroically self-regarding economist. His capacity for equations is not matched by a capacity for working easily with others. When I asked the senior White House official about the relationships between him and Orszag [Obama's budget director], he replied, "There's a little turbulence between Larry and everybody, because that's just the way he is."[24]

Not only has Summers's reputation not hurt him; it has actually helped. If you know you are hiring someone who is difficult, and you do so anyway, you will be *more* committed to the decision—because you will have made the selection *in spite of* whatever flaws the person has. Displaying some negative characteristics, as long as they aren't so overwhelming as to preclude your selection, actually increases your power because those who support you notwithstanding your flaws will be even more committed to you and your success. The process is one of reputational inoculation—people can't complain about traits they know about and will, as in the quote about Larry Summers, come to discount any negative traits as being "just who you are."

Consider the nonexecutive chairman of a publicly traded company making point-of-care ultrasound equipment. A former Marine, the chairman set meeting dates not by consulting with board members on their schedules but by fiat—and woe to anyone who missed meetings, even if they were set at times impossible to attend. He also ran the meetings in an authoritarian fashion. But no harm to him. As one board member commented after agreeing with this characterization, "That's just how he is."

You probably aren't—and don't want to appear in any case—perfect. As long as the quirks you display are irrelevant to the core of your reputation and why people select you—in the case of Summers, for his brilliance in the field of economics—the flaws and foibles can actually strengthen people's commitment to you.

REMEMBER: IMAGE CREATES REALITY

People benefit, or suffer, from the self-reinforcing aspect of reputations. As one analysis of Mike Volpi, former head of business development at Cisco, the network equipment maker, noted:

> He gained a reputation with Chambers [the CEO] and other senior managers for being able to get things done. . . . Volpi began to get a reputation outside of Cisco as well. Favorable press coverage helped to increase his influence within Cisco and with important constituencies outside of the company; reports of his influence became a self-fulfilling prophecy.[25]

You don't have to trade reputation for reality. Volpi was a very successful business development executive. A great reputation can help you achieve great performance and vice versa. The trick is to be sure you do the things to build your reputation, have others tout you, and attract the kind of media coverage and image that can help build your power base.

9

Overcoming Opposition and Setbacks

No matter how worthy your goals, how hard you work, and how talented you are, virtually everyone encounters opposition and setbacks along the path to power. Sandy Weill, who built up several financial services companies before becoming the all-powerful CEO of Citigroup, was turned down by Merrill Lynch, Bache, and Harris Upham when he applied for a job as a stockbroker in the 1950s,[1] and resigned from American Express when he lost a power struggle in 1985—Weill had come to American Express when he sold the company the securities firm, Shearson, he had built.[2] The important question is how you respond to the inevitable opposition and reversals of fortune you will face.

When Laura Esserman, a breast cancer surgeon with an MBA, became head of the Carol Franc Buck Breast Care Center at UCSF in 1997, she had a vision for what needed to happen. First, she wanted to get the relevant specialties together in one attractive, patient-friendly setting so women did not have to go from place to place, in some instances carrying their own medical tests and records. Women frequently confronted delays and inconvenience in the diagnostic process along with uncertainty and fear as they went from having a mammogram to a biopsy to consulting with a surgical oncologist, often in different offices and with days between steps. Esserman wanted to create a facility where women could arrive in the morning referred by their primary care physician with a suspicious lump or another symptom and leave at the end of the day with a treatment plan, having had the necessary tests and evaluation during one day in one nicely designed and decorated place.

Second, Esserman was aware that the cycle time for learning and improving cancer treatments was too long and too expensive, with implications for patient outcomes. As Sue Dubman, now at Genzyme but at one time in the informatics division of the National Cancer Institute, showed me, recruiting patients for clinical trials consumes about 20 percent of the enormous cost of drug development, and the slow pace of signing up doctors and patients causes delays in evaluating new drugs and other treatments. Could these costs and delays be cut? Furthermore, although important information came out of the clinical trials, hundreds of thousands of women were being treated every day and information about what was working and what wasn't from those everyday experiences was being lost. So, Esserman had two other objectives: to build an informatics system to capture more of the data from treatment outcomes and to increase the ease and speed of enrolling patients in clinical trials.

All of these worthy objectives confronted opposition. Although Esserman ran the cancer center, she did not have line authority or budgetary control over the separate academic departments such as surgery and radiology—each with its own budget and priorities—that would need to come together into a single facility to provide the one-stop service she envisioned. Moreover, UCSF was famous for its fundamental scientific research, and patient care was less of a cultural imperative. Academic medical centers faced financial challenges, particularly in California with its high proportion of health-maintenance organizations, which made investment in informatics difficult. Academic physicians were trained to compete for funding and prestige; that individualistic, competitive culture would have to change if patient data from multiple sites were to be combined for analysis about what did and didn't work. To compound her other difficulties, Esserman was, by her own admission, quick to anger, impatient, and often neither able nor particularly interested in seeing things from the perspective of others, particularly those she saw thwarting her efforts. At the time I wrote a case about Laura Esserman in 2003, it was unclear how much of her agenda she would be able to accomplish. Many people who saw the case thought her efforts were doomed.[3]

By 2009, the answer was clear: Laura Esserman was well on her way to doing it all. Already by 2003 she had the facility and brought together the resources that provided patient-centered care and fulfilled the promise of less delay in the diagnostic process from initial symptom through mammography to biopsy and then a plan for treatment. Breastcancertrials.org, a website where patients could enter their own information and get matched with appropriate clinical trials, had been piloted in the San Francisco Bay area in 2008 and was rolling out nationally in 2009, speeding the process and cutting the cost of enrolling patients. And project Athena, an unprecedented effort that brought together five medical facilities throughout the University of California system to build a database covering the treatment of thousands of patients, was well under way, sponsored by the university's system-wide leadership and encouraged by the UC Board of Regents and its chair, Richard Blum. Laura Esserman had also evolved in her leadership skills. In her story, and in the examples of others we will see in this chapter seeking to build influence and get things done, there are important lessons for everyone attempting to acquire the power to make change and the resources to build their reputation and career even as they overcome opposition and setbacks along the way.

OVERCOMING OPPOSITION: HOW AND WHEN TO FIGHT

Because people come from different backgrounds, face different rewards, and see different information, they are going to see the world differently. Consequently, disagreements are inevitable in organizations. Unfortunately, many people are conflict-averse, finding disagreement disagreeable and avoiding surfacing differences of opinion and engaging in difficult conversations with their adversaries. As school leader Rudy Crew has said, "Conflict is just an opportunity for another person's education," for exploring why people think the way they do, and for sharing perspectives so the parties to the conflict can learn about and from each other. Particularly in a leadership position, it is irresponsible to avoid people with whom you have disagreements and to duck difficult situations. There are, of course, better and worse ways to engage in conflict. Here are some ideas to make you more successful in surmounting opposition.

TRY A LITTLE TENDERNESS AND LEAVE PEOPLE A GRACEFUL OUT

Social psychologist Jack Brehm's theory of psychological reactance holds that people rebel against constraints or efforts to control their behavior—force is met with countervailing force.[4] Seeking to dominate the conversation and the decision making and totally control the situation may work on some of your adversaries, but probably not too many. Most will seek to push back, very hard—they will react to your attempts to overpower them by doing things to maintain their power and autonomy. Therefore, one way to deal with opponents is to treat them well and leave them a graceful way to retreat. Sometimes, coopting others and making them a part of your team or organization carries the day by giving them a stake in the current system.

Some years ago at the University of Illinois, a group of women faculty, staff, and students were upset because the university was apparently paying women less than men and jobs held by women paid lower salaries than comparable jobs with similar skills held by men. When this group pressured the university, the administrative response was brilliant and effective: the university established a Committee on the Status of Women, gave the committee some stationery, a budget, and a modest amount of office space—in short, legitimacy and a few resources—and told the committee to study the facts and come up with recommendations. This move effectively coopted the opposition, making the potential protesters part of the university, feeling less estranged and like outsiders. The stridency of the demands diminished and soon people were almost as concerned with the committee's budget for the following year as they were about the status of women on campus.

You can turn enemies into allies, or at least people who are indifferent to you and not in your way, through strategic outplacement—getting them a better job somewhere else where they will not be underfoot. When Willie Brown became speaker of the California Assembly after a tough race against fellow Democrat Howard Berman, Brown showed benevolence to his opponents. Following a decennial redistricting that created more congressional districts, Howard Berman and two other Brown rivals, Mel Levine and Rick Lehman, went to the U.S. Congress with Willie Brown's help. "Other Democratic Assembly rivals, like Wadie Deddeh of San Diego, got safe seats in the state Senate."[5] Brown rewarded his Democratic rivals rather than exacting retribution, and thereby solidified his power. Helping opponents move to another organization where they won't be in your way may not be the first thing you think about doing, but it ought to be high on the list.

"Face" is important for people's self-esteem. Giving adversaries something to make them feel better works to your advantage, particularly if the move doesn't cost you that much. That's why boards and bosses often say nice things about people being shown the door, and even sometimes provide money—seldom from their own pockets—that makes the exit easier to swallow. At a large human resources consulting partnership that elects its leader by a vote of the partners, one partner who had built a large organizational practice and was quite visible in the business media backed the losing candidate. The winner called this partner into his office and told him he had to leave, his value to the firm notwithstanding. But to ease the pain and ensure that he would leave quietly, the newly elected leader gave the departing partner enough money that he didn't have to work for a year. If you make it easy and pleasant for your opponents to depart, they will. By contrast, once people have nothing left to lose, they will have no inhibitions or constraints on what they will do to fight you.

DON'T CAUSE YOURSELF UNNECESSARY PROBLEMS

Conflict arouses strong emotions, including anger, and these strong feelings interfere with our ability to think strategically about what we are really trying to do. You need to continually ask yourself, "What would victory look like? If you had won the battle, what would you want that win to encompass?" People lose sight of what their highest priorities are and get diverted fighting other battles that then cause unnecessary problems.

Laura Esserman was already pushing a large agenda and needed all the support she could get. Even she will now say that appearing at a hearing chaired by a state senator friend of hers to investigate the catastrophic merger, subsequently unwound, between the hospitals at Stanford and the University of California at San Francisco was not the smartest move. As she entered the hearing room, she spotted Mike Bishop, the chancellor of the UCSF campus, who knew who she was and commented on her testifying. The UC hospital merger was not on her critical path to change breast cancer treatment, and testifying against the administration of the place where she worked wouldn't make her many friends.

Zia Yusuf, the former senior executive in SAP, sometimes exasperated his subordinates because in a meeting when he saw that the decision was going against him and his group, he typically did not dig in his heels and fight. "It is important to live to fight another day," he says. Because he did not push too hard against his bosses or his peers, Yusuf defused the emotional tone of meetings and by not creating unnecessary enmity, could often get the decisions he wanted, even if it took some time.

Not creating enemies or turmoil when it isn't necessary requires something I have discussed before—focus. You need to have a clear understanding of where you are going and the critical steps on the way. When you confront opposition on this path, you need to react. But you just waste your time and possibly acquire gratuitous problems if you get involved with any issue or individual that has some connection, regardless of how irrelevant, to you and your agenda.

DON'T TAKE THINGS PERSONALLY—MAKE IMPORTANT RELATIONSHIPS WORK

When Gary Loveman became chief operating officer of Harrah's, the casino company, in 1998, many insiders thought they were more qualified for the job and resented his arrival from his position as an associate professor at Harvard Business School who had done some consulting for the company. One of those potentially difficult people was the chief financial officer of the company, a senior executive, older than Gary, who was unhappy with Loveman's appointment. The CFO position was critically important not just politically but also for accomplishing the organizational improvement that would eventually provide Loveman the CEO position in 2003. Loveman moved quickly to cement his relationship with the CFO. He spent some time with the CFO almost every day, visiting him in his office, kept the CFO informed about what he was doing and why, involved him in decisions and meetings—in short, did everything he could to make the relationship successful. Gary Loveman's advice: after you reach a certain level, there comes a point in your career where you simply have to make critical relationships work. Your feelings, or for that matter, others' feeling about you, don't matter. To be successful, you have to get over resentments, jealousies, anger, or anything else that might get in the way of building a relationship where you can get the resources necessary for you to get the job done.

Zia Yusuf had a strategy for depersonalizing the difficult situations he confronted when he ran SAP's internal consulting team and sometimes had to recommend restructuring or other decisions that caused some senior people to lose resources and power: focus on the data. He pushed himself and his team to get as much objective information as possible, and to be analytically and logically rigorous, so that facts would dominate the discussion and make strategic issues less about personalities and feelings.

The ability to not take opposition or slights personally, think about whose support you need and go after it, regardless of their behavior toward you or your own feelings, and remain focused on the data and impartial analysis requires a high level of self-discipline and emotional maturity. It is a rare skill. But it is crucial in surmounting and disarming opponents.

BE PERSISTENT

I met Richard Blum at a meeting launching the Athena project, the multicampus, information technology–intensive effort to gather clinical data about the effectiveness of breast cancer treatments. Blum, an investment banker and investment manager with vast personal wealth, is chair of the UC Board of Regents and also the husband of California senator Dianne Feinstein. When I asked Blum, who serves on numerous corporate boards and nonprofit foundations as well as running his own vast enterprises, what caused him to turn up for this meeting, he replied, "I have learned that when either my wife or Laura [Esserman] asks you to do something, the best answer is, 'Yes, dear.' Because even if you say no, sooner or later you are going to do it anyway. You might as well save yourself the time and aggravation and agree at the beginning." Laura Esserman describes her success as coming from her dogged persistence and likes to talk about other examples of successful scientists who emphasized the importance of not giving up in the face of setbacks. People who have observed her in action describe her as a force of nature.

Persistence works because it wears down the opposition. Much like water eroding a rock, over time keeping at something creates results. In addition, staying in the game maintains the possibility that the situation will shift to your advantage. Opponents retire or leave or make mistakes. The environment changes. When Esserman entered medicine, breast cancer was, believe it or not, a relatively unsexy medical backwater. Women's advocacy and scientific progress that has enhanced diagnosis and treatment have given the disease and its treatment much more visibility. In a tenured academic position (Esserman) and a safe legislative seat (Brown in San Francisco), being patient and persistent is easier to implement than might be the case in other, less secure situations. Nevertheless, not giving up is a precursor to winning.

ADVANCE ON MULTIPLE FRONTS

When Esserman was thwarted at UCSF, she built a scientific and clinical reputation at the national level with, for instance, the head of informatics at the National Cancer Institute. National visibility and ties could be deployed to build her power locally. She also continued to practice medicine, building a loyal cadre of former patients, some of whom had incredible wealth, talent, and connections. As she put it, when she was thwarted making systemic change, she could work on helping people one at a time. When she was discouraged by what she could do for individual patients—breast cancer remains a deadly disease—she could focus on making systemic changes that would improve care and enhance knowledge. By building her power base nationally and locally, both inside UCSF and with others in the community, Esserman could leverage power from one setting to get influence in another.

It's a long way from breast cancer in San Francisco to cricket in India, but the story of how Lalit Modi gained control of the Board of Control for Cricket in India (BCCI), the most powerful and wealthy body in world cricket, and launched the new Indian Premier League (IPL) also illustrates the importance of moving ahead on many fronts. The son of a wealthy family, Modi attended Duke University, where he learned about sports marketing. Back in India, he signed a deal with Disney to sell licensed merchandise. His first attempt—to set up an Indian cricket league with foreign players that was going to get air time on ESPN—foundered when the BCCI opposed it. Modi used his contacts in large U.S. companies such as Disney and ESPN to convince allies in India that if he could open up the BCCI monopoly and build a more entrepreneurial culture, there was a lot of money to be made by selling merchandise and games. He was extremely patient, beginning more than a decade ago to build the relationships that would enable him to successfully seize power in the

BCCI, relationships that were, in many instances, only tangentially related to cricket and included powerful Indian politicians.[6]

MOVE FIRST—SEIZE THE INITIATIVE

If you move quickly, you can often catch your opponents off guard and secure victory before they even know what is happening. In 2005, Jagmohan Dalmiya stood for reelection as president of the BCCI. Modi, coming out of nowhere as a leader of the Rajasthan Cricket Association, hired numerous lawyers to pursue allegations of corruption and mismanagement against Dalmiya and ran an overtly political campaign to oust him. "Dalmiya could not believe the effort being put in by his opponents. He was caught totally unaware."[7] After winning the election and installing himself as vice president and an ally as president of the association, Modi moved quickly to remove opponents and sell TV rights and merchandise sponsorships at high prices to bring in the resources and show people that siding with him was very much in their economic self-interest.

This dynamic plays out all the time in board of directors and CEO struggles. If the CEO can move first to rid the board of opponents, he can usually be successful and save his job. If the board organizes while the CEO is away on vacation or distracted, the members can often mobilize the support to unseat the CEO before he can mount a counterattack. The lesson: Don't wait if you see a power struggle coming. While you are waiting, others are organizing support and orchestrating votes to win.

USE REWARDS AND PUNISHMENTS TO SHAPE BEHAVIOR

Serving on a publicly traded company's board of directors provides prestige and money. At one medical device company, the chair of the compensation committee got into conflict with the CEO. The board member felt that the company was underperforming, not attaining the profit margins that had been projected as sales grew, and the stock price was stagnant. Meanwhile, the CEO retained outside counsel to help him in his negotiations for a larger compensation package. When the board acquiesced to his demands, the CEO had won. Soon, the compensation committee chair was off the board. Coincidence? Possibly. But a lesson to other board members, nonetheless: if you want to keep your position, go along.

The late John Jacobs, political reporter at the time for the *San Francisco Chronicle* and later the McClatchy chain, told me that when as a young reporter he wrote negative articles about the new speaker of the assembly, Willie Brown, he was told he could be barred from the floor of the assembly. That might make doing his job as a political reporter more difficult. When he wrote a favorable article about something Brown had done, he received a gift basket. The lesson: there would be consequences from the relationship Jacobs developed with Brown.

In companies, in government, even in nonprofits, people who have any resource control use it to reward those who are helpful and punish those who stand in their way. When the charming, gentle, and scrupulously honest John Gardner, founder of Common Cause and a man of distinction, was HEW secretary in the Johnson administration, a time when the programs in health, education, and social welfare were greatly expanded under the Great Society rubric, he told people that it was firmly within their right to oppose what he was doing, but he wanted them to know there would be "consequences." If using power in this way seems tough, it may be. But get over your inhibitions, because many of the people you will meet on your path to power will have less hesitation about rewarding their friends and punishing those who oppose them.

MAKE YOUR OBJECTIVES SEEM COMPELLING

Your path to power is going to be easier if you are aligned with a compelling, socially valuable objective. That doesn't mean you are cynically using some social cause for your own gain—just that to the extent you can associate your efforts with a socially desirable, compelling value, you increase your likelihood of success.

Opposing Laura Esserman's efforts at UCSF was tantamount to turning one's back on breast cancer and its victims and their families. Rudy Crew would invariably talk about the hundreds of thousands of schoolchildren being left behind in New York and then Miami-Dade County by the current educational arrangements, and note that his initiatives were designed to remedy real problems with schools. Robert Moses ruled New York for decades because to oppose him was to oppose parks, and, as he put it, to be on the side of parks was to be on the side of the angels.

Power struggles inside companies seldom seem to revolve around blatant self-interest. At the moment of crisis and decision, clever combatants customarily invoke "shareholders' interests." As in, "It would be in the shareholders' interests to have a new CEO," or a "new board member," or for that matter, new executives in other senior roles. Gary Loveman's rationale, as he removed people after he became COO? "They could not do the new jobs expected of them" under a strategy of data-based marketing necessary to enhance Harrah's performance. For example, the marketing executive who won the chairman's award for excellence the preceding year was a great advertiser and photographer of crab legs and properties: this man was great at what used to be the essence of his job, but he could not do the analytical work required to leverage a large customer database to build share of wallet. Loveman often frequently notes that no one owns a position, not even him—everyone works in the interests of the shareholders, who own the right to put whoever is most effective in the job. Loveman is sincere and he has certainly delivered for the shareholders—a stock price of about $16 when he arrived at Harrah's in 1998 became $90 a share when he completed the last of the big leveraged buyouts before the crash in the fall of 2007. But this talk about shareholder sovereignty is also a framing that works to portray his power at the gaming company in a socially desirable and acceptable fashion.

If you are going to do good—for educational systems, public works, breast cancer, or shareholders—you are going to need to be in power. Otherwise, you won't be able to accomplish as much. The lesson: place your own objectives in a broader context that compels others to support you.

COPING WITH SETBACKS

Most successful people have encountered setbacks along the way, and survived. In entrepreneurship, people expect that not every venture is going to succeed. John Lilly, CEO of Internet browser company Mozilla, was much less successful with his first venture. Reed Hastings, the highly successful founder and CEO of Netflix, had a much less successful experience with his first software start-up, Pure Software, where he tried to fire himself twice. Bad things sometimes happen to good people. The issue becomes how and if they recover.

On the evening of December 1, 1997, Jeffrey Sonnenfeld, a professor at the Emory University School of Business, responded to a message from the campus police and went to the police station, thinking it was a prank. It wasn't. The police accused Sonnenfeld, who had built a leadership institute at the university and was famous for his CEO college that brought together leading chief executives and leaders from the public sector, of vandalizing the new business school building. They said they had videotape evidence and got Sonnenfeld to sign a letter of resignation from his tenured full-professor position on the spot, promising they would not arrest him if he quit. Since Sonnenfeld was leaving after the first of the year to become dean of the business school at Georgia Tech anyway, he didn't care about the Emory position, and he was afraid the possible publicity from an arrest would jeopardize his job at Tech. Within days, Emory's president, William Chace, had called senior people at Georgia Tech about Sonnenfeld; Tech then failed to proceed with the approval of Sonnenfeld's appointment at the state board of regents. Shortly after killing Sonnenfeld's new job, Chace talked to a reporter at the *New York Times* and soon the strange case of Jeffrey Sonnenfeld was all over the media. By the end of December 1997, Sonnenfeld had no job and no prospect of one and his reputation was in tatters. Many doubted that those who had given money to the leadership institute or his academic friends would stand by him, and some worried for his physical and mental health.[8]

Many, although not all, of his supporters and faculty colleagues did remain on Sonnenfeld's side during the protracted struggle with Emory. Today Jeffrey Sonnenfeld is a professor of management practice and associate dean for executive education at the Yale School of Management. He has coauthored a book about overcoming setbacks, using examples from politics and industry. The book also reflects his own experience about how to survive reversals of fortune.[9]

DON'T GIVE UP

When Jon, the successful director of a major American ballet company, lost his position as head of the organization in a falling-out with the board, his first reaction was embarrassment. It didn't matter that he had positively affected a number of quantitative measures of the troupe's operations—he felt uncomfortable talking about the circumstances of his departure. Rudy Crew had trouble admitting in public or even to himself that he had been fired by Rudy Giuliani and the New York City school board. Jeff Sonnenfeld's first reaction to the tempest in Atlanta was to curtail his normally frenetic outreach and networking because he felt bad about what had happened. Embarrassment is the normal reaction to losing one's job, even if it isn't your fault. And why not? We are as subject to the just-world effect—believing that we get what we deserve—as are outside observers, so when people lose a power struggle, the first thing they do is blame themselves.

This reaction may be natural, but it is not helpful. Jon, Rudy Crew, and Jeff Sonnenfeld all had a story to tell—their story, about what happened to them and what it reflected, not just about them but about those taking the actions against them. Telling that story requires getting over any embarrassment and the associated tendency to retreat from view. If you are going to persevere and recover, you need to stop blaming yourself, letting your opponents dominate the discussion of what happened, and feeling bad about your complicity in your demise.

The best way to overcome the embarrassment is to talk about what happened to as many people as possible as quickly as possible. You will probably learn that you have more support than you think, and that others, rather than blaming you, will want to come to your aid. Also, the more you tell the tale, the less the telling will stimulate strong emotions in you. You will become acclimated to the story and desensitized to its effects. Making what happened less emotionally fraught is absolutely essential for your being able to think strategically about your next moves.

CONTINUE TO DO WHAT MADE YOU SUCCESSFUL

People who reach senior-level positions in any field are good at what they do. Even if job performance is not the most important determinant of career success, it does matter and, moreover, once you reach a high-level position, unless you go to sleep, over time you will become more capable at doing the job through your accumulated experience. That means that when you face a setback, don't take the advice of those who advocate finding another area of work. Your experience and contacts are all context-specific—you have human and social capital in a particular job domain. Moving to something else, whatever else the virtues of that new career path, will rob you of the resources and competence you have built doing what you do.

Jeff Sonnenfeld got lots of advice in early 1998 about what he should do. He could go into consulting, or go to work for someone like Bernard Marcus of the Home Depot, who had been one of the strong supporters of his leadership center at Emory. But Sonnenfeld wasn't a full-time consultant and he certainly was not a company executive with experience in day-to-day executive responsibilities. He was an educator. And the thing that had made him famous, putting him on national television and receiving favorable press coverage in *BusinessWeek*, was his CEO college—the meeting that brought together leading CEOs to discuss issues in a candid, off-the-record atmosphere with Sonnenfeld as the very effective moderator and organizer. Although this meeting had been held at Emory, the particular physical location had no implications for the value that the CEOs derived from the get-together.

Sonnenfeld started a nonprofit in Atlanta, the Chief Executive Leadership Institute, and found that many, although not all, of the companies that had supported his center at Emory supported his new endeavor. He took his staff from Emory with him. He maintained his contacts—with NASDAQ and other groups for whom he had done similar meetings. He continued his writing and research. This continuity in activity is what permitted him, along with his eventual exoneration and a favorable CBS *60 Minutes* television segment focused on his plight, to rebuild his reputation and successfully return to academia.

ACT AS IF—PROJECTING POWER AND SUCCESS

A very successful former CEO of a human capital software company took a job as a partner with a foreign venture capital firm. The firm's investments weren't very good, and, more importantly, Steve soon figured out that he could not work effectively with his overseas partners. They parted ways, and Steve's next job was as CEO of a small software company in which he had invested while he was still at the venture capital fund. Even though he had left his previous position and was running a company that was both small and in a precarious financial position, in talking to him you would never know there had been any problem at all. He spoke enthusiastically about his current job and the company's prospects and refused to acknowledge any setback from his venture capital experience. Now an executive vice president at a large international research and consulting firm, Steve's success in landing a great position derives in no small measure from his never appearing as if there had been any career reversal.

Situations are often ambiguous. Did you resign or were you fired? Was your previous job experience successful or not? One of the ways others are going to ascertain how things turned out is by how you present yourself. Are you upbeat? Do you project power and success or the reverse? This is why developing the ability to act in ways that you may not feel at the moment, described in chapter 7, is such an important skill. You want to convey that everything is fine and under your control, even under dire circumstances.

People want to associate with winners. At the very moment when you have suffered a reversal in fortune and most need help, the best way to attract that help is to act as if you are going to triumph in the end. This advice does not mean that you should not tell people what happened and enlist their aid. It does mean you need to show enough strength and resilience that your potential allies will not believe their efforts to help you will be wasted.

For Jeffrey Sonnenfeld, suing Emory University in Atlanta, where you could hardly find a judge or law firm that didn't have some tie to Emory or its law school, was emotionally tough. Having to scramble for money to support the new leadership institute was also difficult. But Sonnenfeld, feeling not only wronged but confident in his abilities as an educator and researcher, was able to show toughness and act as if he was going to eventually prevail. That confidence helped him attract the funding for his new center in the first place—no one is going to donate money to an organization that is not going to be able to collect sufficient resources to fulfill its mission. It's in that sense that the ability to act as if you will win becomes a self-fulfilling prophecy.

10

The Price of Power

IT WAS the late Nobel Prize–winning economist Milton Friedman who famously said, "There is no free lunch." Nothing comes without cost, and that is certainly true of power. As you chart your course and make decisions about what you will and will not do to acquire power, consider carefully what you are striving for and if you really want it. People who seek and attain power often pay some price for the quest, for holding on to their positions, and confronting the difficult but inevitable transitions out of powerful roles. This chapter considers some of the costs incurred by those who successfully pursue a path to power.

COST 1: VISIBILITY AND PUBLIC SCRUTINY

In January 2005, two employees of a large U.S. manufacturing company, one of whom was divorced and one who was still married, began having a consensual affair. There was never any evidence of sexual harassment or unwanted advances—it was a case of mutual attraction. There are thousands, maybe hundreds of thousands, of such incidents each year, most of which have little or no consequence for the professional careers of the people involved and few of which gain any public attention. But not in this case, because the man involved was Harry Stonecipher, the CEO of Boeing, and the woman was a Boeing vice president. The Boeing board of directors asked for, and got, Stonecipher's resignation when the affair was brought to its attention by an internal whistle-blower.[1] An important lesson: if you are going to misbehave in any way, do so before you achieve a high-level position that makes you the object of constant attention by peers, subordinates, superiors, and the media.

It's not just the big things that draw scrutiny when you are in power. Rudy Crew, when he ran the Miami-Dade County school district, faced public commentary on the fact that he drove a Mercedes. One reporter found it important to write that in a self-serve restaurant, he failed to bus his dishes when he had finished eating. As these examples illustrate, holding a position of power means that more than your job performance is being carefully watched—although that happens, too. Every aspect of your life, including how you dress, where you live, how you spend your time, who you choose to spend time with, what your children do, what you drive, how you act in completely non-job-related domains, will draw scrutiny. As A. Bartlett Giamatti, the former president of Yale University, noted, "Not that I've been treated unfairly, but you go from being a private person to suddenly reading descriptions of your face, your clothes, the way your hands look."[2] Organizational behavior scholars Robert Sutton and Charles Galunic note that the public scrutiny experienced by organizational leaders entails persistent attention, close performance monitoring, interruptions, and relentless questions about what is going on. They argue that such scrutiny has many negative consequences for both the leaders and the organizations they lead.[3]

All this scrutiny makes doing your job more difficult. If you ever played a musical instrument, I'm sure you remember your first recital. If you are like most people, playing while others watch is a different and more demanding experience than playing under the gaze of your music teacher or parents or, better yet, alone. A recital is a lot more stressful. That stress leads people to forget their notes—or their lines if they are on stage—and perform a lot worse than when they perform without an audience.

Social psychologists have a term for this widespread and well-studied phenomenon—it is called the "social facilitation effect."[4] When you are in the presence of other people, even if they aren't watching you, you are more motivated and on edge. That's fine, up to a point. The relationship between motivation and performance is curvilinear—positive up to some level as effort increases but then negative as increased tension decreases your ability to process information and make decisions. The social facilitation literature shows that the presence of others, by increasing motivation and psychological arousal, will *enhance* performance of overlearned and simple activities such as running or walking, but will *decrease* performance on tasks that entail new learning or involve novel or difficult activities. What tasks people have mastered varies depending on the person. But generally, simple repetitive motions such as those involved in assembly-line work benefit from the social facilitation effect, while tasks entailing complex intellectual work, such as analyzing complex and multifaceted information to make a decision, are harmed. The negative effect of observers on performance that is not completely routinized through repeated practice is why actors and other performers do so much rehearsing before they have to appear in public.

Another cost of visibility is distraction of effort. People are interested in their reputation and image. Consequently, they spend time on impression management. This need to spend time and other resources on image maintenance increases as public scrutiny increases. And time spent dealing with scrutiny and managing appearances is time that cannot be spent doing other aspects of one's job.

To take the starkest example of how visibility diverts effort, consider the life of a CEO of a publicly traded company. One survey of American CEOs found that they spent 11 percent of their time on corporate governance and administration, which includes investor presentations and conferences, quarterly conference calls, and the like. To put that 11 percent in perspective, this amount of time was as much time as the CEOs reported spending on operations and more time than they spent on product development.[5] A study of 79 CEOs in Japan, even with its less shareholder-obsessed culture, reported that they spent more time on investor relations than they spent on unions, employee training, and outsourcing issues combined.[6]

The distractions caused by the requirements for responding to the demands of visibility can cripple both individual and organizational performance. One biography of Nobel Prize–winning physicist Richard Feynman noted how the attention that came with winning the prize often made it impossible for the winners to continue the research work that brought them distinction in the first place:

> Most scientists knew that not-so-amusing metalaw that the receipt of the Nobel Prize marks the end of one's productive career . . . the fame and distinction tend to accelerate the waning of a scientist's ability to give . . . creative work the time-intensive, fanatical attention that it often requires.[7]

The Wallace Company was the first small manufacturing organization to win the Malcolm Baldrige National Quality Award, which at one time was accompanied by a lot of press and public attention. The visits, press requests, and conferences proved so distracting that the company wound up filing for bankruptcy. An executive commented:

> When you win the Baldrige, there is also an obligation, if not a contractual commitment, to go out and spread the gospel. You also have to open up your business to others who want to see your systems and procedures. That is good, but if you are in the business of trying to survive, it becomes a financial problem and defeats your original purpose of being in business.[8]

There is yet another cost of visibility. Under the pressure to "look good," people and companies are reluctant to take risks or innovate, opting to do what seems safe. This may help to explain the "innovator's dilemma," described by Clayton Christensen.[9] Christensen noted that once companies became large and successful, they seldom introduced the next generation of innovations in their industries, particularly when such innovations were disruptive to their existing business model. This reluctance to innovate occurred even though the large, dominant players typically had the intellectual and financial wherewithal to bring the new technologies to market and in many instances had discovered or developed the new ideas themselves. This process is quite evident in the semiconductor industry, where each generation of new technology has produced different companies that then came to dominate the industry. Under public scrutiny and demands from analysts and the media to perform reliably, industry leaders become unwilling to take the chance of missing a quarter or taking undue risks. Because of the costs of scrutiny, it can pay to be under the radar for as long as possible, and this is true whether you are a company or an individual trying to forge a path to power.

COST 2: THE LOSS OF AUTONOMY

James March, a very distinguished organizational scholar and political scientist, once remarked that you could have power or autonomy, but not both. How right he was. When I asked a former colleague what changed when he became a business school dean, his reply was that he lost control over his schedule. Whereas once he could exercise, take time to think and reflect, and do things that interested him, now there were many people and constituencies wanting to see him. Like many senior leaders, his "office" scheduled his time, and unless he got to them and blocked time for himself before they scheduled every minute, there would be no free time or even time whose allocation he controlled so he could move his agenda forward.

At first, in a powerful role, all the demands for your attention are flattering—after all, it's great that so many people want to see you. Therefore people who have recently been promoted tend to be overwhelmed by the time demands of their more powerful job. Not wanting to refuse requests by groups and individuals whose support they may need and whose attention they value, powerful people can easily find themselves overscheduled and working too many hours, something that drains their energy and leaves them unable to cope with the unexpected challenges of their job. After a while, most of the CEOs and other senior leaders I know block out time for themselves and the activities that they want to do. But all of them talk about the loss of control over how they spend their time as one of the big costs of being in a position of power.

COST 3: THE TIME AND EFFORT REQUIRED

Building and maintaining power requires time and effort, there are no two ways about it. Time spent on your quest for power and status is time that you cannot spend on other things, such as hobbies or personal relationships and families. The quest for power often exacts a high toll on people's personal lives, and although everyone bears some costs, the price seems to be particularly severe for women.

Frances Conley was one of the first female neurosurgeons and, at the time of her retirement, chief of staff for the Veterans Administration hospital in Palo Alto, an associate dean at Stanford University's School of Medicine, and an accomplished researcher whose work had helped start a biotechnology company. Conley's life in academic medicine, described in her autobiography, was demanding.[10] Her husband, Phil, a Harvard MBA, left the corporate world and did investment management for them and for others, playing the role of supportive spouse, doing much of the cooking, and taking care of the house. Phil occasionally resented the fact that, for his wife, patients and work came first. As for having children, Conley wrote, "by the time of my tenure review in 1982, Phil and I had decided . . . that we would not have children. Having children never seemed to fit into our lives—I was always a student, an intern, a resident, or a faculty person, driven to succeed."[11]

Things aren't that different today. An up-and-coming, high-potential, 41-year-old female executive at a large shoe company told me in 2009 that of the top 100 or so women at her company, there were very, very few in traditional marriages with children. Some of the senior women were single, like her; some were married with no children. Speaking of her own situation, she said she had no real personal life: she had moved numerous times for her career, and men often saw her as "threatening" because she was a strong and successful woman. Andrea Wong, the CEO of Lifetime Television and a former executive at ABC, where she developed a number of the early reality shows, is in her early forties and has never married. An executive running retail operations in China for a large oil company is married with children, but her husband does not work. Although there are strong, successful women with similarly successful husbands—Hillary and Bill Clinton would be one notable example—such arrangements are still the exception rather than the rule.

Sociologist Hanna Papanek described women's frequent response to the demands of their husbands' occupations as the "two-person single career."[12] Wives contribute to their husbands' success by providing advice and support, entertaining colleagues, and relieving husbands of many of the routine tasks of daily life. Although it is most often women who fill this role, men can and do so also, as I have already described. I have heard many professional women say that they "need a wife," meaning they need someone to help them in their quest for success. Two talented people working on a single career bring more time and resources to bear, enhancing the odds of success. Because of these career dynamics, studies of the graduates of leading professional school programs in law, medicine, and particularly business document the fact that most women 15 years after graduation have dropped out of the labor force, at least temporarily, at some point in their work lives.

The trade-offs between having a successful career and a family, and the fact that the social policies in most industrialized countries don't provide much help navigating this situation, is one reason why virtually every advanced industrialized country with the exception of France has a below-replacement-level birth rate. Research shows that being married and having children has either no effect or a positive effect on men's careers, while most studies show a negative impact on the careers of women from being married and having children.[13]

Put simply, you can't have it all, and the quest for power entails trade-offs, including in one's personal life. Men also confront the choice of how to spend their time, and for them, too, there are only 24 hours in a day. Being successful exacts a price for men also. I recall Jack Valenti, who ran the Motion Picture Association of America for 38 years, expressing his concern that his ambition had been a "dark thread" throughout his life that had taken him away from his family, and he worried, still keeping a busy schedule into his eighties, that he had not spent enough time with his children. Valenti had a house in the Washington, D.C., area and also an apartment in Los Angeles. His wife had not wanted to move to California and in any event, the arrangement worked well given his job. The studio heads and much of the movie industry were mostly in Los Angeles, while the lobbying of both U.S. and other governments occurred in Washington and overseas, so being bicoastal, although hard because of the travel involved, was very helpful for Valenti's ability to do his job.

Getting and keeping power takes time away from friends and family. This is a price that some people are willing to pay. But it is an inevitable cost of pursuing powerful, high-status positions that require time, energy, and focus for success.

COST 4: TRUST DILEMMAS

Here's a simple truth: the higher you rise and the more powerful the position you occupy, the greater the number of people who will want your job. Consequently, holding a position of great power creates a problem: who do you trust? Some people will be seeking to create an opportunity for themselves through your downfall, but they won't be forthcoming about what they are doing. Some people will be trying to curry favor with you by telling you what they think you want to hear so you will like them and help them advance. And some people will be doing both.

Gary Loveman, the former Harvard Business School professor who is now the CEO of Harrah's Entertainment, commented that the higher you rise in an organization, the more people are going to tell you that you are right. This leads to an absence of critical thought and makes it difficul for senior leaders to get the truth—a problem both for the company and its leaders, as you can't address problems if you don't know about them. Loveman tried to overcome this problem by regularly and publicly admitting the mistakes he made so that others would be encouraged to admit where they had messed up too. He also placed a lot of emphasis on the process by which decisions got made—particularly, the use of data and analytics—and almost no emphasis on *who* was making the decision. Gary was conscious of the tendency for people in power to become deeply self-righteous and believe their own hype. This problem is difficult to overcome as it plays into our natural tendency to want to think highly of ourselves, but Loveman tried to overcome this tendency by seeking the opinions of outsiders with no stake in Harrah's and by encouraging open debate and critical self-reflection within the company.

Loveman's success at Harrah's and his position as a leading executive in the gaming industry insulated him, to some extent, from coup attempts. But no one in a position of power is completely immune from palace revolts. Patricia Seeman, a Swiss executive coach and adviser to numerous high-ranking executives, particularly in the financial services industry, told me that in the typical senior management team, all the people reporting to the CEO believe they could hold the CEO position, many think they could do better than the incumbent, and most direct reports aspire to their boss's job. Some people are going to be willing to take their turn and hope that they will be chosen when the incumbent steps down, but others will be more proactive in their efforts to move up. Therefore, for CEOs to survive in their jobs, they need to be able to discern who is undermining them and be tough enough to remove those people before they themselves lose the power struggle. What's true for CEOs is also true for other senior-level executives with ambitious subordinates.

Ross Johnson, formerly CEO of Nabisco, is justly famous for his role in the first huge leveraged buyout, the RJR Nabisco transaction described so well in the book *Barbarians at the Gate*.[14] But where Johnson really excelled was maneuvering himself into CEO jobs and eliminating rivals who naively trusted him. When Johnson engineered the merger of Standard Brands, where he was CEO, into Nabisco, the huge cookie and cracker manufacturer, he was ostensibly in the number two role and faced numerous internal Nabisco rivals. One was Dick Owens, Nabisco's chief financial officer—at the time of the merger promoted to the title of executive vice president and appointed to the board of directors. "Whatever Owens wanted, Johnson got him. He approved a steady stream of Owens's requests for new aides. . . . In Johnson's warm embrace, Owens's financial fiefdom grew greatly." That is, until Johnson went to the CEO and told him that Owens had built too large and too centralized a financial empire. Owens was then replaced for a time by Johnson himself.[15]

Next, Johnson gracefully pushed the CEO aside, doing it with flattery and kindness. Johnson had Nabisco endow a chair in accounting at Pace University in the name of the CEO, Robert Schaeberle. He ensured that the board named the new Nabisco research center building after the CEO. Soon, Johnson was the CEO of Nabisco. As Johnson's allies realized, "a man who had his name on a building . . . might as well be dead."[16]

When you are in power, you should probably trust no single

person in your organization too much, unless you are certain of their loyalty and that they are not after your job. The constant vigilance required by those in power—to ensure they are hearing the truth and to maintain their position vis-à-vis rivals—is yet another cost of occupying a job that many others want.

COST 5: POWER AS AN ADDICTIVE DRUG

Nick Binkley, a guitar-playing, song-writing (he has produced several music CDs) graduate in political science from Colorado College, with a master's degree in international studies from Johns Hopkins School of Advanced International Studies, made a career in finance when he figured out he could not support himself doing music full-time. Binkley joined Security Pacific Bank in California as an assistant vice president in 1977 and rose through the ranks, moving to the bank holding company's financial services systems division in 1983 and eventually becoming vice chairman of Security Pacific Corporation responsible for all the nonbanking subsidiaries, which included venture capital and personal finance (e.g., personal lines of credit). When Bank of America purchased Security Pacific in the early 1990s, Binkley became vice chairman and a member of Bank of America's board of directors with an extensive portfolio of businesses within the bank.

In his senior positions, first at Security Pacific and then at Bank of America, Binkley had all the perquisites of power. He recounted flying with the Security Pacific CEO in a private jet for a lunch in Japan and then flying back after the lunch. He had access to positions on nonprofit boards, tickets for the opera and symphony when he wanted them, and helicopters, private planes, and limousines to take him around. When Bank of America acquired Security Pacific,

Binkley got a golden parachute to protect him in the event that he lost his job. Although encouraged by Bank of America's CEO at the time, Richard Rosenberg, to stay at the bank, Binkley figured that as a senior outsider, he did not necessarily have the most secure future, so he decided, as his parachute was expiring, to "pull the cord," leaving with some colleagues from the venture capital operation to form Forrest, Binkley and Brown, a venture capital and private equity firm that was backed by the Sid and Lee Bass interests of Fort Worth, Texas.

As Binkley described it, one day he was vice chair of one of the largest banks in the world, and the next day he was not. The transition was, to put it mildly, difficult. He notes that occupying a senior-level corporate position in a large organization requires an enormous amount of energy to get through the day. To be a public figure and perform at a high level requires an intensity that produces, in his words, "a caffeinated high." When you leave such a position and that level of activity ceases, it is almost, as Binkley put it, "like a car going from ninety miles an hour to a dead stop." When the adrenaline rush ceases, there is a visceral, physiological reaction. In addition to the change in activity and intensity level, there is also the change from being the center of a universe of people fawning over you and heeding your every request to a more "normal" and less in-the-limelight existence. As a high-level executive in a large corporation, Binkley observed, you are surrounded by "players"—that is, by people of equally high status. And when you no longer have that job, you lose these associations because most of the people are only interested in your companionship when you hold status and power. This feeling of no longer being a player or a member of the elite is a loss felt intensely by many who have been successful at the power-and-money game.

Nick Binkley described a withdrawal that had physiological as well as psychological components—he was literally ill and had difficulty sleeping. He could not imagine that withdrawal from hard drugs could have been any more difficult. The loss of power, even though voluntary, put stress on his marriage which, in the end, not only endured but became stronger. Today Binkley is a member of the outside financial advisory board of the San Francisco Zen Center; he also serves on corporate boards and is winding down the venture capital firm after some 17 years. He was attracted to the Zen Center's Buddhist meditation and spiritual practices when he sought help in coping with the "power withdrawal symptoms." In the center of frenetic energy and attention, it is difficult not to lose one's identity and values.

While I was visiting the London Business School in 2005, Jack Welch, the former CEO of General Electric, came to give a talk and promote his newest book. As Welch lapped up the adulation of the LBS students, I thought to myself, "Why is he doing this at this stage in his life?" One can reasonably conjecture, not just for Welch but for many other people who have left positions of great power and status and continue to serve on multiple boards and maintain an intense pace, that, accustomed as they were during their work life to days filled with frenetic activity, once out of the job they seek to re-create the same peripatetic life, the same adrenaline high, and if possible, the same level of adulation they once received routinely.

People have a heightened risk of death in the period immediately after they lose their job—and not just because of greater financial stress or the absence of medical insurance. As Michael Marmot, a British researcher on the effects of social standing on health, has written, one reason there is a connection between not working and health is because being out of work "represents loss of a social role and all the things that go with it."[17]

Power is addictive, in both a psychological and physical sense. The rush and excitement from being involved in important discussions with senior figures and the ego boost from having people at your beck and call are tough to lose, even if you voluntarily choose to retire or leave and even if you have more money than you could ever spend. In a power- and celebrity-obsessed culture, to be "out of power" is to be out of the limelight, away from the action, and almost invisible. It is a tough transition to make. And because it is, some executives seek to avoid switching to a less powerful role—Sandy Weill of Citigroup and Hank Greenberg of AIG worked long past normal retirement age and finally were forced out by boards of directors of these large public companies when they refused to anoint successors. Bill Paley of CBS asked his biographer Sally Bedell Smith why he had to die as he maintained control of the media company into his eighties. These examples and numerous others illustrate yet another price of power—the addictive quality that makes it tough to leave powerful positions. But everyone eventually has to step down, and the druglike nature of power makes leaving a powerful position a truly wrenching experience for some.

In the introduction, we saw some of the benefits of achieving power and status—longer life and better health, the potential for monetizing power and fame to create wealth, and the ability to accomplish important organizational and social change. In this chapter, we see the other side of the equation—the costs of achieving and holding powerful positions. You should not necessarily eschew power, but it is important to recognize the potential downsides. The balance between the advantages and the costs is something each individual must weigh in deciding his or her own particular relationship with power.

11

How—and Why—People Lose Power

Even after achieving a powerful, top-level position, staying on top is scarcely guaranteed. The CEO position, particularly in the United States, has become extremely powerful. Incumbent CEOs control enormous financial resources, have carte blanche to bring in supporters and dismiss underlings who challenge their authority, and can influence the selection of boards of directors, ostensibly their bosses. Nonetheless, as consulting firm Booz Allen reported, the annual turnover rate of corporate CEOs increased 59 percent between 1995 and 2006. This increase occurred worldwide, not just in the United States. During that same period, instances where CEOs were fired or pushed out rose by 318 percent.[1]

Things aren't different for leaders in other domains. One study of business school deans noted that among the 100 members of the Association of Business Schools in the United Kingdom, there had been 41 changes of incumbent in the preceding two years.[2] The average tenure of school superintendents in the United States in districts with more than 25,000 students is less than six years.[3] Leaders of health-care organizations now face shorter tenures because of the growing challenges and instability in that sector.[4] Even volunteer organizations such as the American Red Cross have faced leadership turmoil.[5]

If you manage to get to a position of power, it would be nice to keep it for a while. Although each case of lost power has its own peculiarities, there are some common factors that you need to avoid. While it is inevitable that everyone will lose power eventually—we all get old and leave our positions—it is not inevitable that people will lose power as often or as quickly as they do. Jack Valenti ran the Motion Picture Association of America for almost 40 years—and he reported to the major studio heads, not necessarily the nicest or best bosses in the world. Willie Brown was speaker of the California Assembly for more than a decade and would probably still be in the job if term limits had not forced him from the legislature. Alfred Sloan was CEO of General Motors for 23 years and chairman of its board for 19, and Robert Moses held dominion over New York's parks, bridges, and public works for almost 40 years, outlasting numerous powerful and flamboyant mayors and governors. Holding on to power is difficult and becoming more so, but it is not impossible.

OVERCONFIDENCE, DISINHIBITION, AND IGNORING THE INTERESTS OF OTHERS

The old saying "Power corrupts" turns out to be mostly true, although "corrupt" is probably not quite the right word. Berkeley social psychologist Dacher Keltner and his colleagues talk about power leading to "approach" behavior—in that people more actively try to obtain what they want—and diminishing "inhibition," or the tendency to follow social rules and constraints that might limit what people do to obtain their goals.[6] Such behavior is a logical consequence of what happens to people in power. The obsequious and less powerful flatter the powerful to remain on their good side. Those with power have their wishes and requests granted. They get used to getting their way and being treated as if they are special. Although the powerful may be conscious that the special treatment comes from the position they occupy and the resources they control, over time these thoughts fade. As a friend who works at a senior position in British Petroleum and has observed its CEOs at close range told me, "No matter what the original intentions and aspiration, eventually power goes to everyone's head."

Studies of the effects of power on the power holder consistently find that power produces overconfidence and risk taking,[7] insensitivity to others, stereotyping, and a tendency to see other people as a means to the power holder's gratification. In a study all too reminiscent of what goes on in workplaces every day, David Kipnis put research participants in a simulated work situation with a subordinate. Some people in the managerial role had little formal control over resources and had to influence through persuasion, while others were given the power to reward and punish those working for them. The more control participants had over levers of power such as pay increases or decreases, the more attempts they made to influence their subordinates. Moreover, those with more power came to see their subordinates' job performance as resulting from their control and less from the efforts or motivation of those they were supervising. And because the supervisors with power saw themselves as superior to those they were supervising, they evidenced less desire to spend time with their subordinates and wanted to distance themselves from those less powerful—even though in this experimental study who was a supervisor and how much power that person had was randomly determined and temporary.[8]

One lesson from the growing number of studies on the effects of power is how little it takes to get people into a power mind-set where they engage in all kinds of disrespectful and rude behavior. Just having them think about a time when they were in power and able to get what they wanted (in contrast to having them think about a time they had little power and could not) or giving them even modest control over meaningless rewards in temporary groups of strangers seems to be sufficient.

In one of the more well-known and interesting studies of the effects of power, the Berkeley cookie study, groups of three strangers discussed a long and boring list of social issues for 30 minutes. One member of the group was randomly chosen by the experimenter to fill the role of assigning experimental points—which had no substantive consequence—to the other two. When the experimenter arrived with a plate of cookies, each person naturally took one. The individual randomly assigned to give points to the other two was more likely to take a second cookie, more likely to chew with his mouth open, and more likely to scatter crumbs on his face and the table.[9]

Overconfidence and insensitivity lead to losing power, as people become so full of themselves that they fail to attend to the needs of those whose enmity can cause them problems. Conversely, not letting power go to your head and acting as if you were all-powerful can help you maintain your position. Safra Catz came to Oracle in 1999 with an undefined role; today she is president of the large software company. Oracle has regularly gone through high-profile senior leaders, including one former president, Ray Lane, and Marc Benioff, who left a senior vice president position to found Salesforce.com. The company seems to particularly reject senior executives whose profiles get too big. Catz avoids publicity and anything that might upstage Oracle founder and CEO Larry Ellison. And although she is rich and powerful—a profile in *Fortune* listed her as one of the most powerful women executives in the

United States—she has always known her place. As Adam Lashinsky's profile of Catz noted:

> Initially, she didn't even have an office, working instead at a round table near Ellison's. . . . A senior executive from the Oracle unit that sells to the federal government arranged a meeting with Catz to figure out what she did. "I'm here to help Larry," Catz said, according to an attendee.[10]

As they focus on achieving their own or the organization's objectives, those with power pay less attention to those who are less powerful. But this lack of attention can cost leaders their jobs. Bernadine Healy, a cardiologist, lasted just two years as head of the American Red Cross. In many ways, the Red Cross has been a troubled organization. One of the largest providers in the blood banking business, the Red Cross has faced criticism from the Food and Drug Administration over its practices in tracking and screening blood donations. After the September 11 attack on the World Trade Center, the Red Cross was criticized for using the disaster to raise vast sums of money, much of which was spent on general operations or relief for other disasters. Between 1989 and December 2001, when Healy was fired, there had been three leaders and four interim leaders.[11]

Healy came in determined to fix a troubled organization and, she thought, with a mandate to make major change. The Red Cross had a history of decentralization, with local chapter autonomy and a large, 50-person board drawn mostly from local chapters that did not like criticism and was not about to buckle under pressure from the top. Healy's downfall began, ironically, with the discovery of financial impropriety in a small, poor chapter in Hudson, New Jersey, where the director had engaged in embezzlement. "Veteran administrators thought that she should have suspended the employee *with* pay and they objected to involving external auditors."[12]

Having a position of formal authority or even being right is not going to win you the support of those whose mistakes you have called out. It is tough for those in power to see the world from others' perspectives—but if you are going to survive, you need to get over yourself and your formal position and retain your sensitivity to the political dynamics around you.

Patricia Seeman, a consultant and executive coach to senior Swiss executives, says that the best way to hold on to your position is to maintain your perspective and balance. She commented that "unless you understand yourself pretty well, you're going to lose control of yourself." Seeman told me that a former chairman of Swiss Re had this advice for maintaining a sense of perspective about oneself: "What you have to do is every now and then expose yourself to a social circle that really doesn't care about your position." So this brilliant and powerful senior leader would go back to his primary school, somewhere in a village in the Alps—to the people to whom he was just the same person he was when he was seven years old.

Unfortunately, people who arrive at high-level positions with lots of power often do not like to be reminded of what and who they once were and how far they have come. They will sometimes divorce the spouses who were there at the beginning of their careers and take on a trophy companion. They will leave behind associates who can remind them of the time when they did not have so much power. To the extent that you can resist such tendencies and the behavioral changes that come with power, you are more likely to keep your influence.

MISPLACED OR TOO MUCH TRUST

When you are powerful and successful, you are overconfident and less observant—and one specific manifestation of such tendencies is to trust what others tell you and rely on their assurances. As you become less vigilant and paranoid about others' intentions, they have the opportunity to take you out of your position of power.

When NationsBank, based in Charlotte, North Carolina, and the Bank of America, headquartered in San Francisco, merged in 1998, it was to be a merger of equals with shared governance between the managements of the two institutions. David Coulter, the Carnegie-Mellon business school–trained Bank of America CEO, had entered the merger thinking it was great for both companies. Approaching the transaction as an intellectual challenge to increase shareholder value and improve the organization, Coulter believed the assurances about shared power and did not see the power play unfolding. He trusted the promises provided by Hugh McColl, the CEO of NationsBank, about Coulter's significant role in the merged institution. David Demarest, director of White House communications under the first President Bush, was vice president and director of corporate communications at BankAmerica Corporation at the time of the merger. He related what happened:

> It was really an amazing phenomenon. I went to a media roundtable with the *Charlotte Observer*, with David and Hugh in which Hugh almost got teary-eyed talking about how great David Coulter was and how he [Hugh] might just retire a little early because he sees the value of this guy. And it was really quite a performance. And within weeks, many of the commitments about how things were going to be—"we're just going to pick the best person for each slot"—started to unravel. At this point,

> the rumor has it he [Coulter] checked with some legal counsel as to whether we could unravel the deal. And when that got around, that's when Hugh said, "Enough of this" and then you could see the press stories that were coming out from Charlotte about, "Wow, there's this screw up in the old Bank of America and we didn't know that this program was so poorly funded," and you could see the building of the case for why they were going to get rid of Coulter.

David Coulter trusted what Hugh McColl, a man who kept an allegedly live hand grenade on his desk, told him—and it cost him his job. Less than three weeks after the merger, Coulter resigned as president of BankAmerica Corporation. As one press reporter noted, "McColl and his lieutenants blew away the trusting BankAmerica folks, who forgot that war can be brutal."[13]

Coulter's not alone. People will do lots of things to acquire power—but you shouldn't necessarily rely on them to keep their word once they have it. Lee Kuan Yew, the longtime prime minister of Singapore, came to power by latching on to a pro-communist movement, usurping its rhetoric, and seizing control of it. Once in power, he turned on his communist allies, not only discarding them but in some instances jailing them. As he explained:

> First, we had to get rid of the British. . . . To do that, you had to mobilize support from the widest possible group and get as big a majority of the population as you could. . . . First, you've got to get power. Then, having got power, you say, "What's the problem? Have I said these things? If so, let's forget it."[14]

Lee and his political party have maintained power for decades in Singapore by never forgetting his own behavior and, therefore, never becoming complacent about their potential enemies and opposition and excessively trusting the good words of others. Stan Sesser's portrait of Singapore called it a city of fear, and his reporting detailed numerous examples of opposition leaders and others concerned about staying on the good side of Lee and his colleagues.[15]

One way to figure out how much to trust people is to look at what they do. As the saying goes, "Actions speak louder than words." In the BankAmerica-NationsBank merger, McColl prevailed on Coulter to modify the original deal for a board evenly split between members from the two banks' boards and got the headquarters for the combined institution moved to Charlotte. That should have been a signal that he was interested in control, not just shareholder well-being. The 13-to-12 split on the board in favor of NationsBank doomed Coulter in the resulting power struggle.

PEOPLE LOSE PATIENCE

Dr. Modesto Alex "Mitch" Maidique voluntarily stepped down as president of Florida International University in Miami in 2009, having served for 23 years. That term of service made Maidique, a Cuban American, the longest-serving university president in Florida and the second-longest-serving research university president in the United States. Maidique, a prominent member of the Miami community, was involved in the hiring of Rudy Crew—the same Rudy Crew who was fired after being named the best superintendent in the United States. How could Maidique stay in an extremely political position for such a long time while Crew could not? There are many answers to this question, and the jobs each held are clearly different, but part of it has to do with patience.

As Mitch explained to me, being in a powerful position in a

large, visible institution is difficult. You have to attend functions for people you don't necessarily like—weddings, bar mitzvahs, fundraisers, funerals—sometimes when you would rather be doing something else. But you have to be at these events to fulfill social obligations and expectations and also to solidify your relationships with people who are important to your ability to do and keep your job. Moreover, in a visible position such as university president, everybody—students, faculty, alumni, citizens, staff—has an opinion about what you could be doing to do your job better, and many feel free to share their views with you and with the public. Many of these people don't know what they are talking about and all of them take time away from the difficult task of, in this case, running a university of some 38,000 students with rapidly expanding research funding. After a while, it is easy to lose patience and lash out at the sorry fools who are making your job more difficult than it should be—except, as Maidique thoughtfully noted, some of these "sorry fools" can cost you your position. After decades in public education, Rudy Crew had lost patience with the patronage, the pettiness, and the fact that tens of thousands of children were getting left behind. He was simply unwilling to choose his words carefully. Maidique, in all the decades at the helm of FIU, somehow managed to keep his composure and outward demeanor of charm, regardless of what he actually felt.

It's easier to lose your patience when you are in power—power leads to disinhibition, to not watching what you say and do, to being more concerned about yourself than about the feelings of others. But losing patience causes people to lose control and offend others, and that can cost them their jobs.

PEOPLE GET TIRED

It is hard work to keep your ego in check, to constantly be attentive to the actions of others, and obtaining and keeping power requires long hours and lots of energy. After a while, some people get tired; they become less vigilant and more willing to compromise and give in. We always tend to see what we want or expect to see, but as people get burned out, the tendency to project desires onto reality becomes stronger.

Tony Levitan and a classmate, Fred Campbell, knew that they wanted to start a special company with a unique, egalitarian culture. When they graduated from business school in 1993, they began a company that would become eGreetings, which initially sold and then gave away electronic greeting cards on the Internet. Campbell was the CEO, Levitan the co-CEO, but they had a shared leadership model and used unusual job titles—Levitan called himself the creator of chaos—to signal that they wanted to build a place where employees could have fun. Their business, probably ahead of its time given the evolution of the Internet, went public under the symbol EGRT in 1999. The dot-com crash doomed the organization, and it was sold for a modest sum to American Greetings. By the time that all occurred, however, Tony Levitan had already left the company.

The work of launching a start-up is demanding. "I'm the kind of guy that I really just dive into things," said Campbell. "So I spend seven days a week; if I'm not at work, I'm thinking about it. But it also takes a toll on me, and I eventually burn out." When he started working with Levitan, he said he was good for about five years.

Levitan was also getting tired from the stress and the grind. When Campbell announced he was going to leave, Levitan did not press the board of directors to become the sole CEO. Instead, the company hired a search firm to seek an outside successor. But it was a tough time to attract good CEO talent, as the Internet bubble was approaching its height. The search itself went on for seven months—not that unusual, as a high fraction of searches are never completed successfully. The long search process further exhausted people at eGreetings. The company finally hired Gordon Tucker, even though Levitan and others had some apprehensions about his fit with the culture and his management style. Tony was tired and the board felt a sense of urgency. Shortly after Tucker's arrival, Levitan was marginalized and soon left eGreetings. In talking to Tony Levitan about the lessons he learned as a cofounder being forced out of the company he had started, he emphasized that he was just getting too tired to remain on his game, be alert to the maneuverings, and continue to fight.

If you feel yourself getting tired or burned out and you hold a position of substantial power, you might as well leave. There are going to be others who will be willing to wrest your position from you. With reduced energy and vigilance, you won't be able to resist very well in any case.

THE WORLD CHANGES, BUT TACTICS DON'T

When Robert Nardelli was CEO of Home Depot, he ran a shareholders' annual meeting like a despot, with other board members absent and shareholders denied an opportunity to voice questions or concerns as their microphones were turned off. He probably thought he was doing nothing unusual. After all, the age of the imperial CEO was in full flower, and ignoring shareholder activists was neither something new nor unheard of. But his behavior provoked outrage and contributed, among other things, to his losing his job. There is much commentary about the leadership skills of the "new" CEO—

and among such skills are listening, paying attention to multiple constituencies, and displaying less arrogance than CEOs got away with in the past. For Nardelli, times had changed. He had not figured that out, or if he had, he couldn't adjust his style.

Nor did New York parks commissioner Robert Moses, who remained in power for almost 40 years, into his eighties, fully recognize changed circumstances. In 1956, West Side mothers protested his plans to take less than a one-acre parcel out of New York's Central Park to make a parking lot for the Tavern on the Green restaurant. Moses dealt with those mothers as he had dealt with opponents to his construction projects for years. He ignored their opposition and laid plans to cut down the trees during the night. The mothers' protest did not impress him, as Robert Caro's biography makes clear:

> On the seismograph on which Moses recorded public tremors, in fact, the Tavern-on-the-Green protest had barely registered. Twenty-three mothers? He had just finished evicting hundreds of mothers rather than shift a section of his Cross-Bronx Expressway a single block! He was at that very moment in the process of displacing *five thousand* mothers for Manhattantown, *four thousand* for Lincoln Center! A parking lot, and a tiny parking lot at that![16]

In this instance, there was press coverage and public criticism such as Robert Moses had never faced before. He backed down and put in a playground instead of the parking lot. His reputation for always winning had been tarnished and public scrutiny of his actions was heightened. Some of his confidants said that his ability to get his way was never quite the same after that, even though he held his many positions for more than a decade longer. The problem was that the idea of bulldozers and bulldozing had begun to take on a different connotation in the 1950s and 1960s than it had in the 1920s, when the building of parks and other public works was in its infancy and the improvements were more desperately needed.

People—and companies—fall into competency traps. They are successful because they do certain things in a certain way. The U.S. automakers got rich making minivans and then sport utility vehicles. When the market changed to smaller cars, the car companies didn't notice the change, and when they did, they had little expertise in moving to the new market segments. General Electric was lionized for its diversified financial structure that provided some risk mitigation because it operated in so many different economic sectors. When conglomerates fell from fashion, GE was stuck. Al Dunlap became a hero for downsizing the companies he ran, and Frank Lorenzo was cheered in various business schools for his battles with the labor unions, first at Eastern Airlines and then when he ran Continental. Both downsizing and union busting were strategies for a certain time and place, but eventually they lost their effectiveness; neither Dunlap nor Lorenzo seemed to notice. Companies and leaders can fail to see the changes in the social environment that can make old ways less successful than they once were. The tendency of power to diminish the power holder's attention and sensitivity to others with less power compounds this problem. The combination of diminished vigilance and changed circumstances often leads to the loss of power.

LEAVE GRACEFULLY

In the end, of course, everyone loses power. As organizational behavior professor Jeffrey Sonnenfeld noted in his book *The Hero's Farewell*, some individuals make way for their successors. Others hang on past the time when they are effective. Armand Hammer, the CEO and creator of Occidental Petroleum, put in a long-term incentive compensation system for himself with a ten-year payout—when he was in his nineties.

Some senior leaders prepare successors and leave to do other things. Jack Welch had a number of possible replacements when he stepped down from General Electric, and after his retirement as CEO, he became a columnist, author, and speaker about management issues. Bill George, former CEO of Medtronic, went on to a career as a faculty member at Harvard Business School and a writer and speaker on leadership issues.

It is both possible and desirable to, as my wife nicely puts it, "leave before the party's over" and to do so in a way that causes others to remember you fondly. You cannot always completely control how much power you maintain, but you can leave your position with dignity and thereby influence your legacy.

12

Power Dynamics: Good for Organizations, Good for You?

THIS BOOK has been about creating your path to power and, even if you don't want a lot of power, figuring out how to survive the organizational dynamics you will almost certainly experience. Which raises the question I am often asked: "Is all of this political behavior good for the organization, even if it is good for me and my career?"

At first glance, this concern about political behavior in organizations seems justified. One dominant perspective in the research literature on organizations is that "politics is associated with the 'dark side' of workplace behaviour and researchers have described political behaviour as inherently divisive, stressful, and a cause of dissent and reduced performance."[1] The empirical evidence supports this view. Higher levels of perceived politics inside organizations are associated with reduced job satisfaction, morale, and organizational commitment, and higher levels of perceived politics are also correlated with higher intentions to quit.[2]

But I'm not sure you should worry about the effect of your

behavior on the organization, because there is lots of data to suggest that organizations don't care very much about you. In the spring of 2009, *VentureBeat* reported that four partners were leaving the large and venerable venture capital firm Venrock.[3] Tony Sun, a managing partner who had been at the firm for 30 years and over that time had made his partners literally billions of dollars, was going. So, too, was David Siminoff, who had joined Venrock only two years before to much fanfare because of his experience in the digital media space—he had been CEO of Spark Networks, which ran JDate, the Jewish dating cite, and had founded 4INFO, a leading mobile research service. Also leaving were Eric Copeland, who had been at Venrock for 11 years and who had a strong background in engineering with experience in digital communications technologies, and Rich Moran, a former senior Accenture consulting firm executive. Moran had been brought into Venrock after doing consulting work helping improve its decision processes and organizational dynamics.

Although the "official" story was that the departures were voluntary, they were not. Tony Sun was caught off guard by the request for him to step down. When he thought about resisting his ouster, he learned that the partners pushing for his removal had outmaneuvered him. They had already told the limited partners (investors) about the move and lined up their support. Moran, retained for a few months in the transitional role of executive in residence, was also caught off guard by his and the others' ousters. When I asked him why he would be forced out given that he had just recently been brought into the firm to provide "adult supervision" to the ego-driven interpersonal dynamics, his insightful response was that people who were behaving badly didn't want to be reminded of their bad behavior, even by having someone around with the responsibility for improving organizational processes.

It's probably to be expected that at the senior levels in partnerships, people get pushed out in coups and revolts—something that happened even to Pete Peterson, the billionaire cofounder of Black-Rock, the money management firm, when he got into a power struggle with Lew Glucksman, who forced him out of his role as the leader of investment bank Lehman Brothers, at that time a partnership.[4] When he was forced out in a power struggle at the large law firm Jones Day, government contracts lawyer Eldon Crowell took most of the Washington office with him as he founded Crowell and Moring.[5] Numerous managing partners have been unceremoniously ousted from large accounting firms.[6]

The many involuntary departures at partnerships occur with particular frequency when times are tough. Research shows what common sense suggests is true: political struggles are more likely to occur and to be more fierce and power is used more often when resources are scarcer and therefore there is more struggle over their allocation. Studies of budget allocations in universities found that when money was tighter, the relationship between departmental power and the amount of the budget obtained was stronger.[7] As one venture capital partner told me, "When the money was rolling in and times were great, I could more readily tolerate some of the partners behaving like jerks. If they weren't making me a lot of money and we had to shrink the firm, my tolerance for their behavior went way down." An article on the venture capital industry in the summer of 2009 listed the numerous partners leaving the industry as the number of principals shrank from 8,892 to 7,497 in one year.[8] So the turmoil at Venrock was occurring elsewhere in the industry as well, as capital flows decreased, limited partners complained about poor returns, and the number and size of firms declined. The lesson is clear: you should always watch your back, but be particularly wary and sensitive to what is occurring during times of economic stress. That is when political turmoil and the use of power are likely to be at their peak.

You may be thinking, "What does this have to do with me?" When senior-level people get thrown out or lose a power struggle, they leave with more money than most of us ever dreamed of, and power struggles at the upper ranks are common enough to be almost predictable. But these events aren't confined to the senior executive ranks: people can find themselves caught off guard and out of a job, even if they have done what was expected of them. Ray was brought into Unisys, the computer company, to build a leadership development effort. He did so with great success, putting a large number of senior executives through a very highly rated program and earning the approval of the CEO at the time. But when that CEO retired, Ray faced a layoff or reduction in force—of precisely one person, himself. He did not have the support of the staff in the human resources department, which actually resented his independent success and executive access, and they eliminated him as soon as they could.

Nor is it the case that this sort of infighting and political behavior is confined just to men or to male-dominated organizations. In a nonprofit organization in the San Francisco area, when the leader stepped down and some other senior people left their positions for other opportunities at around the same time, a senior woman moved quickly to try to take over control of additional functions and positions and also to eliminate people she perceived as being in the way of increasing her power.

If organizations aren't worrying about you and you can lose your job in a political struggle or on a whim, why should you worry about them? Reciprocity works both ways. This is not a book about broken promises, but the list of companies that have shown little concern for their employees is enormous. Defined-benefit pension plans have been terminated or changed, with retirement risks shifted to employees and benefits cut. Health insurance has been abandoned or premiums and copayments have been dramatically increased.

Meanwhile, people who may have retired thinking they were going to get health insurance find that companies are going through bankruptcy to shed these obligations or, in other cases where they are not contractually guaranteed, simply changing the deal.[9] Not only have layoffs, the offshoring of work, outsourcing, and other forms of "restructuring" (a terrible euphemism) increased over past decades; they are sometimes instigated not in response to financial stress but simply to increase profits or copy what other companies are doing.

The employer-employee relationship has profoundly changed over the past several decades, not just in the United States but in many countries. In ways big and small, both implicitly and explicitly, employers and their leaders have told their employees that they themselves are responsible for their own careers and, in many instances, their own health care and retirement. If people have to fend for themselves on the job, never knowing when or, in the United States with its doctrine of at-will employment, even why they might be let go, then it seems to me they should use every means at their disposal to ensure their organizational survival—and that includes mastering the concepts and skills of power and influence.

More than 20 years ago, Paul Hirsch, now a business school professor at Northwestern, wrote a book titled *Pack Your Own Parachute*, suggesting that managers be less loyal to their companies and adopt free-agent thinking.[10] To survive in the new world of work, managers needed to be visible, marketable, and, above all, mobile. The idea of an economy employing free agents has a sometimes overly rosy and unrealistic view of the upside potential of having to fend for oneself. It also doesn't fully acknowledge the economic and psychological risks of being employed when you can be fired "at will," for any or no reason at all.

So don't worry about how your efforts to build your path to power are affecting your employer, because your employer is probably not worrying about you. Neither are your coworkers or "partners," if you happen to have any—they are undoubtedly thinking about your usefulness to them, and you will be gone, if they can manage it, when you are no longer of use. You need to take care of yourself and use whatever means you have to do so—after all, that has been the message of companies and business pundits for years. Take those admonitions seriously.

POWER AND HIERARCHY ARE UBIQUITOUS

Holding aside the fact that you are probably in an environment where survival of the fittest—the most politically skilled—prevails, even if you wanted to avoid the organizational politics, I don't think it is possible. I have had entrepreneurs tell me they wanted to created businesses free of organizational power dynamics, but there is evidence that suggests this is impossible. So the original question posed at the beginning of this chapter—"Is all of this political behavior good for the organization?"—may be irrelevant because these processes are ubiquitous in social interaction.

At some intuitive level, we understand the inevitability of organizational politics. Management researchers Jeffrey Gandz and Victor Murray surveyed 428 managers working in a variety of companies about their opinions of organizational power dynamics. Some 93 percent expressed strong or moderate agreement with the statement, "The existence of workplace politics is common to most organizations," and 89 percent agreed with the statement, "Successful executives must be good politicians." More than three-quarters agreed with the statement, "The higher you go in organizations, the more political the climate becomes," and about 85 percent thought that powerful executives acted politically.[11]

One of the reasons why power moves and political dynamics are so common is that hierarchy is ubiquitous in animal societies—even among fish! As soon as hierarchy exists, it is natural to want to move up and avoid being at the bottom. Consequently, there are contests for dominance among all animals that travel or congregate in groups. This includes people. In human interaction, even in the absence of formal organizational arrangements, job titles, and differences in resource endowments, differentiation arises among individuals as they interact.[12] Informal leaders with more influence emerge even if groups are just engaged in pleasurable social interaction such as discussing a book or going on an outing. Research evidence also suggests that the larger the group or organization, the greater the degree of differentiation, including hierarchical differentiation, will be. Therefore, hierarchy will be prevalent in larger collectivities such as many work organizations.[13] Even though organizations vary in the extent to which they attempt to practice shared leadership and the people in specific leadership roles change over time, all organizations create hierarchies and the very existence of hierarchy means that there will be competition for who occupies higher-status positions.

It's too bad that hierarchies are present in all social groups, because, as social psychologist Deborah Gruenfeld has told me, many people have trouble with hierarchical relationships. Some people resent having others in superior positions with more power and the authority to tell them what to do; they act on these feelings by becoming counterdependent and rebelling in ways large and small against authority. Some people are uncomfortable with having power over others, feeling that they don't really deserve to be in positions where they get to control others. The people uncomfortable with their authority don't exercise the leadership that others expect, failing to provide direction that leaves those they supervise lost and uncertain about what to do.

Empirical research demonstrates two facts about hierarchies. First, status is "imported" or "carried" from one setting to another. Personal characteristics that define status in the larger society—such as race, gender, age, and educational credentials—get imported into informal and formal organization settings and are used to create status hierarchies.[14] Status, however derived, tends to generalize across the environments in which we interact. Jon Corzine could move from a leadership position in the investment bank Goldman Sachs to the U.S. Senate to the New Jersey governor's mansion because his personal wealth and social ties could be redeployed and also because people assume that if you are smart enough to succeed in one highly competitive domain, you must be competent in other, even unrelated domains as well. One implication of this phenomenon for you is that the specific organization or domain in which you rise to power may matter less than the fact that you manage to achieve high-level status someplace. The prestige and power that come from achieving a senior position will generalize to some extent to other contexts, providing you with status there as well.

The second fact about hierarchies is that people seem to prefer them. In six experimental studies, social psychologist Larissa Tiedens and her colleagues examined the extent to which people perceived others as different from themselves (either higher or lower) in dominance. These perceptions of difference in dominance were motivated by the desire for positive task relationships as demonstrated by the fact that perceptions of difference in dominance were greater when people expected to interact with the other in task-related interactions. The interpretation was that when people expected to interact on a task, and particularly when task performance was important, they voluntarily constructed differences in hierarchy. This behavior shows that people prefer or expect such differences in status in task settings.[15]

Research by New York University social psychologist John Jost provides even stronger evidence that people seem to prefer hierarchical relationships. Jost's research shows that people will voluntarily contribute to their own disempowerment to maintain a stable hierarchical social order. In a series of studies, Jost found that lower-power groups often developed attitudes that justified their own inferior (and others' more favored) position, thereby contributing to the persistence of hierarchical arrangements that disadvantaged them. So, people attending a lower-status university would not bolster their university's status compared to higher-status schools but accepted the fact of the lower status of their educational institution and the implications of that lowered status.[16]

If hierarchy is a fact of organizational life and, in fact, apparently preferred by people, then hierarchical arrangements will be omnipresent. When hierarchy exists, at least some proportion of people are going to want to enjoy the benefits of holding higher- rather than lower-status positions within hierarchies. Consequently, striving for status and power is going to be common in organizations and, because of its foundation in a hierarchical social order that people desire, will be impossible to eliminate.

INFLUENCE SKILLS ARE USEFUL FOR GETTING THINGS DONE

Most people I talk to think they don't have enough power and would love to become more effective at wielding influence. There are many, many jobs—project or product manager would be one good example—where people have tasks to accomplish that require the cooperation of others but do not have the formal authority to order, reward, or punish those whose cooperation they need.

A product manager seeking to introduce a new version may need the help of engineering or research and development to design the new product, manufacturing to get it produced, and sales attention for distributing it into the market. But in many consumer products companies, product managers do not have line authority over any of these critical functions. Similarly, implementing a new information technology system, such as an enterprise resource planning application, often led by a project manager from IT, requires the assistance of those from the operating units who will need to provide data and also use the system and the cooperation of the finance function, although IT people do not have line authority over either operations or finance. Simply put, responsibility and authority don't always coincide. As organizations have become more matrixed, with overlapping and dotted-line chains of command, employ more task forces and teams to bring disparate expertise together to solve problems, and face greater demands for speed, the premium for execution is going up.

Getting things done under circumstances where you lack direct line authority requires influence and political skills—a knowledge of organizational dynamics—not just technical skills and knowledge. Zia Yusuf, the senior SAP executive described in chapter 3, has been extremely successful in working across organizational boundaries—something he had to do in his roles as leader of the internal strategy consulting team and as head of the SAP ecosystems unit. In describing how he has been able to implement ideas even without a technical background and as an outsider to the company, at least initially, Yusuf emphasized two things: first, do excellent quality work, which entails hiring and effectively leading outstanding talent. And second, understand the organizational dynamics—how different people perceive things, what their interests are, how to make a persuasive case, and how to get along with people and build effective personal relationships.

POLITICAL INFLUENCE VERSUS HIERARCHY IN DECISION MAKING

A fourth way to think about the issue of whether political dynamics are good for organizations is to contrast them with the most common and seemingly preferred alternative—hierarchical decision making with its control, discipline, and orderliness. We seem to like markets and democracies for societies, but prefer more dictatorial arrangements inside organizations. Much has been written about the imperial CEO with ever-increasing salaries and perquisites and unchecked authority, including the power to stifle dissent.[17] Senior executives, and even board members who don't support the CEO, are often ousted.

The political contests for power and influence and lobbying for support for one's ideas that constitute power dynamics in companies can appear messy and chaotic. But maybe there are some useful parallels between countries and the organizations that reside within them. As Winston Churchill noted, "It is said that democracy is the worst form of government except all the others that have been tried."[18] Although people take it as axiomatic that regardless of its faults, a democratic system, complete with campaigns designed to influence voter choice, equal weight for everyone's vote, and politicking to affect decisions, is a great way to make societal-level choices, inside companies democracy is the exception. In spite of many studies showing the superior performance achieved through delegating decision-making authority, little devolution of power has occurred inside companies in the last 50 years. "The idea that . . . organizations can be governed as democratic political systems is alien to mainstream management thinking."[19] And even though many commentators speak about the evils of dictatorship, the folly of central planning, and the wisdom of crowds in making forecasts, centralization of control inside organizations in the hands of a few people prevails.

Maybe, as Churchill's quote suggests, democracy is good not only as a form of government for public entities but also as a way of making better decisions in companies and nonprofits. This was the point made by James Surowiecki's book *The Wisdom of Crowds*. Surowiecki reviewed evidence that not only were collections of individuals better at making estimates and predictions than were experts, often aggregating their judgments through simple voting mechanisms; they can also be more effective in figuring out which product ideas to support and what strategies to pursue.[20]

In many instances, people inside organizations have different goals, and even if they share the same objective, they may have different views of how to accomplish that objective. Inside the UCSF Mt. Zion Medical Center, not everyone thought patient care was the highest priority—as an academic medical center, there was great emphasis on cutting-edge research. Some administrators were worried about meeting budgets and the hospital's credit rating. So, even though many could, in principle, agree with Laura Esserman's more patient-centered approach to delivering treatment for breast cancer, there was great disagreement about priorities and issues of implementation. Inside companies there are vigorous disagreements about whether to cut costs or increase the value of the product offering to consumers, move into new markets or retrench to where the company seems to have some advantage.

There are only two ways to resolve the inevitable disagreements about what to do and how to do it—through the imposition of hierarchical authority in which the boss gets to make the decision, or through a more political system in which various interests vie for power, with those with the most power most affecting the final choices. Neither system is perfect, but before we eschew the operation of markets, including markets for power and influence, inside organizations of all types, remember the research summarized by James Surowiecki and the wisdom of Winston Churchill.

In this chapter, we have seen that there are a variety of answers to the question, "Are organizational politics good for you and good for the organization?" One answer is that you need to take care of yourself if you are going to survive and succeed in places where, if you don't look out for yourself, no one else is going to. A second answer is that the question itself is off the mark: the evidence shows that hierarchy is ubiquitous and sought by people and, as a consequence, there are inevitable contests for obtaining the scarce higher-level positions in status hierarchies. In addition, power and influence skills are essential for getting things done in complex, interdependent systems and may be an effective way to make decisions, particularly compared to the more typical hierarchical arrangements. The message is that you need to master the knowledge and skills necessary to wield power effectively. In some circumstances, this may be good for the organization, but in virtually all circumstances, it is going to be good for you.

13

It's Easier Than You Think

It's not difficult to use the ideas in this book to increase your power and your chances of being successful inside organizations. How do I know? Lots of people have told me how helpful these concepts can be. One wrote:

> I just wanted to drop you a line and say hello. . . . I use the material from the Paths to Power course all the time! What I learned made me much more strategic and thoughtful about visibility and positioning myself, especially given that I'm working for a large and somewhat bureaucratic corporation. Here's a nice example. I've got a newly absentee boss—my manager recently switched roles, leaving a management vacuum above me. So I just sort of took over. And I used that as a basis to request frequent meetings with higher levels of management.

What's important about this situation is how completely "ordinary" it is. The power play, so to speak, was nothing very dramatic. What this young woman describes is seizing an available opportunity, the temporary absence of someone above her, to fill a leadership vacuum—and to leverage the situation to build more visibility and relationships at senior levels. Building power does not require extraordinary actions or amazing brilliance. Instead, as comedian, actor, and movie director Woody Allen has noted, "Eighty percent of success is showing up."[1]

The problem with the heroic, almost superhuman leaders whom we see depicted in so many autobiographies and leadership classes and cases is not just that the stories are seldom fully told or completely accurate. And contrary to management author David Bradford's view, nor are we in a "post-heroic" world. Bradford argues that organizations and, for that matter, their employees, would be better off with more collaboration, delegation, and teamwork.[2]

The biggest problem from the tall tales and high expectations established in much of the writing about organizational leadership is that it is too easy for people to ask, "Can I do all this? Is this me, and could it ever be?" Yes, it could be you, and anyone in any role in almost any organization can benefit from the ideas I have presented.

Some people think they don't or won't like playing the power game. But how can they know until they try it? One young woman decided to try out these ideas in a low-risk situation—to see if she could take over a student committee on which she served. The committee was charged with organizing the events for a weekend when the school she attended hosted admitted applicants who were deciding where to pursue their degrees. She devised measures of success—the percentage of communications that flowed through her, her ability to get her way on decisions—and set off on her experiment. She found that she enjoyed acquiring power and that, contrary to her expectations, her efforts did not produce resentment on the part of the other committee members. They were glad to offload the work and responsibility. She received lots of recognition and praise for her work. Most important, she decided that she really did enjoy this power stuff. Sort of like eating some new food, you can't know what you will truly enjoy until you do it and become somewhat proficient at it—we tend to like doing things we are good at doing. Once you engage in activities, including activities involved in acquiring power, those things become part of your identity and repertoire of skills. Don't give up before you begin.

BUILDING YOUR PATH TO POWER

It's important for you to find the right place given your aptitude and interests. Some jobs require more political skill than others. Project or product manager would be one such job—lots of responsibility without a lot of formal authority over the people whose cooperation you need to be successful. Assistant to a senior leader would be another such position, with a lot of visibility, the need to get things done, and not much direct power to reward or punish people for their cooperation or opposition. Although it is possible and desirable to develop your power skills, few people are comfortable changing their likes and dislikes. Yes, you can evolve and change, like the young woman who took over the committee, but only within limits. I suspect that she actually had an aptitude for and interest in power but just had never had a chance to explore how much. Therefore, the first step in building a path to power is to pick an environment that fits your aptitudes and interests—one where you can be successful in both the technical and political aspects, if any, of the work.

This seems like blindingly obvious advice, but it is not often followed. Finding the right place for you requires several steps. First, you must be brutally honest about your strengths, weaknesses, and preferences—and because of the self-enhancement motive discussed previously, not many people are as objective about themselves as they need to be. Second, you can't get trapped into following the crowd and doing something just because everyone else is. As decades-old research in social psychology illustrates, conformity pressures are strong. And so are the pressures of informational social influence: if everyone else is doing something, it must be because that is the right or smart thing to do. For you to do something else is to turn your back on their collective wisdom. So if everyone is going into finance, you go; if everyone is going overseas, you try to find an international position; if high tech is cool, you go there. But this conforming behavior can get in the way of doing what's right for you.

Third, to pick the right place for yourself, you must be objective not only about yourself but about the job and its risks and opportunities. We see what we want to see, and if the job looks attractive because of its compensation package or title, we can fool ourselves or intentionally overlook the fact that it may require more influence skills or being tougher than we like. Harvard Business School professor John Kotter told me that he thought for many people, the biggest obstacle to success was not talent or motivation but the fact that they were in the wrong place—that the power and influence requirements of their job did not fit their personal aptitudes and interests. Although I know of no formal study of this hypothesis, my own experiences and those of many others who have watched careers unfold suggest that it is right.

Because we see what we want to see, we may not accurately assess the political risks of a job—and suffer the consequences. A few years ago a woman graduating from business school told me she was accepting a position as the assistant to the incoming university president at a large private university in the East. For almost 20 years the university had as its leader a tough, very visible, and controversial president, and the board of trustees felt it was time for a change. The outgoing president was going to remain on the board of trustees, and, since the new person would not take over until the academic year began in the fall, the soon to be former president still held formal authority. Was it a good idea, I inquired, to take a job with this degree of political risk? What if the new president, whose assistant she would be, was undermined by his predecessor?

Things turned out worse than even I expected—the new president never assumed his position. The outgoing leader used his relationships with the board and senior administrative people to sabotage his successor before that person could even take office. For the putative president, not a big deal—he got a "package" and had a distinguished reputation that permitted him to quickly land another position. For his prospective assistant, things were not as rosy—no package and more effort required locating a new job. You need to be realistic about the political risks, not just to you but to those to whom you are tied, if you want to build a path to power.

Don't Give Up Your Power

You need to be in a job that fits and doesn't come with undue political risks, but you also need to do the right things in that job. Most important, you need to claim power and not do things that give yours away. It's amazing to me that people, in ways little and big, voluntarily give up their power, preemptively surrendering in the competition for status and influence. The process often begins with how you feel about yourself. If you feel powerful, you will act and project power and others will respond accordingly. If you feel powerless, your behavior will be similarly self-confirming.

Social psychologists Cameron Anderson and Jennifer Berdahl reviewed literature showing that people who had less power or didn't feel powerful exhibited "inhibitive nonverbal behaviors," such as shrinking in, caving in their chests, physically withdrawing, and using fewer and less forceful and dramatic hand gestures.[3] As we know from chapter 7, "Acting and Speaking with Power," one of the ways in which you can claim power is through your demeanor and voice—how you come across. Shrinking in and not behaving in a forceful fashion causes others to attribute less power to you, reinforcing a negative cycle of behavior in which you're not treated as powerful and you further withdraw and act powerless.

Anderson and Berdahl's experiments showed that people higher in personality dominance or given control over resources were more likely to express their true attitudes and to perceive rewards as being available in situations. People lower in personality dominance with less resource control perceived situations as threats not opportunities and hid their true attitudes.

People give up their power in other ways, too. They don't behave strategically toward people with power over them, such as their boss, and instead let their true feelings show. As a very skilled news reporter told me, he expressed his resentment toward his distant bosses who mostly spent their time managing up and did not provide the support to the news-gathering field operations that he and his colleagues wanted. But as a result, he was just perceived negatively and had even less influence. As he so nicely put it, "Either you deal with your boss, or you leave for a different company. In a small, tightly connected industry, sometimes even leaving isn't a very good option. There is no other solution than to work with the cards you are dealt." It may feel good to blow off steam, tell people off, and express your real inner feelings. But if the targets of your behavior are those with power, your good feelings will be quite temporary as the consequences of your actions unfold.

People sometimes give away their power by defining situations as outside of their control, thereby playing the victim role. Being a victim may help you bond with fellow victims as you commiserate about the difficulties you face, and it may excuse you from doing anything about the situation, but it won't get you much power or approval inside companies. Melinda described interviewing two people for a job and asking each, "Among your peers, you have some you work with better than others. What's the difference?" One candidate answered that the people he works well with are easy to work with and the ones he was challenged by were moody and hard to work with. As Melinda explained, "That candidate gave away all his power by defining the problem externally and as something he couldn't influence. When we tell ourselves that our problems are caused by others, we spend time on why we can't be successful. When instead we focus on what we *can* do, we spend time on being successful." With that level of insight, it is no wonder that Melinda is enjoying a very successful career herself. Her wisdom applies not just to job applications but to all organizational situations.

People give away their power by not trying. If you don't try, you can't fail—which protects your self-esteem. But not trying guarantees failure to win the competition for power and status. Sometimes people don't want to "play the game," or think they won't be good at it, or can't see themselves following the strategies of successful, more political individuals. I am convinced that we are frequently our own biggest barriers to having as much power as we would like simply because we don't make sufficient effort to build ourselves up. When we stop thinking of ourselves as powerless victims and cease eschewing doing the things that will bring influence, our chances of success increase dramatically. As Eleanor Roosevelt said, "No one can make you feel inferior without your consent."[4] It is much more difficult for others to take away your power if you aren't complicit in the process.

Take Care of Yourself—Don't Expect Justice

A few years ago, Bob, the CEO of a private, venture-backed human capital software company, invited me to serve on the board of directors as the company began a transition to a new product platform and sought to increase its growth rate and profitability. Not long after I joined the board, in the midst of an upgrading in management talent, the CEO hired a new chief financial officer, Chris. Chris was an ambitious, hardworking, articulate individual who had big plans for the company—and himself. Chris asked Bob to make him chief operating officer. Bob agreed. Chris asked to join the board of directors. Bob agreed. I could see what was coming next, so I called Bob and said, "Chris is after your job." Bob's reply was that he was only interested in what was best for the company, would not stoop to playing politics, and thought that the board had seen his level of competence and integrity and would do the right thing.

You can guess how this story ended—Bob's gone, Chris is the CEO. What was interesting was the conference call in which the board discussed the moves. Although there was much agreement that Chris's behavior had been inappropriate and harmful to the company, there was little support for Bob. If he was not going to put up a fight, no one was going to pick up the cudgel on his behalf. People who are complicit in their own beheading don't garner much sympathy or support.

Taking care of yourself sometimes means acting in ways that may seem selfish. A woman who worked in a nonprofit organization valued collaboration—so much so that she failed to press an advantage in gaining influence over an important strategic planning exercise:

> The executive director asked me to set up some time with her to discuss the plans for the strategic planning session. I knew that if I alone were the one to have this initial meeting with her, I

> would be the main person involved in setting the direction of the project and would be viewed as the key point person; I would be the leader and my colleague would be there to help get the work done. I wrestled with whether or not I could actually just schedule the meeting without my colleague, but I couldn't bring myself to do it, despite the voice in my head saying it was all right. This is an indication for me of the areas where I am most challenged in acquiring power.

One wonders if her colleague would have been as considerate. And remember, in hierarchical settings, colleagues are also competitors for promotions and status.

It's not just that the world is not always fair so you should stop counting on the triumph of your merit. People align with who they think is going to win. If you don't stand up for yourself and actively promote your own interests, few will be willing to be on your side. Since observers will see you as not trying to triumph and therefore losing, they will either not join you side or desert you, making your organizational demise more certain. Therefore, although self-promotion and fighting for your interests can seem unattractive, the alternative scenario is invariably much worse.

Pay Attention to the Small Tasks

Throughout this book we have seen that it's often the little things that matter. Just as companies sometimes overemphasize grand strategy and overlook the mundane details of execution, individuals often neglect the small steps they can take that can provide them with control over vital resources, visibility, and the opportunity to build important relationships. The people who pay attention to these small things have an edge in creating power.

When Matt joined a major consulting company, he was one of many talented individuals in the entering cohort. How to stand out and build a reputation? When new associates come into the firm, there are often many in the entering "class." The partners need to know who the new people are who can be assigned to projects, and the entering associates need to know about the partners and the projects in the office. In the past, there had been some informal methods—like meals and seminars—that had brought the various people together. Matt asked the managing partner whether he could formalize this process of ensuring that everyone knew about everyone else to make project assignments and also the new associates' integration into the office easier. "Of course," he was told. The task required Matt to interview the partners in the office to obtain their biographies and interests, and also to interview the new associates to ascertain their skills and specific consulting interests. By the time he had completed this activity, Matt knew a lot about lots of people; he had also developed deeper relationships with people throughout the office.

Will these activities make Matt a partner some day? Unlikely just by themselves. But coupled with hard and effective work, they will provide Matt with the reputation and visibility that gives an advantage. And the personal relationships can be further deepened and maintained to provide even more influence in the system.

SURVIVING AND SUCCEEDING IN ORGANIZATIONS

I hope I have convinced you that power and political processes in organizations are ubiquitous—not just in certain industries, or in the private sector, or only in the United States. Organizational politics is everywhere. You may wish it weren't so, but it is. And because of fundamental human psychology, there isn't much prospect of power and politics disappearing from organizational life.

Not only can you survive, but you can even succeed if you learn the principles and the rules and are willing to implement them in your daily organizational life. That's what this book has been about—exposing you to the ideas, the research, and the numerous examples of how to create a path to power for yourself.

So don't complain about how life isn't fair, or that your organizational culture isn't healthy, or that your boss is a jerk.[5] You have both the responsibility and the potential to change your situation, either in your present job or in some new place. Stop waiting for things to get better or for other people to acquire power and use it in a benevolent fashion to improve the situation. It's up to you to find—or create—a better place for yourself. And it's up to you to build your own path to power. As former Bay Area radio personality Scoop Nisker used to say, "If you don't like the news, go out and make some of your own."

If you wonder if this power seeking is worth the aggravation and effort, remember the research I described in the introduction on the relationship between having power over and in your work environment and sickness and mortality. Michael Marmot's study of 18,000 British civil servants—all people working in office jobs in the same society—uncovered that people at the bottom of the hierarchy had *four times* the risk of death from heart disease as did those at the top.[6] Controlling for risk factors such as smoking or obesity did not make the social gradient in health disappear, nor did statistically controlling for the longevity of one's parents. As Marmot concludes, "Social circumstances in adult life predict health."[7]

So seek power as if your life depends on it. Because it does.

ACKNOWLEDGMENTS

For more than 35 years, I have been researching and teaching about power. This is my third book on the subject. In my work on power and throughout my career, I have benefited enormously from the people who have collaborated with me in my teaching and research. I firmly believe that performance reflects more than just individual ability and motivation—it also owes a great deal to one's environment. I have taught at Stanford since 1979 and I never take the intellectual and financial resources afforded me for granted. My colleagues in organizational behavior throughout the campus, including Jim March and Dick Scott, and the school's administration in the person of the deans and associate deans I have worked with over the years, have been wonderfully generous with their friendship, advice, and support. I thank them all. My assistant, Nanci Moore, does so many things to make my life easier and is a delight to work with.

The elective course I teach at Stanford, called "The Paths to Power," owes a great deal, including its title and organizing framework, to my dear friend and colleague Roderick Kramer. Rod has taught sections of the course, contributed materials, and stimulated my thinking about the subject. Rod's articles about power and trust are invariably insightful, and I owe a huge debt of gratitude to his intellectual partnership. I also want to acknowledge the contributions to the class of the late Gene Webb, a member of my doctoral dissertation committee all those many years ago, who taught sections of the course in the early 1990s. My able course assistants have provided help, feedback, and ideas important to the class and my teaching. So many thanks to Nate Fast, Christina Fong, Caitlin Hogan, Ena Inesi, Senia Maymin, and Tanya Menon.

Other colleagues, both at Stanford and elsewhere, who study aspects of power and influence have profoundly influenced my writing and thinking. I owe a huge debt of gratitude to Cameron Anderson, Ron Burt, Bob Cialdini, Gerald Ferris, Frank Flynn, Adam Galinsky, Deborah Gruenfeld, Morten Hansen, Joel Podolny, Barry Staw, and Lara Tiedens. Each of these individuals can, I hope, see the influence of their ideas on these pages. My empirical research on power was done mostly with the late Jerry Salancik. Jerry was an incredible friend, colleague, and mentor who taught me a great deal about social science and life. For as long as I live I will miss his infectious laugh and amazing insights.

Over the years I have had the privilege of writing cases about and learning more informally from a simply amazing range of talented people. I have also been able to watch at close range, sometimes painfully close, some very effective organizational power players. A partial list of those to whom I owe much of my insight and understanding of organizational power includes Janet Abrams, Caryl Athanasiades, Shanda Bahles, Beth Benjamin, Adi Bittan, Nikki Blane, Nuria Chinchilla, Steve Ciesinski, Frances Conley, Kirby Cramer, Rudy Crew, David Demarest, Bill English, Laura Esserman, Keith Ferrazzi, Rashi Goel, Kevin Goodwin, Ignacio Gorupicz, Ishan Gupta, Burt Herman, Ian Hill, Ray Jackson, Michael Kahn, Rob Lawson, Tony Levitan, Bernard Looney, Gary Loveman, Meagan Marks, Chris Marsh, Melissa McSherry, Marcelo Miranda, Rich Moran, Kara Nortman, Jenny Parker, Josh Raffaelli, Carole Robin, Heidi Roizen, Jim Roth, John Russ, Andrew Saltoun, Patricia Seeman, Pepe Shabot, Jeffrey Sonnenfeld, Kenji Tateiwa, Amanda

Tucker, Jack Valenti, Ross Walker, Steve Westly, Zia Yusuf, and all the students in the many sections of the course over the years who have been kind enough to share their stories, ideas, and most important, their energy.

My amazingly wonderful agents, Christy Fletcher and Don Lamm, provided support, advice, and encouragement every step of the way. Don also provided unstinting editorial advice and friendship as well as telling me the truth about this project, even when I didn't want to hear it. Over the years, Don has become a dear friend and I value his wisdom. I have worked with a number of editors over the years, but have never encountered anyone better than Ben Loehnen of HarperCollins. Ben offered support and thoughtful comments and had an uncanny ability to help me produce text that was better than I thought I was capable of writing. Ben deserves enormous credit for helping me see how to improve the early drafts and for providing just the right mix of critique and support.

Charles O'Reilly and Bob Sutton deserve a special place in my heart. Close friends as well as coauthors and colleagues, they are unselfish with their time, advice, feedback, and support. Chip Heath, as always, was insightful and generous with his suggestions about titles. It is an honor and privilege to work with all of these people.

My dear friend and former Sloan student, Stuart Young, provided much indirect inspiration for this book. Stuart, a radiologist already retired for several years in his early sixties, lives in a huge house in Portola Valley and drives a Bentley. Stuart was someone who made his money from biotech companies that not only were never profitable, they never even had revenues. Our "grumpy old men" lunches are a source of continuing delight, and the very fact of his financial success renders an analysis of power in organizations all the more relevant.

When I met Kathleen Frances Fowler at approximately 10 P.M.

on January 19, 1985, at a party in San Francisco, it changed my life forever, although I didn't fully understand in what ways and how much that evening. After we started going out, she wanted to read something I had written. I gave her an autographed copy of my first book on this subject, *Power in Organizations*, which she found way too academic. On the other hand, she married me on July 23, 1986. It was Kathleen's encouragement that I write something that regular people could read that produced *Managing with Power* and many other things such as the various magazine columns I have written over the years. This book will, hopefully, be even more to her liking—if nothing else, it is shorter! Now, as we approach the 25th anniversary of the evening we met, I realize that she has taught me more than I know, or at least act on. Kathleen remains my best friend as well as the most beautiful human being I have ever encountered. This book, like everything in my life, is dedicated to her.

NOTES

Introduction

1. David C. McClelland and David H. Burnham, "Power Is the Great Motivator," *Harvard Business Review* 81 (2003): 117–126.
2. Gerald R. Ferris, Darren C. Treadway, Robert W. Kolodinsky, Wayne A. Hochwarter, Charles J. Kacmar, Caesar Douglas, and Dwight D. Frink, "Development and Validation of the Political Skill Inventory," *Journal of Management* 31 (2005): 126–152.
3. M. G. Marmot, H. Bosma, H. Hemingway, E. Brunner, and S. Stansfeld, "Contribution of Job Control and Other Risk Factors to Social Variations in Coronary Heart Disease Incidence," *The Lancet* 350 (1997): 235–239.
4. Mark J. Martinko and William L. Gardner, "Learned Helplessness: An Alternative Explanation for Performance Deficits," *Academy of Management Review* 7 (1982): 195–204.
5. This and other, related research is summarized in Michael Marmot, *The Status Syndrome: How Social Standing Affects Our Health and Longevity* (New York: Times Books, 2004).
6. Mike McIntire, "Clintons Made $109 Million in Last 8 Years," *New York Times*, April 5, 2008.
7. John W. Gardner, *On Leadership* (New York: Free Press, 1993).
8. David C. McClelland, *Power: The Inner Experience* (New York: Wiley, 1976); McClelland and Burnham, "Power Is the Great Motivator."
9. Matthew Montagu-Pollock, "Why Jim Walker Walked," *Asiamoney* (December 2000).
10. Melvin J. Lerner, *The Belief in a Just World: A Fundamental Delusion* (New York: Plenum, 1980).
11. C. R. Snyder, "Social Motivation: The Search for Belonging and Order," *Psychological Inquiry* 7 (1996): 248.
12. Murray Webster Jr., book review of *The Belief in a Just World*, by Melvin J. Lerner, *American Journal of Sociology* 88 (1983): 1048.
13. Ibid., 1049.

14. Ibid.

15. Jim Collins, *Good to Great* (New York: HarperCollins, 2001), 12.

16. Rudolph W. Giuliani, *Leadership* (New York: Hyperion, 2002).

17. This process was described more than 30 years ago by Barry M. Staw, "Attributions of the 'Causes' of Performance: A General Alternative Interpretation of Cross-Sectional Research on Organizations," *Organizational Behavior and Human Performance* 13 (1975): 414–432. It was applied to the leadership literature that same year by Terence R. Mitchell, James R. Larson, and Stephen G. Green, "Leader Behavior, Situational Moderators, and Group Performance: An Attributional Analysis," Defense Technical Information Center, Accession No: AD1021285. The fundamental idea—that positive attributes will be construed as occurring together even if they don't, undergirds the argument in Phil Rosenzweig, *The Halo Effect* (New York: Free Press, 2007).

18. These and other data on the extent of misrepresenting qualifications on resumés can be found in Jeffrey Pfeffer, *What Were They Thinking? Unconventional Wisdom About Management* (Boston: Harvard Business School Press, 2007), ch. 13.

19. See, for instance, E. E. Jones and S. Berglas, "Control of Attributions About the Self Through Self-Handicapping Strategies: The Appeal of Alcohol and the Role of Underachievement," *Personality and Social Psychology Bulletin* 4 (1978): 200–206.

20. Michael J. Strube, "An Analysis of the Self-Handicapping Scale," *Basic and Applied Social Psychology* 7 (1986): 211–224.

21. Frederick Rhodewalt and James Davison Jr., "Self-Handicapping and Subsequent Performance: Role of Outcome Valence and Attributional Certainty," *Basic and Applied Social Psychology* 7 (1986): 307–322.

1. It Takes More Than Performance

1. Christine Armario, "Miami Ousts Nationally Recognized School Leader," Associated Press, September 11, 2008.

2. Amy C. Edmondson, Brian R. Golden, and Gary J. Young, "Turnaround at the Veterans Health Administration (A)," Case no. 9-607-035, Boston: Harvard Business School Publishing, July 20, 2007.

3. Catherine Arnst, "The Best Medical Care in the U.S.," *BusinessWeek*, July 17, 2006.

4. Amy C. Edmondson and Brian R. Golden, "Turnaround at the Veterans Health Administration (B)," Case no. 9-608-062, Boston: Harvard Business School Publishing, August 14, 2007.

5. F. David Schoorman, "Escalation Bias in Performance Appraisals: An Unintended Consequence of Supervisor Participation in Hiring Decisions," *Journal of Applied Psychology* 73 (1988): 58–62.

6. James L. Medoff and Katherine G. Abraham, "Experience, Performance, and Earnings," *Quarterly Journal of Economics* 95 (1980): 705–736.

7. Thomas J. Dohmen, "Performance, Seniority, and Wages: Formal Salary Systems and Individual Earnings Profiles," *Labour Economics* 11 (2004): 741–763.

8. Abraham Carmeli, Revital Shalom, and Jacob Weisberg, "Considerations in Organizational Career Advancement: What Really Matters," *Personnel Review* 36 (2007): 190–205.

9. Dimitrios Spyropoulos, "Analysis of Career Progression and Job Performance in Internal Labor Markets: The Case of Federal Civil Service Employees," unpublished master's thesis, Naval Postgraduate School, School of Business and Public Policy, Monterey, CA, March 2005; http://www.stormingmedia.us/71/7132/A713234.html.

10. S. C. Gilson, "Management Turnover and Financial Distress," *Journal of Financial Economics* 25 (1989): 241–262.

11. C. Edward Fee and Charles J. Hadlock, "Management Turnover Across the Corporate Hierarchy," *Journal of Accounting and Economics* 37 (2004): 3–38.

12. Eddie Harmon-Jones and John J. B. Allen, "The Role of Affect in the Mere Exposure Effect: Evidence from Psychophysiological and Individual Differences Approaches," *Personality and Social Psychology Bulletin* 27 (2001): 889–898.

13. Angela Y. Lee, "The Mere Exposure Effect: An Uncertainty Reduction Explanation Revisited," *Personality and Social Psychology Bulletin* 27, no. 10 (2001): 1255–1266.

14. Robert B. Zajonc, "Mere Exposure: A Gateway to the Subliminal," *Current Directions in Psychological Science* 10, no. 6 (2001): 224–228.

15. Elizabeth Kolbert, "How Tina Brown Moves Magazines," *New York Times Magazine*, December 5, 1993.

16. For a review of this literature, see John R. Chambers and Paul D. Windschitl, "Biases in Social Comparative Judgments: The Role of Nonmotivated Factors in Above-Average and Comparative-Optimism Effects," *Psychological Bulletin* 130 (2004): 813–838.

17. John T. Jones, Brett W. Pelham, Mauricio Carvallo, and Matthew C. Mirenberg, "How Do I Love Thee? Let Me Count the Js: Implicit Egotism and Interpersonal Attraction," *Journal of Personality and Social Psychology* 87 (2004): 665–683.

18. Jennifer Crocker and Ian Schwartz, "Prejudice and Ingroup Favoritism in a Minimal Intergroup Situation: Effects of Self-Esteem," *Personality and Social Psychology Bulletin* 11 (1985): 379–386.

19. Robert B. Cialdini, *Influence: Science and Practice*, 4th ed. (Boston: Allyn and Bacon, 2001).

20. Connie Bruck, "The Personal Touch," *The New Yorker*, August 13, 2001.

21. Ibid.

22. Jack Valenti, *This Time, This Place: My Life in War, the White House, and Hollywood* (New York: Harmony Books, 2007).

2. The Personal Qualities That Bring Influence

1. "Ronald Meyer," http://en.wikipedia.org/wiki/Ronald_Meyer.
2. Daniel R. Ames and Lara K. Kammrath, "Mind-Reading and Metacognition: Narcissism, Not Actual Competence, Predicts Self-Estimated Ability," *Journal of Nonverbal Behavior* 28 (2004): 187–209.
3. James Richardson, *Willie Brown: A Biography* (Berkeley: University of California Press, 1996).
4. "Creativity Step by Step: A Conversation with Choreographer Twyla Tharp," *Harvard Business Review* (April 2008): 49.
5. Marshall Goldsmith and Mark Reiter, *What Got You Here Won't Get You There: How Successful People Become Even More Successful* (New York: Hyperion, 2007).
6. See, for instance, Justin Kruger and David Dunning, "Unskilled and Unaware of It: How Difficulties in Recognizing One's Own Incompetence Lead to Inflated Self-Assessments," *Journal of Personality and Social Psychology* 77 (1999): 1121–1134; David Dunning, Kerri Johnson, Joyce Ehrlinger, and Justin Kruger, "Why People Fail to Recognize Their Own Incompetence," *Current Directions in Psychological Science* 12 (2003): 83–87.
7. Quoted in Dunning et al., "Why People Fail," 83.
8. See, for example, David Mechanic, "Sources of Power of Lower Participants in Complex Organizations," *Administrative Science Quarterly* 7 (1962): 349–364.
9. Alan Ehrenhalt, "Little Caesar," review of *American Pharaoh*, by Adam Cohen and Elizabeth Taylor, *New York Times Book Review*, June 4, 2000.
10. Doris Kearns Goodwin, *Team of Rivals: The Political Genius of Abraham Lincoln* (New York: Simon and Schuster, 2005).
11. G. Wayne Miller, *Toy Wars* (New York: Times Books, 1998), 214.
12. Sally Bedell Smith, *In All His Glory: The Life of William S. Paley* (New York: Simon and Schuster, 1990), 394.
13. Sara Mosle, "The Stealth Chancellor," *New York Times Magazine*, August 31, 1997.
14. The literature on emotional contagion is vast, and encompasses field research, experiments, and even neuroimaging studies. See, for instance, Christopher K. Hsee, Elaine Hatfield, John G, Carlson, and Claude Chemtob, "The Effect of Power on Susceptibility to Emotional Contagion," *Cognition and Emotion* 4 (October 1990): 327–340; Daniel Goleman, Richard Boyatzis, and Annie McKee, "The Emotional Reality of Teams," *Journal of Organizational Excellence* 21 (Spring 2002): 55–65.
15. Robert A. Caro, *The Path to Power* (New York: Knopf, 1982), ch. 13.

16. Dean Keith Simonton, "Talent and Its Development: An Emergenic and Epigenetic Model," *Psychological Review* 106 (1999): 435–457.

17. Fay Hansen, "Data Bank: CEO Profile," *Workforce Management*, June 22, 2009, 16.

18. Brenda Major and Ellen Konar, "An Investigation of Sex Differences in Pay Expectations and Their Possible Causes," *Academy of Management Journal* 27 (1984): 777–792; Brenda Major, Dean B. McFarlin, and Diana Gagnon, "Overworked and Underpaid: On the Nature of Gender Differences in Personal Entitlement," *Journal of Personality and Social Psychology* 47 (1984): 1399–1412.

19. William Ickes, ed., "Introduction," in *Empathic Accuracy* (New York: Guilford Press, 1997), 2.

20. See, for example, Denise Salin, "Ways of Explaining Workplace Bullying: A Review of Enabling, Motivating and Precipitating Structures and Processes in the Work Environment," *Human Relations* 56 (2003): 1213–1232; Tim Field, "Workplace Bullying: The Silent Epidemic," *British Medical Journal* 326 (2003): 776–777.

21. Ryan Lizza, "The Gatekeeper: Rahm Emanuel on the Job," *The New Yorker*, March 2, 2009.

22. Michael Powell and Russ Buetnner, "In Matters Big and Small, Crossing Giuliani Had Price," *New York Times*, January 22, 2008.

23. Stan Sesser, "A Reporter at Large: A Nation of Contradictions," *The New Yorker*, January 13, 1992.

24. David Halberstam, *The Reckoning* (New York: William Morrow, 1986), 149.

25. See, for instance, John E. Hunter and Frank L. Schmidt, "Intelligence and Job Performance: Economic and Social Implications," *Psychology, Public Policy, and Law* 2 (1996): 447–472.

26. Tarmo Strenze, "Intelligence and Socioeconomic Success: A Meta-Analytic Review of Longitudinal Research," *Intelligence* 35 (2007): 401–426. The quoted number comes from page 411.

27. Ibid. Their meta-analysis finds a correlation of just .09 between academic performance and income, meaning that less than 1 percent of the variation in income can be attributed to variation in academic performance while in school.

28. Walter Kirn, "Life, Liberty and the Pursuit of Aptitude," *New York Times Magazine*, July 5, 2009, 11–12.

29. See, for instance, Stephane Cote and Christopher T. H. Miners, "Emotional Intelligence, Cognitive Intelligence, and Job Performance," *Administrative Science Quarterly* 51 (2006): 1–28.

30. Tim Weiner, "Robert S. McNamara, Architect of a Futile War, Dies at 93," *New York Times*, July 7, 2009.

3. Choosing Where to Start

1. William L. Moore and Jeffrey Pfeffer, "The Relationship Between Departmental Power and Faculty Careers on Two Campuses: The Case for Structural Effects on Faculty Salaries," *Research in Higher Education* 13 (1980): 291–306.
2. John E. Sheridan, John W. Slocum Jr., Richard Buda, and Richard C. Thompson, "Effects of Corporate Sponsorship and Department Power on Career Tournaments," *Academy of Management Journal* 33 (1990): 578–602.
3. Jeffrey Pfeffer, *Managing with Power* (Boston: Harvard Business School Press, 1992), 58.
4. Jeffrey Pfeffer, "The Importance of Being in the Right Unit," ibid.
5. The material on Zia Yusuf comes from a case I wrote. See "Zia Yusuf at SAP: Having Impact," Stanford, CA: Graduate School of Business, Case no. OB-73, February 3, 2009.
6. John Hagel and John Seely Brown, "How SAP Seeds Innovation," *Business-Week*, July 23, 2008.
7. Finance's rise to power at Ford Motor is described in David Halberstam's book, *The Reckoning* (New York: William Morrow, 1986).
8. Ibid., 256.
9. Pfeffer, "The Importance of Being in the Right Unit."
10. Ibid.; see also D. J. Hickson, C. R. Hinings, C. A. Lee, R. E. Schneck, and J. M. Pennings, "A 'Strategic Contingencies' Theory of Intraorganizational Power," *Administrative Science Quarterly* 16 (1971): 216–229; C. R. Hinings, D. J. Hickson, J. M. Pennings, and R. E. Schneck, "Structural Conditions of Intraorganizational Power," *Administrative Science Quarterly* 19 (1974): 22–44; Gerald R. Salancik and Jeffrey Pfeffer, "The Bases and Use of Power in Organizational Decision Making: The Case of a University," *Administrative Science Quarterly* 19 (1974): 453–473.
11. Neil Fligstein, "The Intraorganizational Power Struggle: Rise of Finance Personnel to Top Leadership in Large Corporations, 1919–1979," *American Sociological Review* 52 (1987): 44–58.
12. Halberstam, *The Reckoning*.
13. Andrew M. Pettigrew, *Politics of Organizational Decision-Making* (London: Tavistock Institute, 1973).
14. David Krackhardt, "Assessing the Political Landscape: Structure, Cognition and Power in Organizations," *Administrative Science Quarterly* 35 (1990): 342–369.
15. Jeffrey Pfeffer, *Competitive Advantage Through People* (Boston: Harvard Business School Press, 1994), 52.
16. John W. Dean III, *Blind Ambition* (New York: Simon and Schuster, 1976), 29–30.

4. Getting In

1. Victoria Chang and Jeffrey Pfeffer, "Keith Ferrazzi," Case no. OB-44, Stanford, CA: Graduate School of Business, Stanford University, October 2003, 4.

2. An excellent short biography of Lewis can be found at http://www.africanamericanculture.org/museum_reglewis.html.

3. Reginald F. Lewis, Blair S. Walker, and Hugh B. Price, *Why Should White Guys Have All the Fun? How Reginald Lewis Created a Billion-Dollar Business Empire* (New York: John Wiley, 1994), 52.

4. Francis J. Flynn and Vanessa K. B. Lake, "If You Need Help, Just Ask: Underestimating Compliance with Direct Requests for Help," *Journal of Personality and Social Psychology* 95 (2008): 128–143.

5. Kate Zernike and Jeff Zeleny, "Obama in the Senate: Star Power, Minor Role," *New York Times*, March 9, 2008.

6. Ishan Gupta and Rajat Khare, *Make the Move: Demystifying Entrepreneurship* (New Delhi: Unicorn Books, 2007).

7. Jerry M. Burger, Nicole Messian, Shehani Patel, Alicia del Prado, and Carmen Anderson, "What a Coincidence! The Effects of Incidental Similarity on Compliance," *Personality and Social Psychology Bulletin* 30 (2004): 35–43.

8. Larissa MacFarquhar, "Mrs. Kennedy Regrets," *The New Yorker*, February 2, 2009.

9. Walter Isaacson, "Harvard: The Ambitious Student, 1947–1955," in *Kissinger: A Biography* (New York: Simon and Schuster, 1992).

10. "Mr. Sony's Struggle," *Fortune*, November 22, 1999, 237–248.

11. Malcolm Gladwell, "How David Beats Goliath: When Underdogs Break the Rules," *The New Yorker*, May 11, 2009.

12. Robert B. Cialdini, *Influence: Science and Practice*, 5th ed. (Boston: Allyn and Bacon, 2008).

13. Susan T. Fiske, Amy J. C. Cuddy, and Peter Glick, "Universal Dimensions of Social Cognition: Warmth and Competence," *Trends in Cognitive Sciences* 11 (2007): 77–83.

14. Teresa M. Amabile, "Brilliant But Cruel: Perceptions of Negative Evaluators," *Journal of Experimental Social Psychology* 19 (1983): 146–156.

15. Amy J. C. Cuddy, "Just Because *I'm Nice*, Don't Assume *I'm Dumb*," *Harvard Business Review* (February 2009): 24.

16. Jacob Heilbrunn, "Consent and Advise," *New York Times Book Review*, January 20, 2008.

17. R. B. Cialdini, R. J. Borden, A. Thorne, M. Walker, S. Freeman, and L. Sloan, "Basking in Reflected Glory: Three (Football) Field Studies," *Journal of Personality and Social Psychology* 34 (1976): 366–375.

18. Gary Weiss, "The Re-Education of Tim Geithner," *Portfolio* (May 2009): 93.

19. Jane Mayer and Jill Abramson, *Strange Justice: The Selling of Clarence Thomas*, (Boston: Houghton Mifflin, 1994), 223.
20. Leon Festinger, *Conflict, Decision, and Dissonance* (Stanford, CA: Stanford University Press, 1964).
21. Robert Caro, *The Power Broker: Robert Moses and the Fall of New York* (New York: Vintage Books, 1975), 217.

5. Making Something out of Nothing

1. James Richardson, *Willie Brown: A Biography* (Berkeley: University of California Press, 1996); see particularly ch. 19, "The Play for Power."
2. Dalton Conley and Brian McCabe, "Bribery or Just Desserts? Evidence on the Influence of Congressional Voting Patterns on PAC Contributions from Exogenous Variation in the Sex Mix of Legislator Offspring," Cambridge, MA: National Bureau of Economic Research Working Paper No. W13945, March 2008.
3. Henry L. Tosi, Steve Werner, and Luis R. Gomez-Mejia, "How Much Does Performance Matter? A Meta-Analysis of CEO Pay Studies," *Journal of Management* 26 (2000): 301–339.
4. Jeffrey Sonnenfeld, *The Hero's Farewell: What Happens When CEOs Retire* (New York: Oxford University Press, 1988).
5. Richardson, *Willie Brown*, 250.
6. Sally Bedell Smith, *In All His Glory: The Life of William S. Paley* (New York: Simon and Schuster, 1990), 156.
7. Ibid., 152.
8. Information on Schwab and the World Economic Forum is widely available. See, for instance, Craig R. Whitney, "Political and Corporate Elite Soak Up Big Ideas at Davos," *New York Times*, January 28, 1997; "What Does It Cost to Get into Davos?" DealBook Blog, *New York Times*, January 23, 2008; Adrienne Gaffney, "Politics and Power: Getting to Know Klaus Schwab, the Man Behind Davos," *Vanity Fair*, January 30, 2009.
9. Whitney, "Political and Corporate Elite Soak Up Big Ideas at Davos."

6. Building Efficient and Effective Social Networks

1. Nicole Tempest and Kathleen McGinn, "Heidi Roizen," Harvard Business School Case no. 9-800-228, September 11, 2000.
2. Hans-Georg Wolff and Klaus Moser, "Effects of Networking on Career Success: A Longitudinal Study," *Journal of Applied Psychology* 94 (2009): 196–197.
3. Ibid., 198.
4. See, for example, M. L. Forret and T. W. Dougherty, "Networking Behaviors

and Career Outcomes: Differences for Men and Women?" *Journal of Organizational Behavior* 25 (2004): 419–437; P. H. Langford, "Importance of Relationship Management for the Career Success of Australian Managers," *Australian Journal of Psychology* 52 (2000): 163–168.

5. Wolff and Moser, "Effects of Networking," 196–206.

6. Ronald S. Burt and Don Ronchi, "Teaching Executives to See Social Capital: Results from a Field Experiment," *Social Science Research* 36 (2007): 1158.

7. Mark S. Granovetter, *Getting a Job: A Study of Contacts and Careers* (Cambridge, MA: Harvard University Press, 1974).

8. Mark S. Granovetter, "The Strength of Weak Ties," *American Journal of Sociology* 78 (1973): 1360–1380.

9. Joel M. Podolny, "A Status-Based Model of Market Competition," *American Journal of Sociology* 98 (1993): 829–872.

10. For a review of this literature, see, for instance, Katherine J. Klein, Beng-Chong Lim, Jessica L. Saltz, and David M. Mayer, "How Do They Get There? An Examination of the Antecedents of Centrality in Team Networks," *Academy of Management Journal* 47 (2004): 952–963.

11. Daniel J. Brass, "Being in the Right Place: A Structural Analysis of Individual Influence in an Organization," *Administrative Science Quarterly* 29 (1984): 532.

12. Seymour M. Hersh, *The Price of Power: Kissinger in the Nixon White House* (New York: Summit Books, 1983).

13. See, for instance, Ronald S. Burt, *Structural Holes: The Social Structure of Competition* (Cambridge, MA: Harvard University Press, 1992); and Ronald S. Burt, *Brokerage and Closure: An Introduction to Social Capital* (Oxford: Oxford University Press, 2005).

14. Ronald S. Burt, "Secondhand Brokerage: Evidence on the Importance of Local Structure for Managers, Bankers, and Analysts," *Academy of Management Journal* 50 (2007): 119–148.

15. See Morten T. Hansen, Joel M. Podolny, and Jeffrey Pfeffer, "So Many Ties, So Little Time: A Task Contingency Perspective on Corporate Social Capital in Organizations," in S. Gabbay and R. Leenders, eds., *Research in the Sociology of Organizations*, vol. 18 (Amsterdam: Elsevier, 2001), 21–57; Morten Hansen, "The Search-Transfer Problem: The Role of Weak Ties in Sharing Knowledge Across Organizational Subunits," *Administrative Science Quarterly* 44 (1999): 82–111.

7. Acting and Speaking with Power

1. "Oliver North, Businessman? Many Bosses Say That He's Their Kind of Employee," *Wall Street Journal*, July 14, 1987.

2. Anthony DePalma, "Stanford President at Brunt of Storm," *New York Times*, May 10, 1991.

3. "Stanford, Government Agree to Settle Dispute over Research Costs," Stanford University News Service News Release, October 18, 1994.
4. Harriet Rubin, "Shall I Compare Thee to an Andy Grove?" *Strategy+ Business* no. 49 (Winter 2007): 26–31.
5. Much of the information on Rubenstein comes from Wikipedia and from Stephanie Rosenbloom, "Calling All Alpha Kitties," *New York Times*, October 4, 2007.
6. John Helyar, "Playing Ball: How Peter Ueberroth Led the Major Leagues in the 'Collusion Era,'" *Wall Street Journal*, May 20, 1991.
7. From the transcript of a talk given by Andy Grove at a Harvard Business School publishing conference, Cupertino, California, October 3, 2002.
8. Rubin, "Shall I Compare Thee to an Andy Grove?"
9. Sigal G. Barsade, "The Ripple Effect: Emotional Contagion and Its Influence on Group Behavior," *Administrative Science Quarterly* 47 (2002): 644–675.
10. Daniel J. Howard and Charles Gengler, "Emotional Contagion Effects on Product Attitudes," *Journal of Consumer Research* 28 (2001).
11. Ryan Lizza, "The Gatekeeper: Rahm Emanuel on the Job," *The New Yorker*, March 2, 2009.
12. Larissa Z. Tiedens, "Anger and Advancement Versus Sadness and Subjugation: The Effect of Negation Emotion Expressions on Social Status Conferral," *Journal of Personality and Social Psychology* 80 (2001): 87.
13. Larissa Z. Tiedens, Phoebe C. Ellsworth, and Batja Mesquita, "Sentimental Stereotypes: Emotional Expectations for High- and Low-Status Group Members," *Personality and Social Psychology Bulletin* 26 (2000): 560–575.
14. Tiedens, "Anger and Advancement Versus Sadness and Subjugation," 86–94.
15. These quotes are from Roderick M. Kramer, "The Great Intimidators," *Harvard Business Review*, February 2006, 92.
16. Lisa Belkin, "The Feminine Critique," *New York Times*, November 1, 2007.
17. Victoria L. Brescoll and Eric Luis Uhlmann, "Can an Angry Woman Get Ahead? Status Conferral, Gender, and Expression of Emotion in the Workplace," *Psychological Science* 19 (2008): 268–275.
18. Ursula Hess, Reginald B. Adams Jr., and Robert E. Kleck, "Who May Frown and Who Should Smile? Dominance, Affiliation, and the Display of Happiness and Anger," *Cognition and Emotion* 19 (2005): 515–536.
19. See http://www.quotationspage.com/quote/21094.html.
20. There are scores of studies on this issue. See, for instance, Anne Case and Christina Paxson, "Stature and Status: Height, Ability and Labor Market Outcomes," *Journal of Political Economy* 116 (2008): 499–532; Nicola Persico and Andrew Postlewaite, "The Effect of Adolescent Experience on Labor Market Outcomes: The Case of Height," *Journal of Political Economy* 112 (2004): 1019–1053.

21. Markus M. Mobius and Tanya S. Rosenblat, "Why Beauty Matters," *American Economic Review* 96 (2006): 222–235.

22. Helyar, "Playing Ball."

23. Harvey Molotch and Deidre Boden, "Talking Social Structure: Discourse, Dominance and the Watergate Hearings," *American Sociological Review* 50 (1985): 273–288.

24. A great discussion of political language can be found in Murray Edelman, *The Symbolic Uses of Politics* (Urbana: University of Illinois Press, 1964).

25. Harold Evans, "His Finest Hour: Roy Jenkins Chronicles the Life of the Prime Minister Who Led Britain to Victory over the Nazis," *New York Times Book Review*, November 11, 2001.

26. Ibid., 13.

27. Max Atkinson, *Our Masters' Voices: The Language and Body Language of Politics* (London: Methuen, 1984), 40.

28. Ibid., 54.

29. Ibid., 57.

30. From a transcript of a video conference presentation on March 15, 2002.

31. Said on Michael Krasny's KQED Forum program, San Francisco, June 19, 2008, in the first hour between 9 A.M. and 10 A.M.

32. Stanley Fish, "The Candidates, Seen from the Classroom," *New York Times*, September 24, 2004.

8. Building a Reputation

1. The information on John Madden and Bill Walsh comes from their Wikipedia entries.

2. Sandy J. Wayne and K. Michele Kacmar, "The Effects of Impression Management on the Performance Appraisal Process," *Organizational Behavior and Human Decision Processes* 48 (1991): 70–88.

3. Rakesh Khurana, *Searching for a Corporate Savior: The Irrational Quest for Charismatic CEOs* (Princeton, NJ: Princeton University Press, 2002).

4. Boris Groysberg, Andrew N. McLean, and Nitin Nohria, "Are Leaders Portable?" *Harvard Business Review* 84 (2006): 92–101.

5. Janine Willis and Alexander Todorov, "First Impressions: Making Up Your Mind After a 100-ms Exposure to a Face," *Psychological Science* 17 (2006): 592–598.

6. Nalini Ambady and Robert Rosenthal, "Thin Slices of Expressive Behavior as Predictors of Interpersonal Consequences: A Meta-Analysis," *Psychological Bulletin* 111 (1992): 256–274.

7. Nalini Ambady and Robert Rosenthal, "Half a Minute: Predicting Teacher

Evaluations from Thin Slices of Nonverbal Behavior and Physical Attractiveness," *Journal of Personality and Social Psychology* 64 (1993): 431–441.

8. T. W. Dougherty, D. B. Turban, and J. C. Callender, "Confirming First Impressions in the Employment Interview: A Field Study of Interviewer Behavior," *Journal of Applied Psychology* 79 (1994): 659–665.

9. For a discussion of these processes, see Philip E. Tetlock, "Accountability and the Perseverance of First Impressions," *Social Psychology Quarterly* 46 (1983): 285–292.

10. Varon's talk, "Genome Out of the Bottle," is available on video. See http://www.charlievaron.com/genome.html.

11. Ryan Lizza, "Making It: How Chicago Shaped Obama," *The New Yorker*, July 21, 2008.

12. See, for instance, *Financial Times*, December 2, 2002.

13. Nuria Chinchilla's influence and rise to power is described in Megan Elisabeth Anderson and Jeffrey Pfeffer, "Nuria Chinchilla: The Power to Change Workplaces," Stanford, CA: Graduate School of Business, Case no. OB-67, January 2008.

14. Ibid., 13.

15. Lee Iacocca with William Novak, *Iacocca: An Autobiography* (New York: Bantam Books, 1984).

16. Robert Lacey, *Ford: The Men and the Machine* (New York: Ballantine Books, 1986); see especially pp. 602–614.

17. Albert J. Dunlap and Bob Andelman, with John Mahaney, *Mean Business* (New York: Crown Business, 1996).

18. John A. Byrne, *Chainsaw: The Notorious Career of Al Dunlap in the Era of Profit-at-Any-Price* (New York: HarperCollins, 1999), 351.

19. Jack Welch and John A. Byrne, *Jack: Straight from the Gut* (New York: Business Plus, 2001).

20. Thomas F. O'Boyle, *At Any Cost: Jack Welch, General Electric, and the Pursuit of Profit* (New York: Random House, 1998).

21. D. T. Kenrick, S. L. Neuberg, and R. B. Cialdini, *Social Psychology: Unraveling the Mystery* (Boston: Allyn and Bacon, 2002), 129.

22. See, for instance, C. Wortman and J. Linsenmeier, "Interpersonal Attraction and Techniques of Ingratiation in Organizational Settings," in B. M. Staw and J. R. Salancik, eds., *New Directions for Organizational Behavior* (Chicago: St. Clair Press, 1977), 133–178; D. R. Forsythe, R. Berger, and T. Mitchell, "The Effects of Self-Serving v. Other-Serving Claims of Responsibility on Attraction and Attribution in Groups," *Social Psychology Quarterly* 44 (1981): 59–64.

23. Jeffrey Pfeffer, Christina T. Fong, Robert B. Cialdini, and Rebecca R. Portnoy,

"Overcoming the Self-Promotion Dilemma: Interpersonal Attraction and Extra Help as a Consequence of Who Sings One's Praises," *Personality and Social Psychology Bulletin* 32 (2006): 1–13.

24. Ryan Lizza, "Money Talks," *The New Yorker*, May 4, 2009.
25. L. Holson, "Young Deal Maker Is Force Behind Company's Growth," *New York Times*, November 19, 1998.

9. Overcoming Opposition and Setbacks

1. Judith Ramsey Ehrlich and Barry J. Rehfeld, *The New Crowd: The Changing of the Jewish Guard on Wall Street* (Boston: Little, Brown, 1989).
2. David B. Hilder, "American Express Chief Keeps Tight Grip—Still, Nearly All the Company's Units Have Difficulty, *Wall Street Journal*, June 28, 1985.
3. "Dr. Laura Esserman (A)," Stanford, CA: Graduate School of Business, Stanford University, Case no. OB42-A, September 30, 2003.
4. Jack W. Brehm, *A Theory of Psychological Reactance* (New York: Academic Press, 1966).
5. James Richardson, *Willie Brown: A Biography* (Berkeley: University of California Press, 1996), 279.
6. Tom Rubython, "Cricket's Rainmaker: Lalit Modi Has Successfully Monetised the Indian Game," *SportsPro*, July 2008, 64–82.
7. Ibid., 68.
8. "Jeffrey Sonnenfeld (A): The Fall from Grace," Stanford, CA: Graduate School of Business, Case no. OB-34(A), September 2000.
9. Jeffrey A. Sonnenfeld and Andrew J. Ward, *Firing Back: How Great Leaders Rebound After Career Disasters* (Boston: Harvard Business School Press, 2007).

10. The Price of Power

1. Stanley Holmes, "The Affair That Grounded Stonecipher," *BusinessWeek*, March 8, 2005.
2. T. R. Horton, *The CEO Paradox: The Privilege and Accountability of Leadership* (New York: AMACOM, 1992), 38–39.
3. Robert I. Sutton and D. Charles Galunic, "Consequences of Public Scrutiny for Leaders and Their Organizations," in Barry M. Staw and Larry L. Cummings, eds., *Research in Organizational Behavior*, vol. 18 (Greenwich, CT: JAI Press, 1996), 201–250.
4. See, for instance, Russell G. Geen, "Social Motivation," *Annual Review of Psychology* 42 (1991): 377–399; Robert Zajonc, "Social Facilitation," *Science* 149 (1965): 269–274.

5. The CEO Project, "Interviews with CEOs of Fast-Growth Companies, Summary of Findings, Preliminary Results as of 10/16/04," Scottsdale, AZ: The CEO Project, 14.

6. Patricia Robinson and Norihiko Shimizu, "Japanese Corporate Restructuring: CEO Priorities as a Window on Environmental and Organizational Change," *Academy of Management Perspectives* 20 (2006): 44–75.

7. J. Gleick, *Genius: The Life and Science of Richard Feynman* (New York: Pantheon, 1992), 382; cited in Sutton and Galunic, "Consequences of Public Scrutiny."

8. R. C. Hill, "When the Going Gets Tough: A Baldrige Award Winner," *Academy of Management Executive* 7 (1993): 75–79.

9. Clayton M. Christensen, *The Innovator's Dilemma: When New Technologies Cause Great Firms to Fail* (Boston: Harvard Business School Press, 1997).

10. Frances K. Conley, *Walking Out on the Boys* (New York: Farrar, Straus and Giroux, 1998).

11. Ibid., 57.

12. Hanna Papanek, "Men, Women, and Work: Reflections on the Two-Person Career," *American Journal of Sociology* 78 (1973): 852–872.

13. See, for instance, Jeffrey Pfeffer and Jerry Ross, "The Effect of Marriage and a Working Wife on Occupational and Wage Attainment," *Administrative Science Quarterly* 27 (1982): 66–80; Eng Seng Loh, "Productivity Differences and the Marriage Wage Premium for White Males," *Journal of Human Resources* 31 (1996): 566-589; Jacqueline Landau and Michael B. Arthur, "The Relationship of Marital Status, Spouse's Career Status, and Gender to Salary Level," *Sex Roles* 27 (1992): 665–681; Catherine Kirchmeyer, "Gender Differences in Managerial Careers: Yesterday, Today, and Tomorrow," *Journal of Business Ethics* 37 (2002): 5–24.

14. Bryan Burrough and John Helyar, *Barbarians at the Gate: The Fall of RJR Nabisco* (New York: Harper and Row, 1990).

15. Ibid., 34.

16. Ibid., 37.

17. Michael Marmot, *The Status Syndrome: How Social Standing Affects Our Health and Longevity* (New York: Henry Holt, 2004), 130.

11. How—and Why—People Lose Power

1. Chuck Lucier, Steven Wheeler, and Rolf Habbel, "The Era of the Inclusive Leader," *Strategy + Business*, no. 47 (Summer 2007): 43–53.

2. Linda Anderson, "Search for a Dean: Improbable Mix of Talents Sought," FT.com, March 18, 2002.

3. Robert J. Clark, "The Superintendent as a Temp," *The School Administrator*, April 2001, 40–41.

4. Stewart Gabel, *Leaders and Health Care Organizational Change* (New York: Springer Verlag, 2001).

5. Deborah Sontag, "Who Brought Bernadine Healy Down? The Red Cross: A Disaster Story Without Any Heroes," *New York Times Magazine*, December 23, 2001.

6. Dacher Keltner, Deborah H. Gruenfeld, and Cameron Anderson, "Power, Approach, and Inhibition," *Psychological Review* 110 (2003): 265–284.

7. Cameron Anderson and Adam D. Galinsky, "Power, Optimism, and Risk-Taking," *European Journal of Social Psychology* 36 (2006): 511–536.

8. David Kipnis, "Does Power Corrupt?" *Journal of Personality and Social Psychology* 24 (1972): 33–41.

9. This particular study is described in Keltner, Gruenfeld, and Anderson, "Power, Approach, and Inhibition." There are numerous studies of a similar form showing how power leads to less inhibition in behavior. See, for instance, Cameron Anderson and Jennifer L. Berdahl, "The Experience of Power: Examining the Effects of Power on Approach and Inhibition Tendencies," *Journal of Personality and Social Psychology* 83 (2002): 1362–1377.

10. Adam Lashinsky, "The Enforcer," *Fortune*, September 28, 2009, 120.

11. Sontag, "Who Brought Bernadine Healy Down?"

12. Ibid., 35.

13. "NationsBank Struck with Brutal Military Precision," http://www.sfgate.com, October 25, 1998.

14. Stan Sesser, "A Reporter at Large: A Nation of Contradictions," *The New Yorker*, January 13, 1992.

15. Ibid., 57.

16. Robert A. Caro, *The Power Broker: Robert Moses and the Fall of New York* (New York: Knopf, 1977), 986.

12. Power Dynamics

1. Jo Silvester, "The Good, the Bad, and the Ugly: Politics and Politicians at Work," in G. P. Hodgkinson and J. K. Ford, eds., *International Review of Industrial and Organizational Psychology*, vol. 23 (Chichester, UK: John Wiley, 2008), 107.

2. Ibid., 112.

3. Camille Rickets, "China-Focused VCs Depart Posts—Asia Capital Crunch to Blame?" http: //venturebeat.com/2009/020/04/china-focused-vcs-depart-posts-asia-capital-crunch-to-blame, February 4, 2009.

4. Ken Auletta, "The Fall of Lehman Brothers: The Men, the Money, The Merger," *New York Times Magazine*, February 24, 1985.

5. Nicholas Lemann, "The Split: A True Story of Washington Lawyers," *Washington Post Magazine*, March 23, 1980.

6. See, as just one of many such tales, Alison Leigh Cowan, "The Partners Revolt at Peat Marwick," *New York Times*, November 18, 1990.
7. Frederick S. Hills and Thomas A. Mahoney, "University Budgets and Organizational Decision Making," *Administrative Science Quarterly* 23 (1978): 454–465; Jeffrey Pfeffer and William L. Moore, "Power in University Budgeting: A Replication and Extension," *Administrative Science Quarterly* 25 (1980): 637–653.
8. Pui-wing Tam, "Venture Capitalists Head for the Door," www.smsmallbiz.com/capital/Venture_Capitalists_Head_for_the_Door, June 5, 2009.
9. Many of these changes are detailed in "More Mr. Nice Guy: Why Cutting Benefits Is a Bad Idea," in Jeffrey Pfeffer, *What Were They Thinking: Unconventional Wisdom About Management* (Boston: Harvard Business School Press, 2007).
10. Paul Hirsch, *Pack Your Own Parachute: How to Survive Mergers, Takeovers, and Other Corporate Disasters* (Reading, MA: Addison-Wesley, 1988).
11. Jeffrey Gandz and Victor V. Murray, "The Experience of Workplace Politics," *Academy of Management Journal* 23 (1980): 237–251.
12. See, for instance, Fred L. Strodtbeck, Rita M. James, and Charles Hawkins, "Social Status in Jury Deliberations," *American Sociologial Review* 22 (1957): 713–719.
13. See, for instance, Peter M. Blau, "A Formal Theory of Differentiation in Organizations," *American Sociological Review* 35 (1970): 201–218; Marshall W. Meyer, "Size and Structure of Organizations: A Causal Analysis," *American Sociological Review* 37 (1972): 434–440.
14. A research program called expectation states theory has produced much evidence on this point. The empirical literature on expectation states is extensive. A good review and overview can be found in Joseph Berger, Cecilia Ridgeway, M. Hamit Fisek, and Robert Z. Norman, "The Legitimation and Delegitimation of Power and Prestige Orders," *American Sociological Review* 63 (1998): 379–405.
15. L. Z. Tiedens, M. M. Unzueta, and M. J. Young, "An Unconscious Desire for Hierarchy? The Motivated Perception of Dominance Complementarity in Task Partners," *Journal of Personality and Social Psychology* 93 (2007): 402–414.
16. John T. Jost and Mahzarin R. Banaji, "The Role of Stereotyping in System-Justification and the Production of False Consciousness," *British Journal of Social Psychology* 33 (1994): 1–27.
17. See, for instance, Rakesh Khurana, *Searching for a Corporate Savior* (Princeton, NJ: Princeton University Press, 2002).
18. See http://www.quotationspage.com/quote/364.html.
19. David Butcher and Martin Clarke, "Organizational Politics: The Cornerstone for Organizational Democracy," *Organizational Dynamics* 31 (2002): 35.
20. James Surowiecki, *The Wisdom of Crowds: Why the Many Are Smarter Than the*

Few and How Collective Wisdom Shapes Business, Economics, Societies, and Nations (New *York*: Doubleday, 2004).

13. It's Easier Than You Think

1. See http://www.quotationspage.com/quote/1903.html.
2. David L. Bradford and Allen R. Cohen, *Power Up: Transforming Organizations Through Shared Leadership* (New York: John Wiley, 1998).
3. Cameron Anderson and Jennifer L. Berdahl, "The Experience of Power: Examining the Effects of Power on Approach and Inhibition Tendencies," *Journal of Personality and Social Psychology* 83 (2002): 1362–1377.
4. See http://quotationspage.com/quote/137.html.
5. Robert I. Sutton, *The No Asshole Rule: Building a Civilized Workplace and Surviving One That Isn't* (New York: Business Plus, 2007).
6. Michael Marmot, *The Status Syndrome: How Social Standing Affects Our Health and Longevity* (New York: Times Books, 2004), 39.
7. Ibid., 53.

FOR FURTHER READING AND LEARNING

If you are interested in learning and reading more about power and influence in organizations, here are some suggestions.

Each year during the winter quarter I teach a class titled "The Paths to Power." The course outline is publicly available. Go to my personal home page, http://faculty-gsb.stanford.edu/pfeffer/. There is a link on the left-hand side of the page that will take you directly to the most recent version of the course.

Cases

Over the years I have written a number of cases for the power class. These are available either through the Stanford Graduate School of Business or through Harvard Business School Case Services, which distributes Stanford's cases. They are short biographies of interesting people doing interesting things entailing the use of power and influence.

Jeffrey Sonnenfeld (A): The Fall from Grace, Case no. OB-34 (A), September 2000.

Jeffrey Sonnenfeld (B): The Road to Redemption, Case no. OB-34 (B), September 2000.

Dr. Laura Esserman (A) and (B): Case no. OB-42, September 2003.

Keith Ferrazzi: Case no. OB-44, October 2003.

Gary Loveman and Harrah's Entertainment: Case no. OB-45, November 2003.

Nuria Chinchilla: The Power to Change Workplaces, Case no. OB-67, January 2008.

Zia Yusuf at SAP: Having Impact, Case no. OB-73, February 2009.

All of these people, with the exception of Jeffrey Sonnenfeld, as well as some others mentioned in the book, including Rudy Crew and Jack Valenti, have spoken in my class, in some instances multiple times. Edited versions of their presentations are available as video cases through the Stanford Graduate School of Business or through Harvard Business School Case Services. Search on their names in the section of the websites under "Cases." Seeing them in person provides great additional insight and learning.

Other Reading

You can learn a lot—and also have a great experience—reading wonderful biographies. Some of my personal favorites are:

Robert A. Caro, *The Power Broker: Robert Moses and the Fall of New York* (New York: Vintage Books, 1975) (winner of the Pulitzer Prize).

Robert A. Caro, *The Years of Lyndon Johnson: The Path to Power* (New York: Knopf, 1982).

Robert A. Caro, *Master of the Senate* (New York: Knopf, 2002).

Seymour M. Hersh, *The Price of Power: Kissinger in the Nixon White House* (New York: Summit Books, 1984).

James Richardson, *Willie Brown: A Biography* (Berkeley: University of California Press, 1996).

Other books with interesting insights about power dynamics and influence strategies include:

Robert B. Cialdini, *Influence: The Psychology of Persuasion* (Boston: Allyn and Bacon, 2001).

David Halberstam, *The Reckoning* (New York: William Morrow, 1986).

Max Atkinson, *Our Masters' Voices: The Language and Body-Language of Politics* (New York: Routledge, 1984).

INDEX